Photoshop® Elements 2 Special Effects

AL WARD

PHOTOSHOP® ELEMENTS 2 SPECIAL EFFECTS

WILEY

Wiley Publishing, Inc.

Photoshop® Elements 2 Special Effects

Published by
Wiley Publishing, Inc.
909 Third Avenue
New York, NY 10022

www.wiley.com

Copyright © 2003 by Wiley Publishing, Inc., Indianapolis, Indiana

Library of Congress Control Number: 2002114775

ISBN: 0-7645-2597-2

Manufactured in the United States of America

10 9 8 7 6 5 4 3 2 1

1V/RY/QS/QT/IN

Published by Wiley Publishing, Inc., Indianapolis, Indiana
Published simultaneously in Canada

WILEY is a trademark of Wiley Publishing, Inc.

To my wife Tonia and to my wonderful kids Noah and Ali. Tonia is my true love and balance, Ali and Noah my joy and inspiration. A man is blessed if he has one person to share life with, to encourage and be encouraged by, to love unconditionally and be loved in the same manner. In this I've been blessed thrice. I can think of no other people who I would rather go through the day to day trials with, and I look forward to every tomorrow knowing that I can share that time with them.

Special thanks also to Richard Lynch. Conversations with Richard inspired me to tackle this project, and he has been a great source of knowledge and become a good friend along the way.

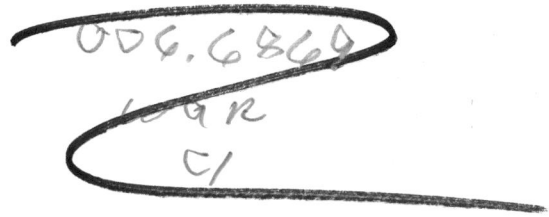

FOREWORD

Not long after I met Al Ward in a friendly e-mail he sent, we got to tossing around ideas about our respective Photoshop projects. We talked about books we'd like to do and how we thought we could make something better for the reader than what was already out there. It was good to discuss things with Al because he'd always get the point and have helpful suggestions for projects and proposals. He quickly became someone I could rely on for expert advice. I learned about as fast that he wasn't like a lot of people who specialize in Photoshop effects. He could really nail an effect that worked — rather than just getting an effect to work in a specific situation or with a specific image. He really knows his Photoshop stuff.

During those first few months of sporadic e-mails, Al was hard at work on one project or another, and I'd been approached with a project having to do with Elements. As a serious Photoshop users for years, I don't know that I was taking Elements too seriously at the time. I mentioned it to Al, and he felt a little like I did. Everyone, including Adobe and other authors, was touting the Elements program as something for beginners: It was missing this or that function or couldn't do some important thing. I got the demo and started looking at the program anyway.

It didn't take long to discover Effects, Styles, and what was then the Recipe palette (now How To). I saw these as areas in the Elements program, and they seemed to have Al's styles written all over them. I sent him an e-mail and told him he should have a look . . . maybe there was something to Elements after all.

It wasn't but a few days and a few e-mails later that Al and I came to the same conclusion 1,500 miles apart: Elements was a lot more powerful and could do a lot more than anybody was letting on. In fact it could do about anything that Photoshop could. What that meant was that years of work that went into all the styles, actions, and effects Al had created and compiled for Photoshop — stuff he did before Elements ever existed — could be adjusted to work in Elements. Getting that stuff into the hands of Elements users would be a huge advantage. This book is a result of what Al compiled.

There's no one who does effects like Al Ward — unless they read his books. You can it see from his Web site to the attention to detail in effects: He doesn't just look to get an effect done any-which-way, but he works hard at getting it to look *right*. The best part about all of Al's hard work is that it makes creating effects that much easier for you. Even better, not only is it easier, but you get top quality effects at the same time.

If you like effects, use Elements, and you are looking for a book to help you out, there is only one tiny scrap of information you need: Buy this book if you haven't already. There are great tutorials, effects, and styles throughout, and a ton more stuff on the CD that you'll find invaluable. Al has put together a unique, must-have collection, and it is definitely one you shouldn't be without. Get it and start applying new effects to your images right away!

Richard Lynch
author, *The Hidden Power of Photoshop Elements 2*
`http://hiddenelements.com`
Elements Newsletter: `hpe-subscribe@yahoogroups.com`

PREFACE

Something I've never been accused of is having an underactive imagination. I chalk it up to two things: growing up on 1,200 acres as a boy with only my brother as a playmate, and developing an interest in reading at an early age. My brother and I turned that old ranch into space ports and battlefields, and central Montana would not be complete without a good western shoot out or two. Somewhere along the line I picked up an interest in fantasy novels, further driving my craving for the fantastic. In a world of "you can't," I developed an attitude of "why not?".

True, there are acceptable boundaries to every action and attitude. The trick is to stretch those boundaries, or maximize the potential of the limits that constrain you. Are you lost yet? Hold on, and I'll try to make my point.

Take a marble, for example. It has a contained weight, density, and dimension. Most people would not be overly enthused about the object . . . it is, after all, just a piece of glass. But that marble can bring the biggest person crashing to the ground simply because of its shape; a transparent marble can be used to focus light and cause a fire, or create a prism effect and divide light into an entire spectrum of colors. Many marbles working together can be used to transport objects of great weight or rotate the inner workings of machinery. How many more examples can you think of? I've barely touched the surface.

So to say that Adobe Elements is merely a basic photo correction program is like telling me the only attribute of a marble is that it is round. Adobe Elements 2 is far more powerful than people give it credit for, and extremely versatile in that it needn't only be used for image correction. This book will take you far beyond that misconception, and delve into the realm of special effects that before may have seemed beyond reach. In the end, I hope that you not only know the tools and commands available to you with this software, but that you also have an understanding of how to use them to your advantage. So sit back and, with Adobe Elements 2 open, let's have some fun expanding the boundaries. Who says every box has to be square?

SOMETHING TO KNOW IN ADVANCE

Although the effects in this book may appear advanced, the approach throughout the text is step-by-step, and written in tutorial style so that the end result can be achieved with minimal description and anecdotes. An intermediate to advanced knowledge of Adobe Elements 2 or image manipulation is not required. The author recommends only that you have a desire to learn, the ability to follow instructions, and an active imagination.

WHAT MAKES THIS BOOK DIFFERENT

The author, and therefore this book, proceed with the assumption that Adobe Elements is far more than a simple photo-editing program. In it, you will be introduced to techniques and effects previously attributed to Adobe Photoshop. Because Elements has many of the original Photoshop tools (and a couple extras not resident in Photoshop), many of the effects seen here have sprung from the author's work in Adobe Photoshop. Not to worry. You can create these effects using Elements, despite its reputation as the "simpler" program.

The approach of this book is step-by-step, going from point A to finished image in an easy to follow manner. If you are new to Elements, do not let the end result images intimidate you. By the end of each technique, you will have both a finished image resembling the example and a firm grasp on how it was created.

WHAT COMPUTER HARDWARD AND SOFTWARE WILL YOU NEED?

FOR WINDOWS 9X, WINDOWS 2000, WINDOWS NT4 (WITH SP 4 OR LATER), WINDOWS ME, OR WINDOWS XP:

- PC with a Pentium processor running at 120 Mhz or faster
- At least 32 MB of total RAM installed on your computer; for best performance, we recommend at least 64 MB
- Ethernet network interface card (NIC) or modem with a speed of at least 28,800 bps
- A CD-ROM drive

FOR MACINTOSH:

- Mac OS computer with a 68040 or faster processor running OS 7.6 or later
- At least 32 MB of total RAM installed on your computer; for best performance, we recommend at least 64 MB
- A CD-ROM drive

CONVENTIONS USED IN THIS BOOK

To make this book easy to use so that you can re-create the effects, I used a special format that focuses on the actual steps you need to take.

I break each tutorial into major steps and explain what the step accomplishes. Follow the bullet points and figures to complete the tutorial on your own. If the figure is shown in the color section, the figure number includes a color plate number, such as **CP2**, in parentheses, so you can quickly find the image in color. I refer you to the files on the CD-ROM you'll use in the tutorial.

Throughout the book, figure numbers appear in bold type, as in **Figure 2.1**. Bold type also designates items you interact with and any text or numbers to be typed.

Adobe Elements has keyboard shortcuts for most of the tools, commands, and settings. Where applicable, the shortcuts have been inserted in the text for the reader's benefit. Both the Mac and PC shortcuts are included. For example, **View ➤ Rulers (⌘/Ctrl+R)** indicates that the rulers may be turned on from the View menu, by pressing the ⌘ key and the R key on a Mac, or by pressing the Ctrl key and the R key on a PC.

ACKNOWLEDGMENTS

This is the one portion of the book that is hardest to write as I feel obligated to mention everyone I ever knew but inevitably will forget someone. There are a few people who absolutely deserve my undying gratitude for this particular work, so after careful trimming of the list, here we go.

My personal thanks to Richard Lynch, an excellent author and teacher in his own right. Richard convinced me to approach Elements in the first place. He's been a source of not only knowledge, but inspiration and encouragement as well. I value his insight, but even more so, his friendship.

Special thanks to the following:

To Scott Kelby and the gang behind the National Association of Photoshop Professionals. Scott gave me my start in this business, and I'm forever in his debt.

To Colin Smith, my frequent collaborator and comrade-in-arms.

To Tonia, Noah, and Ali. They put up with far more than they should and return more love than I deserve.

To my extended family and friends far and wide: Mom, Dad, Ole, Linda, everyone at MLMBC, and all the rest. Too many to mention, but you know who you are and you are in my thoughts always.

CONTENTS AT A GLANCE

CONTENTS

CHAPTER 1: KNOWING THE WORKSPACE: TOOLS, PALETTES, AND SHORTCUTS

CHAPTER 2: 3D OBJECTS IN A 2D WORLD

CHAPTER 3: UNNATURALLY NATURAL ELEMENTS

CHAPTER 4: GETTING TECHNICAL: INDUSTRIAL EFFECTS

CHAPTER 5: SHOCK VALUE: ELECTRONICS

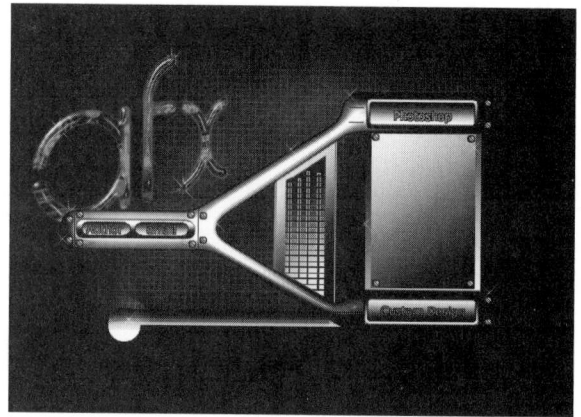

CHAPTER 6: GETTING A GRASP ON INTANGIBLES: VAPORS, RAYS, AND ELECTRICITY

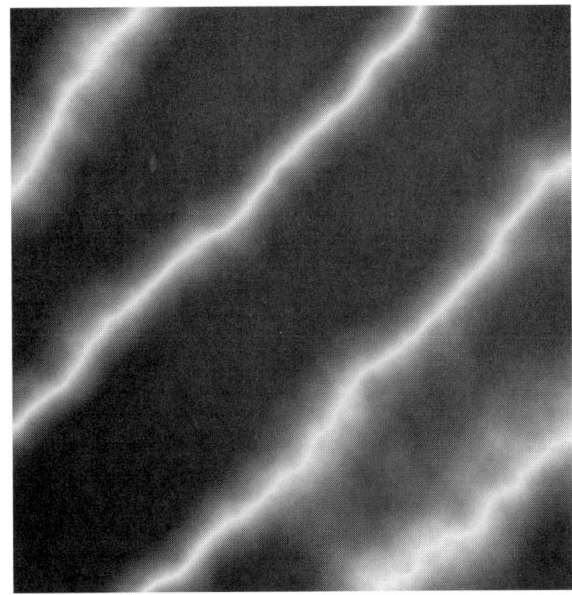

CHAPTER 7: I SHOULD HAVE BEEN A DOCTOR: ALTERING HUMANS AND CRITTERS

CHAPTER 8: INTERFACING WITH THE WEB

CHAPTER 9: HOW CAN YOU SAY THAT? TYPE TREATMENTS

1

KNOWING THE WORKSPACE: TOOLS, PALETTES, AND SHORTCUTS

Before you can begin learning any program, you need to know some vital information on the tools involved. Adobe Elements uses the same standard set of tools that is used by other Adobe products, maintaining a layout and design (called the Common User Interface) that is both user-friendly and intuitive. Well, that is, if you are familiar with the layout, tools, palettes, bars, and so on. This book and, therefore, this chapter assume that you are not familiar with the Adobe mindset and have never looked at, let alone utilized, one of their playing fields before. Be at ease; Adobe Elements is not nearly as intimidating as it looks.

In this chapter, you will familiarize yourself with the tools and settings that will soon have you creating special effects like a pro. The first section covers the Toolbox — everything from Marquee tool selections to gradients to setting the foreground and background colors. The second section demonstrates how to control your tools via a neat little contraption called the Options bar. Every tool has several options that you can adjust (sort of like changing drill bit types and sizes), so these options are discussed here. The third section talks about palettes; you can use

these to alter and modify your images. The fourth section provides valuable shortcuts and key combinations to speed up the process of creating and editing your work. As you work through the tutorials found in the other chapters, you may find yourself referring back to this chapter time and again. That's fine . . . it is all part of the learning process.

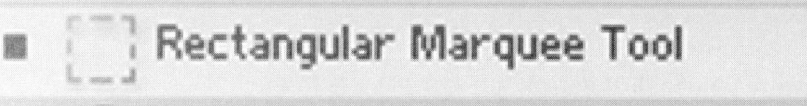

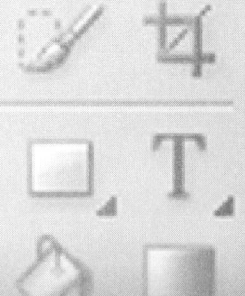

| ■ | [ ] Rectangular Marquee Tool | M |
| ○ | Elliptical Marquee Tool | M |

Window

Images

THE TOOLBOX: TOOLS OF THE TRADE

Image editing can seem like magic to those unfamiliar with the process. A person versed in Adobe Elements 2 can repair a damaged photo, give a new photo the appearance of age, or generate a coffee cup from a blank slate. Someone unfamiliar with process or with the software will stand amazed at the results. The digital magician, however, simply knows the tools of the trade and applies them skillfully to trick the eye. A bit of artistry is definitely helpful but not necessarily required.

Before you can do the tricks, you need to familiarize yourself with the Adobe Elements tools. **Figure 1.1** shows the Toolbox that Adobe Elements utilizes, which follows the standard Adobe format.

Tools are represented in the Toolbox as buttons with small icons indicating their function. Some buttons represent a single tool, but others that have a small arrow in the lower-right corner, indicating that more tools are hidden beneath the button. Clicking the tool button and holding the left mouse button down reveals the other tools available in a small pop-up that expands from the tool button. Also, simply clicking the tool's button reveals the options for that tool in the Options bar (covered shortly). The additional tools are present as well, and you may select the additional tools.

The Toolbox is divided into sections that represent categories of tools. For example, the top portion down to the first indented line contains the Selection and Move tools. The next section contains the drawing, painting, and typing tools, called the Artistic tools. The third section contains tools that allow you to alter specific regions of the image with blurring, smudging, and contrasting effects. Adobe calls these Toning tools. The last batch contains the Focus and Cloning tools. The bottom portion of the toolbar shows the foreground and background colors.

1.1

Many of the tools have shortcut keys assigned to them. I discuss the shortcut key combinations later in this chapter. What is pertinent to know now is that when you select a tool button or simply hover the mouse over the tool button, the shortcut for that tool or tool group pops up alongside the tool name, as shown in **Figure 1.2**.

One more note before I dive into tool descriptions. Clicking the flower at the top of the Toolbox takes you to the Adobe Elements page on the Adobe Web site. This only works if you are online, of course, and the information you find on the Web site on Elements is sparse. However, if you need to purchase a full version or upgrade, you may do so here.

The Toolbox has five sections, indicated by a recessed line embedded into the Toolbox and separating groups of tool icons. Starting at the top just below the Flower icon are the buttons for the Selection tool group.

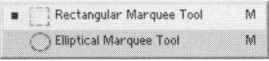

1.2

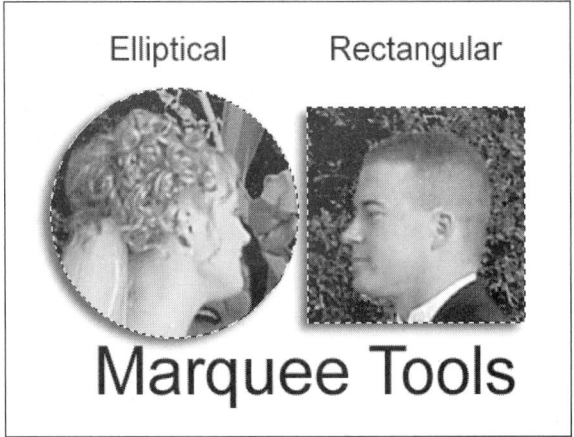

1.3

MARQUEE TOOLS (M)

The first tool button found on the Toolbox is the **Marquee** tool. Two tools are available — the **Rectangular Marquee** tool (squared edges) and the **Elliptical Marquee** tool (rounded edges), both seen in action in **Figure 1.3**. With these tools, you can create a selection out of portions of the canvas and affect only the area within the selection when you edit.

MOVE TOOL (V)

Next to the Marquee tool button is the **Move** tool. With this tool, you can reposition the contents of a layer or a selection in an image.

LASSO TOOLS (L)

The **Lasso** tools allow you to create a freehand or straight-edged selection. These tools are more versatile than the Marquee tools, and give the user the ability to remove people or objects from their background to place on another layer or in another photo.

- **Lasso tool:** Draw freehand selections
- **Polygonal Lasso tool:** Draw straight-edged selections
- **Magnetic Lasso tool:** Draw a border that snaps to the distinctive edge of a subject (combination of the first two Lasso tools)

MAGIC WAND TOOL (W)

The **Magic Wand** tool, when clicked on a layer or within an image, selects an area based on the color values of that area and the adjacent colors. For example, if I select a brown tone, a selection of all browns connected to the area clicked is selected, so long as the color variation is within the tolerance levels. The lower the tolerance, the more restrictive the color selection. Higher tolerance broadens the range of color selected. The tolerance levels for the Magic Wand are selected in the Options bar for that tool. **Figure 1.4** gives an example of the Magic Wand in action.

SELECTION BRUSH TOOL (A)

The **Selection Brush** is an extremely cool tool! With it you can actually paint a selection, or rather outline an area defined by selecting a soft- or hard-edged brush and, with the mouse, painting the area you want selected. Though the Selection Brush is not as exact as the Lasso tools, it gives the user a quick selection, whereas the Lasso tools can be time consuming. You can drag the brush to make a selection or use the selection to define a mask of unselected areas.

CROP TOOL (C)

Occasionally, you may come across a photo that has a bit too much picture surrounding the subject. In this instance the **Crop** tool is for you. With the Crop tool you can select an area of the photograph to keep (see **Figure 1.5**). Everything outside of that area is discarded when you press Return/Enter (see **Figure 1.6**). With a bit of practice and imagination, the Crop tool can be used to great creative effect in other areas of design also.

1.5

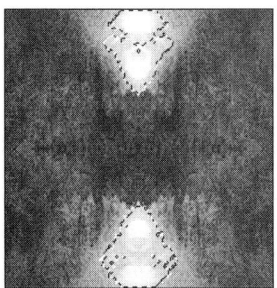

1.4

1.6

SHAPE TOOLS (U)

The **Shape** tools enable the user to create vector shape layers. Vector shape layers are handy for creating buttons for Web graphics, bubbles for text that you might see in a comic book, and navigation bars.

As with the standard Type tool, the Shape tools use vector graphics as opposed to raster graphics. Therefore, you can scale the shape without losing resolution. The shape retains crisp, clearly defined lines, as opposed to the jagged edges and blurry distortions found when a rasterized layer is resized.

Shapes are created by selecting a Shape tool and then by clicking and dragging within a layer. A new layer is created to hold the shape so that it may be manipulated separately from the rest of the image. To select a

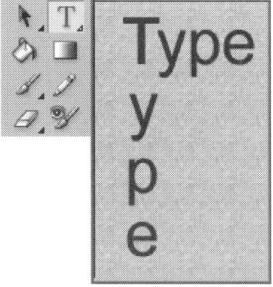

1.7

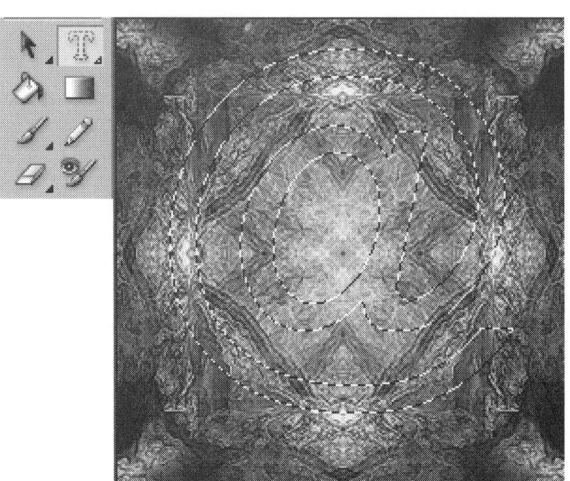

1.8

Shape tool, choose one from the Toolbox (several are hidden; clicking and holding the mouse button down while hovering over the Shape tool reveals them). You may also click the Shape tool and select the type of shape you want to create in the Options bar.

The types of Shape tools available are:

- **Rectangle tool:** Squares and rectangles
- **Rounded Rectangle tool:** Great for buttons
- **Ellipse tool:** Rounded or circular shapes
- **Polygon tool:** Triangles, polygons, hexagons, and so forth
- **Line tool**
- **Custom Shape tool:** Predefined shapes such as bubbles, fruit, stars, and so on.
- **Shape Selection tool:** Enables you to select a shape with one click to resize or move them to other areas of the layer.

TYPE TOOL (T)

The **Type** tools work just how they sound — they allow you to apply text to a layer. Four tools are in this group (see **Figure 1.7**).

- **Horizontal Type tool**
- **Vertical Type tool**
- **Horizontal Type Mask tool**
- **Vertical Type Mask tool**

The **Horizontal Type** and **Vertical Type** tools work like shapes in that they use vector graphics. Each line you enter is independent from other lines. Every time you click a new area and enter text, a new type layer is created.

The **Type Selection** tools enable you to create a type shaped selection, as shown in **Figure 1.8**. You can then fill the selection with a color, gradient, patterns, and so forth, or apply filters as you would any other selection. Only the area within the selection is affected, with some bleed over if you use a feathered selection.

PAINT BUCKET (K)

The **Paint Bucket** allows you to fill a layer or selection with the foreground color, a pattern, or the default colors. This tool is useful when you have large areas that require the same color or pattern.

GRADIENT TOOL (G)

The **Gradient** tool allows you to fill an area or layer with a gradual or stark color change. More than one color may be used, and at varying levels of transparency. This tool has multiple options, each useful in its own way. I devote a lot of time to gradients in the rest of the book, so you will see this tool in action in a wide variety of applications. For now, here's a list of tools available in this group.

- **Linear Gradient:** Gradual linear color changes
- **Radial Gradient:** Gradual circular color changes
- **Angle Gradient:** Gradient in counter-clockwise sweep from starting point. (Great for stereo knobs)
- **Reflected Gradient:** Shades the gradient gradually on either side of the starting point
- **Diamond Gradient:** Creates a diamond-shaped gradation in color, with the starting point as the center, and the endpoint one tip of the diamond

BRUSH TOOLS (P)

Beneath the **Brush** tool you find two types of Brush tools — the standard **Paintbrush** tool, used for painting solid colors or patterns, and the **Impressionist Brush** tool.

- **Paintbrush tool:** You can select from a wide variety of brush tips and alter the dimension of the selected brush. This tool automatically selects the foreground color as the paint color.
- **Impressionist Brush tool:** Applies paint in patterns reflecting different impressionist styles. With a bit of experimentation, you can duplicate texture and stroke style of famous paintings. This brush does not add new color to the area painted but rather alters the blend of the image's own tones.

PENCIL (N)

The **Pencil** tool acts like . . . well, a pencil. With it you can draw hard-edged lines across your image using the foreground color. You can draw freehand, or straight lines when you hold down the Shift key while drawing. The Shift key trick also works with the Brush tool.

ERASER TOOLS (E)

The **Eraser**, **Background Eraser**, and **Magic Eraser** are the three tools that you find in this group.

- **Eraser:** Erases pixels from a layer. You may change the size of the eraser in the same manner in which you would change the size of a brush.
- **Background Eraser:** Allows you to separate a subject in an image by sampling the colors beneath the eraser and deleting them, creating a transparency around the central figure. This brush can be difficult to use. My recommendation is to increase the zoom on the image and select a small eraser to create a fine line of transparency around the subject first (see **Figure 1.9**), and then erase the rest of the background.

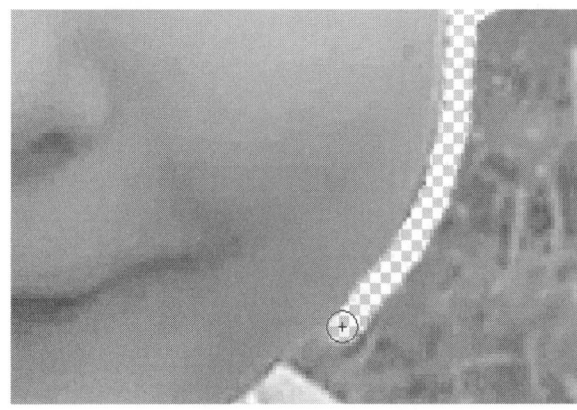

1.9

■ **Magic Eraser:** This tool wipes out all similar pixels with a single click. Though not as exact as the Background Eraser, large areas of similar color can be deleted quickly. Adjusting the tolerance in the Options bar determines how much color variation the Magic Eraser removes.

RED EYE BRUSH TOOL (Y)

The **Red Eye Brush** helps the user with one of the recurring problems associated with photography — red eye. This occurs when light from a flash reflects off the back of a person's eyeball, displaying a red tint on the eye when none is desired.

The process is rather simple. First, you sample a color by selecting the tool. Then Alt+click a portion of the eye with good color and replace the color with the sample.

BLUR TOOL (R)

The **Blur** tool helps you reduce hard edges, giving the area blurred a softer appearance. You can use this to

1.10 (CP2)

help reduce the effect called *jaggies* or to blur out detail in portions of the image.

SHARPEN TOOL (P)

The counterpoint to the Blur tool, the **Sharpen** tool increases the contrast in blurred areas.

SPONGE TOOL (Q)

The **Sponge** tool alters the saturation where applied, slightly altering the appearance by either increasing or decreasing tone. This tool has two modes, **Saturate** and **Desaturate**. Saturate increases hue (pink becomes a brighter shade), whereas Desaturate takes away color. **Figure 1.10** (CP2) demonstrates the effect of each mode. Color was removed from one subject and the background enhanced on the second subject.

SMUDGE TOOL (F)

The **Smudge** tool has the effect of smearing the area to which it is applied. By clicking the mouse and dragging, you stretch the pixels with the drag, effectively smudging the image as your finger might when you paint. You are not restricted to using the color of the image. You may also smear the foreground and background colors onto the area.

DODGE (O) AND BURN (J) TOOLS

The **Dodge** and **Burn** tools run in conjunction with each other and are the two primary toning tools. The primary thought behind these two tools stems from darkroom techniques of applying or removing exposure from areas of photographs.

■ **Dodge:** Lightens the area where it is applied. (Great for bringing detail out of shadows and creating reflections on photo-realistic objects)

■ **Burn:** Darkens the area where it is applied.

These tools are similar to the Sponge but are a bit more advanced in that you can select the tonal range you want to lighten or darken. You have three options — **Shadows**, **Midtones**, and **Highlights**. You also set the exposure desired in the Options bar.

CLONE STAMP TOOL (S)

The **Clone Stamp** is one of my favorite tools and is essential for photo cleanup and restoration. This tool offers the ability to snatch a portion of an image and stamp it into another. For example, say that you have wedding photos taken of a family member, only to find after the film has been developed that the bride has chocolate cake on the front of her gown. With the Clone Stamp, you can sample an unstained portion of the dress and stamp it seamlessly over the stain, restoring the photo to a glory that was originally intended.

PATTERN STAMP TOOL (S)

The **Pattern Stamp** tool is grouped with the Clone Stamp and can either be found beneath the Clone Stamp in the Toolbox or in the Options bar when the Stamp tools are selected. The Pattern Stamp operates in a manner similar to the Clone Stamp, but instead of sampling a portion of the image to stamp into areas that need corrected, the Pattern Stamp applies predefined patterns.

EYEDROPPER TOOL (I)

The **Eyedropper** tool takes a sample of the color where clicked and places that color in the foreground color slot. This is especially useful for retrieving the tone's number values. Sample the color, double-click the foreground color in the Toolbox, and the Color Picker pops up with the number values for that hue.

HAND TOOL (H)

The **Hand** tool is used when you have an image larger than the view window. The Hand tool lets you grab the image and slide it over to view the unseen areas.

ZOOM TOOL (Z)

As the name implies, this tool increases or decreases the percentage view of the image. The amount of zoom is displayed in the image's title bar.

FOREGROUND-BACKGROUND COLORS (D SETS DEFAULT)

On the bottom of the Toolbox, you find what appear to be two squares, one overlaying the other. These squares represent the active foreground and background colors. You can change these manually by double-clicking one of the panels and choosing a color manually in the Color Picker pop-up, enter number values by hand in the Color Picker, sample colors directly off the image, and so on.

The default colors for Elements are black in the foreground and white in the background. You can return to the default settings at any time by pressing the D key. The X key swaps the foreground and background colors.

I provided this summary to help you get acquainted with all of the tools available in Adobe Photoshop Elements 2. As you work through the tutorials in the book, you will find that some tools are used extensively, whereas others you may not touch beyond this point. It is essential that you have a foundation in the tools and recall where to find those needed for specific steps. Now, open the second drawer of the Toolbox, and take a look at the options available for the tools.

PHILLIPS OR STRAIGHT HEAD? TOOL SETTINGS AND THE OPTIONS BAR

Say a friend asks you to hand him a screwdriver. A simple question on the surface, but if you are familiar with that tool family, you know that you have a few options from which to choose, depending on the job. You can choose from a variety of screwdrivers, including type (Phillips or straight head), size, length, and so on. There is a correct tool for every job, but how do you know which one is correct?

Adobe Elements provides an answer. Each tool has options that are located in the Options bar at the top of the workspace. After you select a tool, you then proceed to the Options bar. The next section gives you a quick overview of how to use the Options bar.

WHERE ARE THE OPTIONS?

Selecting the Marquee tool displays the options for that tool (see **Figure 1.11**).

Starting on the left side, you first notice the tools in the Marquee tool group. Clicking either the Rectangular Marquee or Elliptical Marquee enables that tool, and you can then set options for the one selected.

Each tool has a set of options. Throughout this book, you are asked to change settings in the Options bar.

MARQUEE TOOL OPTIONS

Unfortunately, covering each tool's options in depth would take up an entire volume. This run-through is merely an example to get you familiar with options. Further questions can be answered using the Hints palette (covered later in this chapter), the Help files, or your Adobe Elements 2 manual.

Starting from the left, the first icons indicate the tools in that tool group. You may either select them from the Toolbox or click the tool group in the Toolbox and change the tool there.

To the right of the Marquee tools you can choose from the following four options.

- **New Selection:** Creates a new selection every time you draw a selection with the mouse. Any previously-made selections disappear.
- **Add To Selection:** Allows you to make a new selection and add it to an existing selection.
- **Subtract From Selection:** By drawing over an existing selection, the portion drawn over is removed from the active selection.
- **Intersect With Selection:** Overlapping two selections with this option removes all but the overlapped portion. The rest of the selection becomes inactive.

The next option in the Options bar is the **Feather** setting. This option enables you to soften the edges of a selection, creating a blend of pixels to transparency. When Feather is set to 0, no feathering exists, which creates a stark edge between the contents within the selection and those without. **Figure 1.12** shows the difference between two filled selections. The first

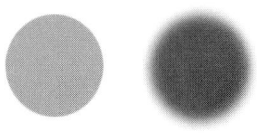

1.12

1.11

selection has a feather of 0, and the second has a feather set to 5 pixels.

In Elements, you can set the Feather radius up to 250 pixels.

The **Anti-aliasing** checkbox, next in line in the list of options, is similar to the Feather setting in that it blends the contents of the selection with the area surrounding the selection. The primary difference is anti-aliasing only blends a 1-pixel thickness. This tool is excellent for softening jagged edges.

The last portion of the Marquee tool options is the **Style** setting. You have three options from which to choose in the Style setting.

- **Normal:** Clicking and dragging creates a new, unconstrained shape selection.
- **Fixed Aspect Ratio:** Clicking and dragging creates a new constrained shape. The Width/Height ratios are set by the user in corresponding boxes found to the right of the Style setting box.

- **Fixed Size:** Generates a fixed size selection. The size is determined by the user's settings in the Width/Height boxes.

Every tutorial found in this book and, I dare say, every technique that you will ever perform using Elements will involve the Options bar. As you work through the book, you will become familiar with the options of many tools. For example, I'm certain that by the time you turn the last page, you will have the Gradient options committed to memory. At face value Elements has 30 to 40 tools, but with options for each tool, your little toolkit just became a full-fledged repair shop.

PALETTES: DOORWAYS TO DYNAMIC EFFECTS

Adobe has created a system for applying additional effects, creating and selecting layers, and providing one-on-one training. A system of information and tool-packed palettes is used to assist the designer in learning and to broaden the scope of effects attainable by Adobe Elements 2.

Palettes (see **Figure 1.13**) are windows that hold commands and information. Unlike the Toolbox and Options bar, palettes impart information with a system of text, links, and images. They assist in editing images by supplying presets in the form of layer styles, prerecorded steps in the form of effects, or tutorials as supplied by the Recipes palette. Palettes also allow you to create and edit layers, apply filters, browse images in folders, and much more.

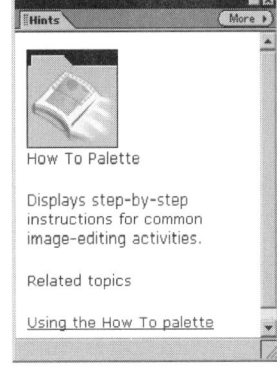

1.13

PALETTE ORGANIZATION

Several palettes are available in Adobe Elements, but before I cover what palettes are at your disposal, I want to show you how to organize them. The first step is viewing a palette.

Figure 1.14 displays the default locations for the palettes when you first open Adobe Elements.

There are two active palettes in this arrangement — the Hints palette, which gives access to the Help files, and the How To palette, which contains Recipes, or tutorials, for techniques. You can find the rest of the palettes in the Palette Well, located above the Hints palette. Note the helpful folder tab style navigation system. Clicking a tab opens the palette, making it active and allowing the user to perform functions or to retrieve information associated with that palette. By docking the palettes in a well (either by the palette's menu or dragging and dropping the palette to the well with the mouse), the clutter of having six extra windows is reduced, tidying up the workspace while giving ready access to the commands and information in each.

1.14

To open a palette, you can simply click the tab, or click **Window** (see **Figure 1.15**) and select the palette you want to activate.

You can move a palette by clicking and dragging the tab to any portion of the active window. They can be separate or several may be docked together outside the Palette Well (see **Figure 1.16**). To dock two palettes together, simply click and drag the tab to overlay another palette.

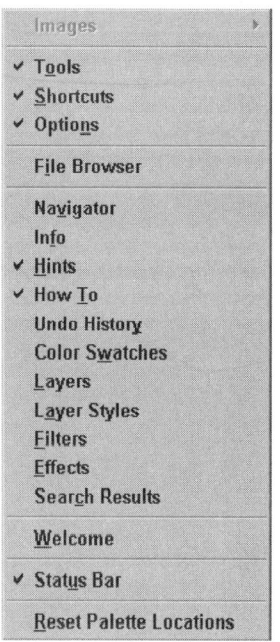

1.15

1.16

PALETTES AT YOUR DISPOSAL

■ **File Browser:** Enables you to locate a file quickly or peruse the images in a given folder.

■ **Navigator:** Allows for thumbnail viewing of large images. Includes a zoom feature.

■ **Info:** Tracks the dimensions, coordinates, transformation, and color value information of the image.

■ **Hints:** Quick tips about the Elements item selected with links to Help files.

■ **How To:** Wizards and tutorials (Recipes) for applying techniques.

■ **Undo History:** Allows you view previous steps applied to an image and delete steps that are unwanted.

■ **Color Swatches:** Load foreground and background colors from presaved color groups. Also allows for additional colors to be included in the swatch.

■ **Layers:** Allows you to view the layers with thumbnails, add and remove layers, select layers to activate them, and duplicate and link layers together. You may also change blending modes and alter opacity of a selected layer.

■ **Layer Styles:** Dynamic effects that can be applied to a layer with one click. These include Drop Shadow, Bevels, Overlays, and Glows.

■ **Filters:** Lists various filters for adding effect to a layer or cleaning up defects. Double-clicking the thumbnail of a filter applies it to the active layer.

■ **Effects:** Prerecorded effects that you can apply to your image. (Similar to Actions in Photoshop 6 and 7.)

■ **Search Results:** Another handy palette for viewing Help files.

Some palettes have corresponding palette menus, which include additional items, commands, and information associated with that palette (see **Figure 1.17**). Those with menus have an icon in the upper right corner of the palette. Clicking this icon opens the menu and allows you to choose additional items associated with the palette.

This section by no means tells you everything about the palette system and all that you can do with it. I cover more on palettes during the course of working through the book, so you will have a firm grasp on them by the time you turn the last page.

Keep in mind that, should you have any questions on tools, palettes, or performing certain functions in Elements, the Help files provided with the software are invaluable. With the Hints palette at your fingertips, you are only one or two clicks from some of the best technical support available.

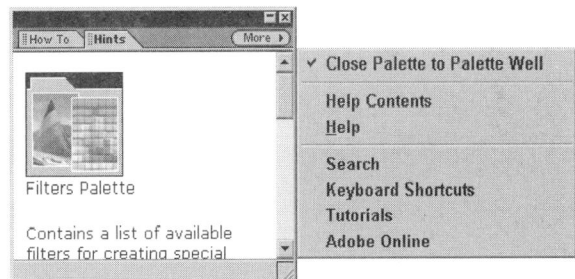

1.17

INTERFACING WITH ELEMENTS: KEYBOARD SHORTCUTS AND KEY COMBINATIONS

Time is a precious commodity. Adobe recognizes this and has followed the example of other software packages in giving their customers quick and easy shortcuts to apply specific tasks or activate tools.

Tables 1.1 through 1.8 are a helpful section in this book. You are likely to refer to them frequently.

TABLE 1.1   VIEWING SHORTCUTS (WINDOWS)

VIEWING SHORTCUT	DESCRIPTION
Double-click Hand tool or Ctrl+0 (zero)	Fits image on screen
Double-click Zoom tool, or Alt+Ctrl+0 (zero)	100% magnification
Ctrl+Plus key	Zooms in
Ctrl+Minus key	Zooms out
Ctrl+spacebar (zoom in) or Alt+spacebar (zoom out)	Selects Zoom tools
Shift+Enter in Navigator palette	Highlights the zoom percentage text
Ctrl+drag over preview in Navigator palette	Zooms in on specified area of an image
Spacebar+drag or drag view area box in Navigator palette	Scrolls image with Hand tool
Page Up or Page Down	Scrolls up or down one screen
Shift+Page Up or Page Down	Scrolls left or right one screen
Shift+Page Up or Page Down	Scrolls up or down 10 pixels
Shift+Ctrl+Page Up or Page Down	Scrolls left or right 10 pixels
Home or End	Moves view to upper-left corner or lower-right corner

TABLE 1.2   VIEWING SHORTCUTS (MAC OS)

VIEWING SHORTCUT	DESCRIPTION
Double-click Hand tool, or Command+0 (zero)	Fits image on screen
Double-click Zoom tool, or Option+ Command+0 (zero)	100% magnification
Command+Plus key	Zooms in
Command+Minus key	Zooms out
Command+spacebar or Option+spacebar	Select Zoom tools
Shift+Return in Navigator palette	Highlights the zoom percentage text
Command+drag over preview in Navigator palette	Zooms in on specified area of an image
Spacebar+drag or drag view area box in Navigator palette	Scrolls image with Hand tool
Page Up or Page Down	Scrolls up or down one screen
Command+Page Up or Page Down	Scrolls left or right one screen

VIEWING SHORTCUT	DESCRIPTION
Shift+Page Up or Page Down	Scrolls up or down 10 pixels
Shift+Command+Page Up or Page Down	Scrolls left or right 10 pixels
Home or End	Moves view to upper-left corner or lower-right corner

TABLE 1.3   SELECTING AND MOVING OBJECTS (WINDOWS)

SHORTCUT COMBINATIONS	DESCRIPTION
Any Marquee tool+spacebar+drag	Repositions marquee or shape while selecting or drawing
Any selection tool+Shift or Alt+drag	Adds to or subtracts from selection
Any selection tool+Shift+Alt+drag	Intersects a selection
Shift+drag	Constrains marquee or shape to square or circle
Alt+drag	Draws marquee or shape from center
Shift+Alt+drag	Constrains shape and draws marquee from center
Ctrl (except when Hand tool or any shape tool is selected)	Switch to Move tool
Alt+drag	Switches from Magnetic Lasso tool to Lasso tool
Alt+click	Switches from Magnetic Lasso tool to Polygon Lasso tool
Move tool+Alt+drag selection	Moves copy of selection or shape
Any selection+an arrow key (hold Shift key to move 10 pixels)	Moves selection area or shape 1 pixel
Move tool+an arrow key (hold Shift key to move 10 pixels)	Moves selection, shape, or layer 1 pixel
Ctrl+an arrow key (hold Shift key to move 10 pixels)	Moves layer 1 pixel when nothing selected on layer
Magnetic Lasso+[or]	Increases or decreases detection width
Crop tool+Enter or Esc	Accepts cropping or exits cropping

TABLE 1.4   SELECTING AND MOVING OBJECTS (MAC OS)

SHORTCUT COMBINATIONS	DESCRIPTION
Any Marquee tool+spacebar+drag	Repositions marquee or shape while selecting or drawing
Any Selection tool+Shift or Option+drag	Adds to or subtracts from selection
Any selection tool+Shift+Option+drag	Intersects a selection
Shift+drag	Constrains marquee or shape to square or circle
Option+drag	Draws marquee or shape from center
Shift+Option+drag	Constrains shape and draws marquee or shape from center
Command (except when Hand tool or any shape tool is selected)	Switch to Move tool
Option+drag	Switches from Magnetic Lasso tool to Lasso tool
Option+click	Switches from Magnetic Lasso tool to Polygon Lasso tool
Move tool+Option+drag selection	Moves copy of selection or shape
Any selection+an arrow key (hold Shift key to move 10 pixels)	Moves selection area 1 pixel
Move tool+an arrow key (hold Shift key to move 10 pixels)	Moves selection, shape, or layer 1 pixel
Command+an arrow key (hold Shift key to move 10 pixels)	Moves layer 1 pixel when nothing selected on layer
Magnetic Lasso tool+[or]	Increases or decreases detection width
Crop tool+Return or Esc	Accepts cropping or exits cropping

TABLE 1.5   PAINTING (WINDOWS)

KEYS	DESCRIPTION
Any painting tool/shape tool+Alt (except impressionist brush)	Switch to Eyedropper tool
Eyedropper tool+Alt+click	Selects background color
Any painting or editing tool+number keys (0 = 100%, 1 = 10%, 6 then 5 in quick succession = 65%)	Sets opacity, pressure, or exposure for painting mode
Shift+Plus/Minus keys	Cycles through blending modes
Alt+(Backspace or Delete), or Ctrl+(Backspace or Delete)	Fill selection/layer with foreground or background color
Shift+Backspace	Displays Fill dialog box
/	Lock transparent pixels on/off, or last applied lock
Any painting tool+Shift+click	Connects points with a straight line

TABLE 1.6   PAINTING (MAC OS)

KEYS	DESCRIPTION
Any painting tool or shape tool+Option (except impressionist brush)	Switch to Eyedropper tool
Eyedropper tool+Option+ click	Selects background color
Any painting or editing tool+number keys (0 = 100%, 1 = 10%, 6 then 5 in quick succession = 65%)	Sets opacity, pressure, or exposure for painting mode
Shift+Plus/Minus keys	Cycles through blending modes
Option+Delete, or Command+Delete	Fills selection/layer with foreground or background color
Shift+Delete	Displays Fill dialog box
/	Locks transparent pixels on/off, or last applied lock
Any painting tool+Shift+click	Connects points with a straight line

TABLE 1.7   TYPE EDITING (WINDOWS)

KEYS	DESCRIPTION
Ctrl+drag text when Type is selected	Moves text in image
Type tool or Type Selection tool+ Shift+Ctrl+L, C, or R	Aligns left, center, or right
Vertical Type tool or Vertical Type Selection tool+Shift+Ctrl+L, C, or R	Aligns top, center, or bottom
Shift+an arrow key, or Shift+Ctrl+Left/Right arrow key	Selects one character left/right, one line down/up, or one word left/right
Shift+click	Selects characters from insertion point to mouse click point
Left/Right arrow key, Up/Down arrow key, or Ctrl+Left/Right arrow key	Moves one character left/right, one line down/up, or one word left/right

KEYS	DESCRIPTION
Shift+click	Designates new origin over existing text
Double-click or triple-click	Selects word or line
Ctrl+H	Shows/Hides selection on selected text created with a Type Mask tool
Shift+Ctrl+U	Toggles Underlining on/off
Shift+Ctrl+/	Toggles Strikethrough on/off
Shift+Ctrl+< > (Hold down Alt to decrease/increase 10 times)	Decreases/increases font size of selected text 2 points/pixels.

TABLE 1.8   TYPE EDITING (MAC OS)

KEYS	DESCRIPTION
Command+drag text when type is selected	Moves text in image
Type tool or Type Mask tool+Shift+Command+L, C, or R	Aligns left, center, or right
Vertical Type tool or Vertical Type Mask tool+ Shift+ Command+L, C, or R	Aligns top, center, or bottom
Shift+an arrow key, or Shift+Command+Left/Right arrow key	Selects one character left/right, one line down/up, or one word left/right
Shift+click	Selects characters from insertion point to mouse click point
Left/Right arrow key, Up/Down arrow key, or Command+Left/Right arrow key	Moves one character left/right, one line down/up, or one word left/right
Shift+click	Designates new origin over existing text
Double-click or triple-click	Selects word or line
Command+H	Shows/Hides selection on selected text created with a Type Mask tool
Shift+Command+U	Toggles Underlining on/off
Shift+Command+/	Toggles Strikethrough on/off
Shift+Command+< > (Hold down Alt to decrease/increase 10 times)	Decreases/increases font size of selected text 2 points/pixels

Though not a chapter that dealt with special effects, this chapter is necessary in that, in order to work through the following tutorials, at least a cursory knowledge of tools, palettes, and shortcuts is required. Again, you may want to keep this chapter bookmarked, because the information here will definitely come into play later on.

So without further ado, create some Special Effects!

CHAPTER **2**

3D OBJECTS IN A 2D WORLD

From a digital artist's point of view, photorealism is creating a digital image on a computer that appears as though it could actually exist in the physical realm. To do this, you need to understand a few important aspects of what makes an object appear real. After you have this understanding, the approach to faux realism is quite a bit easier to grasp, and the results are far more satisfying than, say, trying to build a house without any knowledge of carpentry. Just as houses require foundations, digital designs also have a few foundational requirements.

For example, picture a yellow crescent shape in your mind. Now imagine a banana side by side with your yellow shape. What distinguishes the banana from the crescent? You may notice more variation in color in the banana. Is the banana in your mind not quite ripe yet? You may find a few green hues blending with the yellow. Has it aged a bit? Then some spots of black may be visible. Place the banana on a table. Do you see a shadow? If so, then there is a light source, so a portion of the banana's surface is a bit brighter than the rest. Also, the shadow appears on the opposite side of the fruit from the light source. The banana may also have some surface texture, an attribute that is more apparent with age. The crescent remains two-dimensional while the banana lies there ready to be peeled.

In this chapter, you create illusory three-dimensional surfaces and objects in a program whose roots are in two-dimensional image correction.

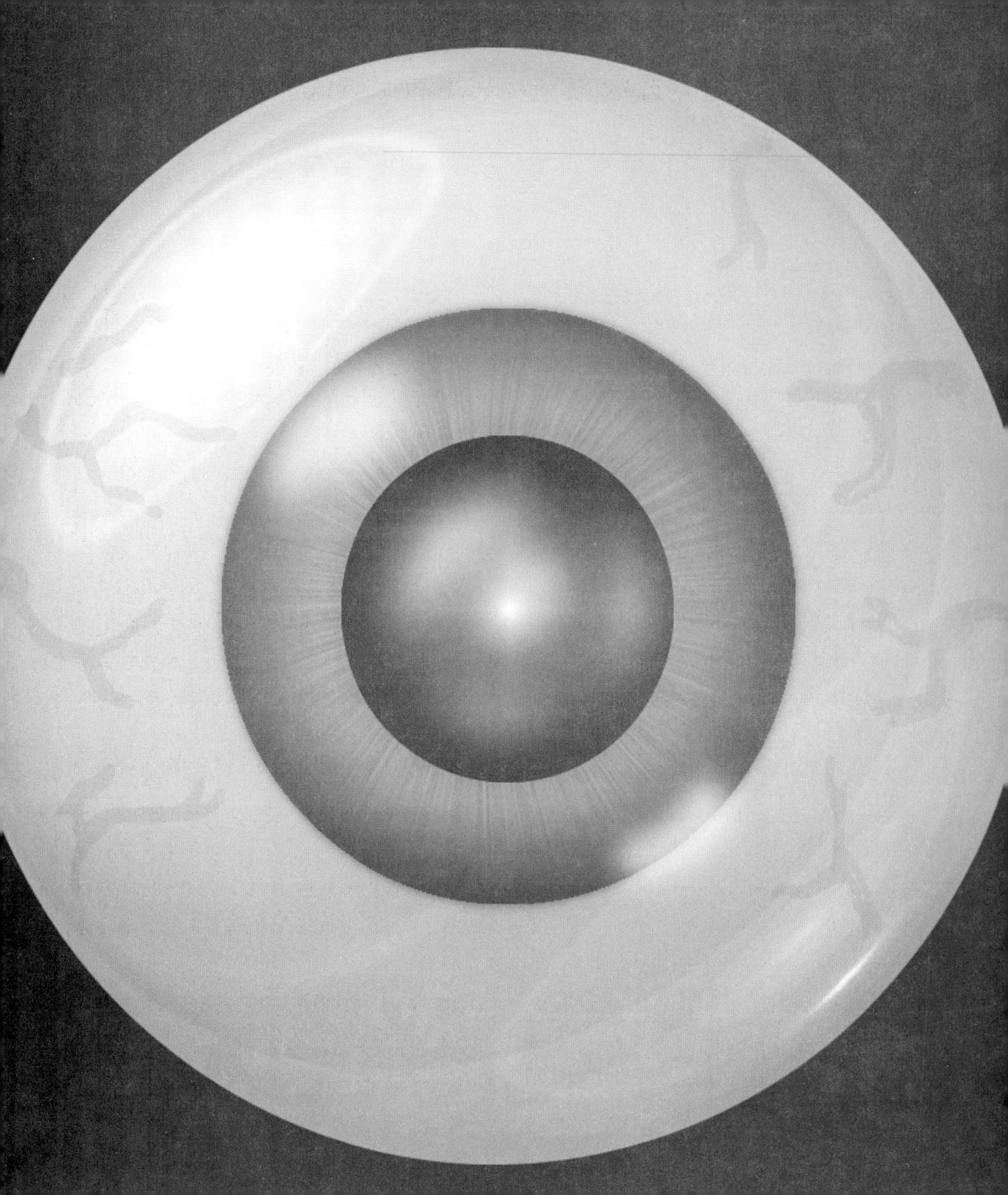

CREATING A POOL BALL

I n the first tutorial, I demonstrate how to create a basic real world object by transforming a simple circle into a billiard ball. These same techniques you'll use to apply depth can also be used to create fruit, ball bearings, a light bulb, and nearly any reflective sphere you can imagine.

STEP 1: PERFECT CIRCLE SELECTION

Prior to making a sphere, you need a circular selection. Using Elements, you can create perfect circles with just a few short clicks. Here is a short demonstration of the process.

- Create a new image by choosing **File ➢ New**. The New dialog box is shown in **Figure 2.1**. Click **OK**.
- In the Toolbox, select the **Elliptical Marquee** tool.
- In the Options bar, check the **Anti-aliased** check box. Click the arrow to the right of the Style box and choose **Fixed Aspect Ratio** from the menu that appears. Enter a **1** in both the Width and Height boxes.

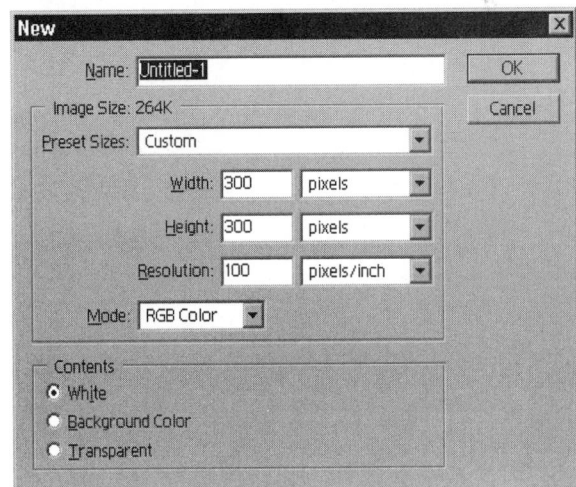

2.1

■ Starting in the upper-left corner, click and drag the mouse diagonally down to the right. When you finish, you have a selection that is perfectly round (see **Figure 2.2**).

STEP 2: OPEN THE BACKGROUND

Realism is the primary goal of any special effect. To achieve the greatness factor, the effect has to have

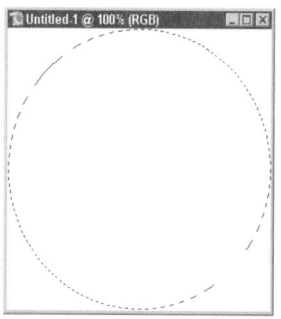

2.2

2.3

some attribute that gives it the illusion that it could exist in the real world.

For this tutorial, I created a pool table on which to set the object. You can find the pool table image on the CD-ROM. See **Figure 2.3**.

■ Chapter2-PoolTable.jpg
■ Open **Chapter2-PoolTable.jpg** in the Project Images folder on the CD-ROM.

STEP 3: CREATE THE SELECTION

The first step was merely practice. This step basically re-creates the circle selection you previously created, but this time, you are creating the object on the pool table canvas as opposed to a sterile background.

■ Click the **Create a New Layer** icon on the bottom of the Layers palette.
■ Click the **Elliptical Marquee** tool. In the Options bar, click the **Anti-aliased** check box and choose **Fixed Aspect Ratio** from the Style drop-down menu.
■ Draw your selection (see **Figure 2.4**).

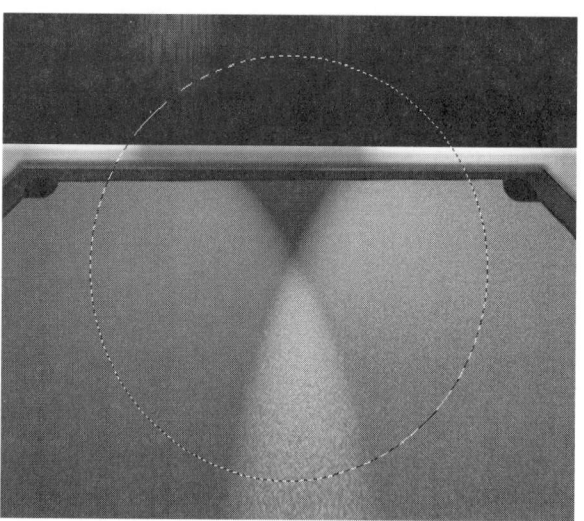

2.4

STEP 4: FILL THE CIRCLE WITH GRADIENT COLOR

- Click the **Gradient** tool in the Toolbox.
- Hold the mouse arrow over the Gradient window in the Options bar. A message appears, saying Click to edit the gradient. Click in the Gradient window. The Gradient Editor opens, as shown in **Figure 2.5**, displaying two main sections: Presets (those gradients that have been loaded into Elements already); and an editing area where you can create and save new gradients.

Note the color stops beneath the Gradient Editor bar. To change the color, double-click a stop. Doing so opens the Color Picker window. Simply select the color you want for the color stops (see **Figure 2.6**).

- Select a light orange, almost white color as the first in the gradient. Then select the stop at the far

end of the Gradient Editor and choose a deeper orange/yellow. After the colors are selected, you may want to name the gradient and save it for later use.
- Click **OK**.
- Select the **Radial** gradient in the Options bar. Check the **Reverse** checkbox. Starting in the upper-left quadrant of the selection, draw the gradient to the lower right of the selection. After the ball is filled, choose **Select ➢ Deselect** (see **Figure 2.7**).

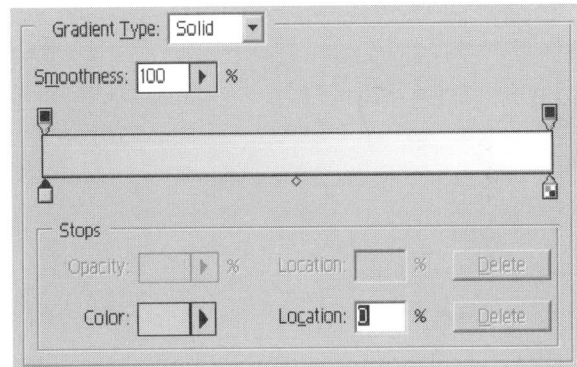

2.6

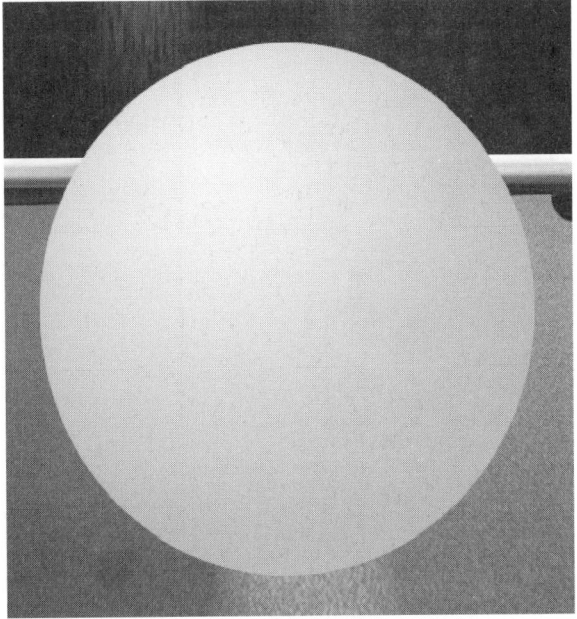

2.5

2.7

STEP 5: ADD THE NUMBER

- Create a new layer above the gradient layer.
- On the new layer, create a smaller circular selection centered over the original sphere and fill the selection with white, as shown in **Figure 2.8**.
- Create a new layer and deselect the active circle.
- Select the **Type** tool.
- Press the **D** key to reset your foreground and background colors to black and white, respectively.

- Type the number you want to affix to the pool ball into the new type layer. Make sure that you use a font size that fits within the white area but covers enough to be legible. In this example, the Verdana font set to 100 points seems to fit just right (see **Figures 2.9** and **2.10**).

STEP 6: APPLY THE NUMBER TO THE CURVED SURFACES

- In the Layers palette, hold the mouse pointer over the type layer and right-click. A menu appears with a few selections on it. Choose **Simplify Layer** from the menu.
- Choose **Layer ➢ Merge Layers** to combine the type with the white circle. Alternatively, you can simply use the shortcut keys. Press ⌘+**E** on a Mac or **Ctrl+E** on a PC to merge the selected layer with the one directly below it.

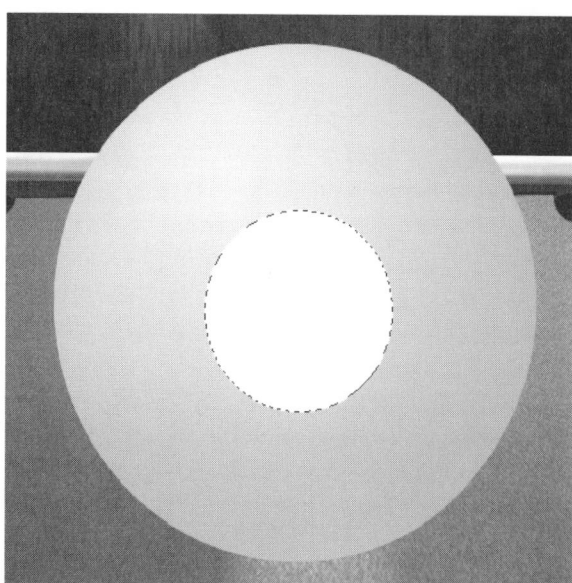

2.8

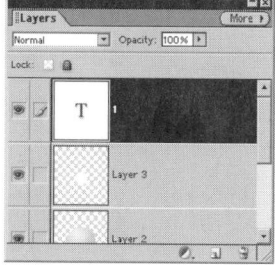

2.9

2.10

■ With your newly merged layer selected, choose **Filter** ➤ **Render** ➤ **3D Transform** (see **Figure 2.11**).

Transforming your type with the 3D Transform tool may be tricky the first few times you use it, especially if you are unfamiliar with the process.

When the 3D Transform dialog box appears:

■ Click the **Sphere** tool. (It is the second button down in the right column of buttons.)

■ With the mouse, click and drag from the upper left of the 3D Transform window to the lower right of the 3D Transform window, making a circle around the number in the viewer roughly the size of the sphere.

■ Select the **Trackball** tool. Click directly on the number in the viewer and drag it to the left. The number begins to warp, as though it is moving on the face of a sphere (see **Figure 2.12**).

■ After you have the number placed where you want it in the viewer, click **OK**. Your image now looks similar to **Figure 2.13**.

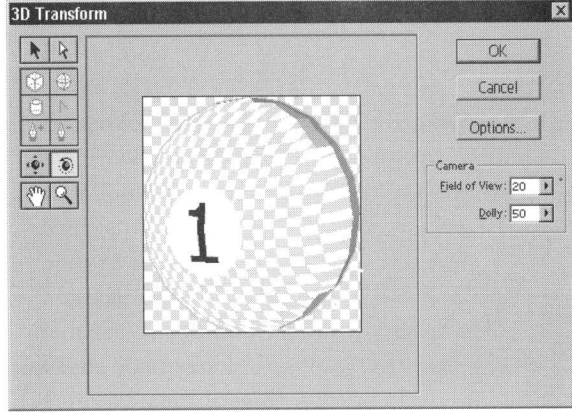

2.12

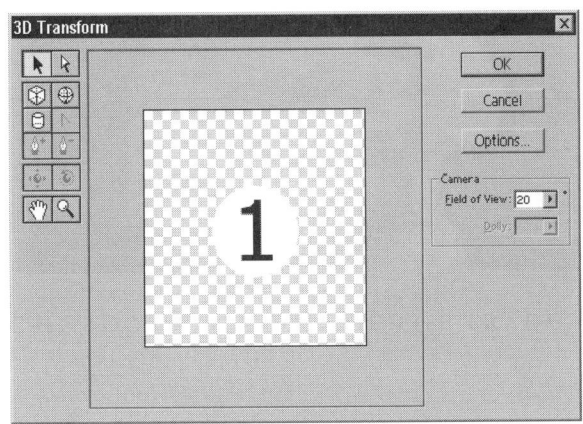

2.11

2.13

- In the Toolbox, click the **Eraser** tool.
- In the Options bar, set the mode to **Brush** and choose a feathered brush set to **100**. Erase the unwanted color left by the 3D transform from the number layer (see **Figure 2.14**).

STEP 7: ADD SHADOW

- Reactivate the spherical selection. You can do this by pressing ⌘+click (Mac) or by pressing **Ctrl**+click (PC) on the original sphere layer.
- Create a new layer, placing it just above the sphere layer and just below the number layer.
- In the Toolbox, click the foreground color. When the Color Picker opens, select a deep brown tone and click **OK.**

- Click the **Brush** tool.
- In the Options bar, select the **Airbrush**.
- For size and shape, select a feathered brush and set the size to **100** or so.
- Set the opacity to **60%**, because you want some of the original color to bleed through the paint.
- As soon as the brush is set up, you can start painting. Because the sphere was created with the primary light source coming from the upper left of the ball, you need to shade the right side and lower portion. Start painting along these areas of the selection but try not to stay in one area too long. Just lightly move the mouse around the right and lower perimeter when applying the paint (see **Figure 2.15**).

2.14

2.15

STEP 8: ADD HIGHLIGHTS

■ Select white as your foreground color and spray a bit in the upper-left region of the sphere where you started the first gradient, as shown in **Figure 2.16**. You need to add just a few highlights, so don't apply too liberally; a couple spot sprays should do.

■ Create a new layer just above the current layer. Spray a bit more liberally here in a somewhat circular motion following the contour of the ball. Do this in several spots, as shown in **Figure 2.17**.

■ Apply a Gaussian Blur by choosing **Filter ➢ Blur ➢ Gaussian Blur**. Use a setting of **24** pixels or so. Deselect the sphere.

STEP 9: ADD TABLE SHADOW

■ Press **D** to reset the default colors.

■ Create a new layer above the background layer.

■ Spray around the base of the ball in the new layer with the **Brush** tool settings used in Step 7, creating the shading and highlights shown in **Figure 2.18**.

■ Choose **Filter ➢ Blur ➢ Gaussian Blur** one more time to blur any deep areas in the shadow painting. Use a setting of **13** to **14**.

2.17

2.16

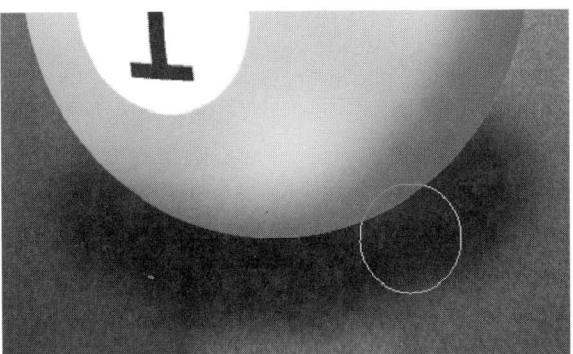

2.18

When you finish, your pool ball looks similar to **Figure 2.19 (CP3)**.

With a little imaginative use of filters, gradients, and airbrushing techniques, you can take a simple circle and make objects that have depth and character, almost as though they have a place in the 3D world.

2.19 (CP3)

CREATING AN EYEBALL

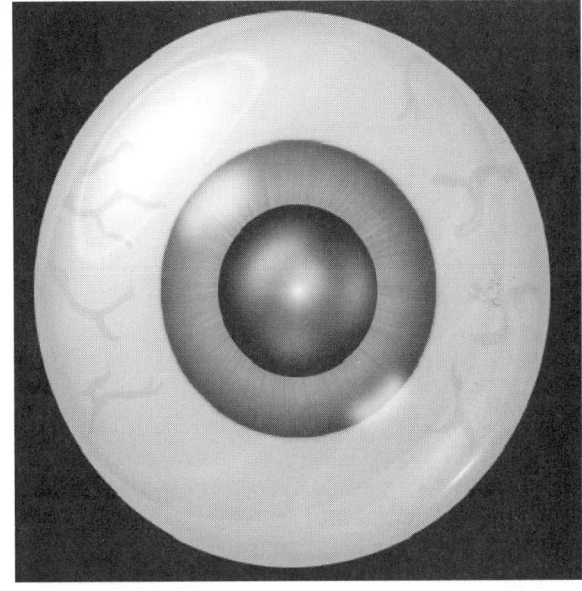

This tutorial takes a different approach to generating spheres than did the previous tutorial. Adobe Elements has filters that, when applied in the correct order, create near-perfect glossy spheres every time. This is an extremely cool effect, so please perform this section sitting down!

STEP 1: CREATE A NEW IMAGE

- Choose **File ➢ New**.
- Name the new file **Eyeball**.
- Set the dimensions of the new document to **8 x 8** inches; Resolution, **100** pixels per inch; **RGB**; **transparent**.
- Choose **Edit ➢ Fill** and then fill the new image with black at **100%** opacity.
- Depending on your screen resolution, you may want to set the zoom to **50%** to see the entire image.
- Duplicate the filled background layer. Name the new layer **Sphere**, as shown in **Figure 2.20**.

2.20

STEP 2: GENERATE THE SPHERE

- Choose **Filter** ➢ **Render** ➢ **Lens Flare**.
- Using the default location for the flare center, set the Flare Brightness to **120%**. Set the Lens Type to **50-300mm** Zoom. See **Figure 2.21**.
- Choose **Filter** ➢ **Distort** ➢ **Polar Coordinates**.
- Select **Polar to Rectangular**.
- Click **OK**.
- Choose **Image** ➢ **Rotate** ➢ **Flip Vertical**.
- Again, choose **Filter** ➢ **Distort** ➢ **Polar Coordinates**. Change the setting to **Rectangular to Polar**.

- Click **OK**. You should now have a glossy sphere that is nearly identical to the one in **Figure 2.22**.

This step is almost finished. Note that the sphere is still attached to a background. The background will need to be removed to proceed, so that the eye can be edited separately from the background.

- Select the **Elliptical Marquee** tool. In the Options bar, use the following settings:
  - Feather = **0**
  - Anti-aliased = **Checked**
  - Style = **Fixed Aspect Ratio**
  - Width and height = **1** for both
- Starting in the upper-left of the image, click and drag to the lower-right corner to create a selection. Doing this covers almost the entire sphere.
- Choose **Select** ➢ **Inverse**.
- Press the **Delete** key. You should now have a sphere independent of its background, as shown in **Figure 2.23**.

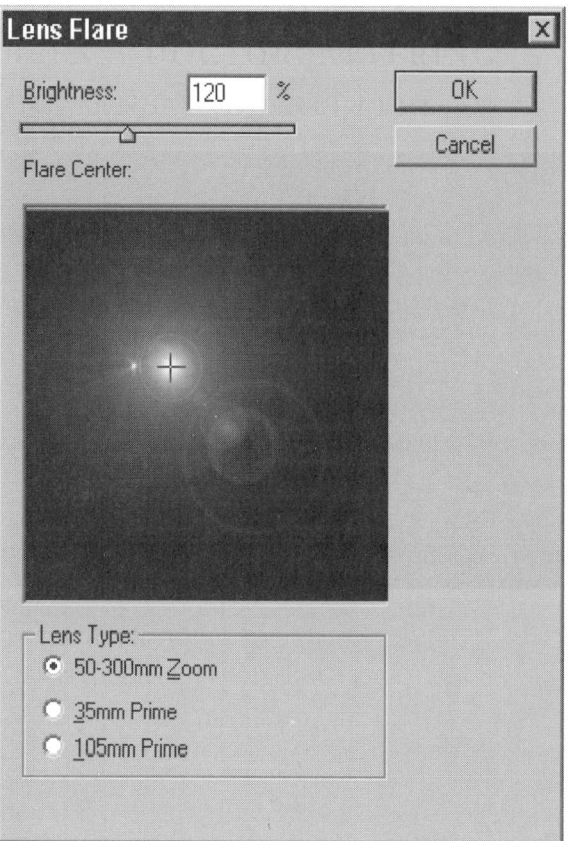

2.21

2.22

STEP 3: COLOR THE SCLERA

After the sphere is generated, you now have an excellent foundation for a wide variety of effects. Because this tutorial is based on the creation of an eyeball, the following steps focus on one variation to achieve that result. The sphere created in the steps above can have a wide variety of applications (crystal ball, snow globe, and so forth). Use your imagination!

Next, color the sclera, the white portion of the eye.

- Select the sphere by ⌘/**Ctrl**+clicking the sphere layer.
- Three icons are on the bottom of the Layers palette. Click the first one. As you hover the mouse over this icon, a message appears, saying Create new fill or adjustment layer. Click this icon and choose **Gradient** from the menu that appears.
- The Gradient Fill dialog box opens. Click within the gradient example to open the Gradient Editor.
- Create a new gradient. Set the color of the first color stop to #757474, or R = **117**, G = **116**, and B = **116**.

- Set the second color stop to white.
- Set the white stop's location to **40%**.
- Set an opacity stop to **40%** also, changing the opacity value to **75%**. The resulting gradient created by the editor is seen in **Figure 2.24**.
- You may want to name and save the gradient. If so, type in a name and click **New** to add this gradient to the loaded set.
- Click **OK**.
- In the Gradient Fill dialog box, enter the following settings:
  - Style = **Radial**
  - Angle = **90%**
  - Scale = **100%**
  - Reverse = **Checked**
  - Dither = **Unchecked**
  - Align with layer = **Checked**
- Click **OK**.

2.23

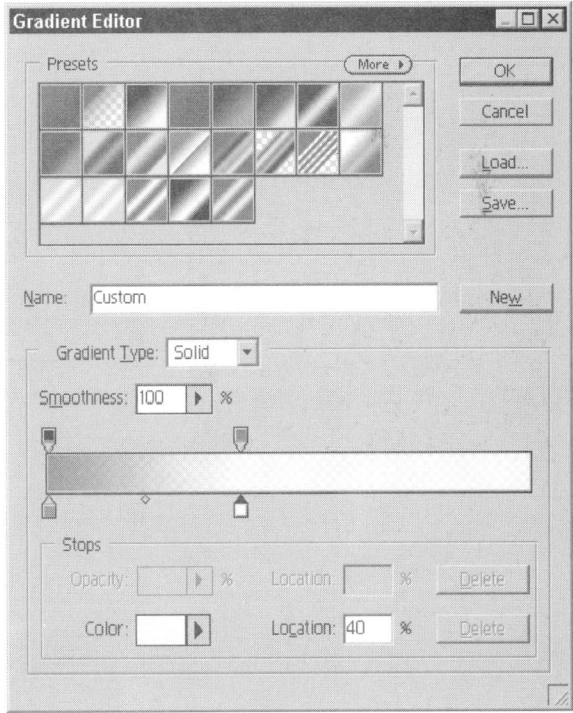

2.24

- Starting at the center of the sphere, draw the gradient outward to the edge of the sphere.
- In the Layers palette, set the blending mode of the gradient fill layer to **Screen**, and set the opacity to **95%**. See **Figure 2.25**.

STEP 4: CREATE THE IRIS

- Create a new layer above the gradient fill.
- Select the **Elliptical Marquee** tool in the Toolbox.
- In the Options bar, use the following settings:
  - Selection Type = **New Selection**
  - Feather = **0** (zero)
  - Anti-aliased = **Checked**
  - Style = **Fixed Aspect Ratio**
  - Width and Height = **1** for both
- Create new selection, roughly ½ the size of the original sphere. Center it on the image.

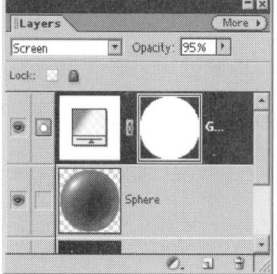

2.25

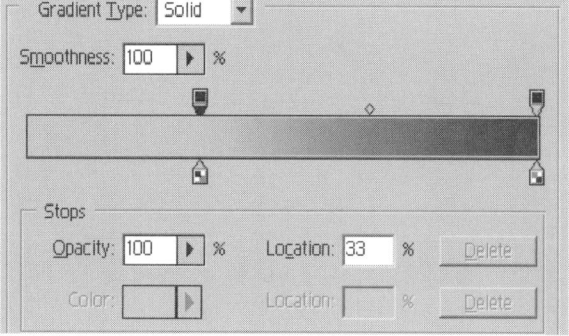

2.26

- In the Toolbox, click the **Gradient** tool.
- On the bottom of the Toolbox, click the background color. I'm partial to blue eyes, so that is what I'll be creating. Select a dark-blue color for the background color. In this example the color is **#1901AC**, or R = **25**, G = **1**, and B = **172**.
- Click **OK**.
- Click the foreground color. The setting for this example is **#7ED2FD**, or R = **126**, G = **210**, and B = **253**.
- Select the **Gradient** tool. In the Options bar, click in the Gradient window to open the Gradient Editor.
- Select the **Foreground to Background** gradient, usually found in the first position in the Presets. Uncheck the **Reverse** option.
- In the Gradient Editor, change the location of both the first color stop and the first opacity stop to **33%**, as shown in **Figure 2.26**.
- Starting in the center of the selection, draw the gradient to the outside of the selection to a point between the selection edge and the edge of the sphere. See **Figure 2.27**.
- Set the opacity for the iris layer to **90%**.

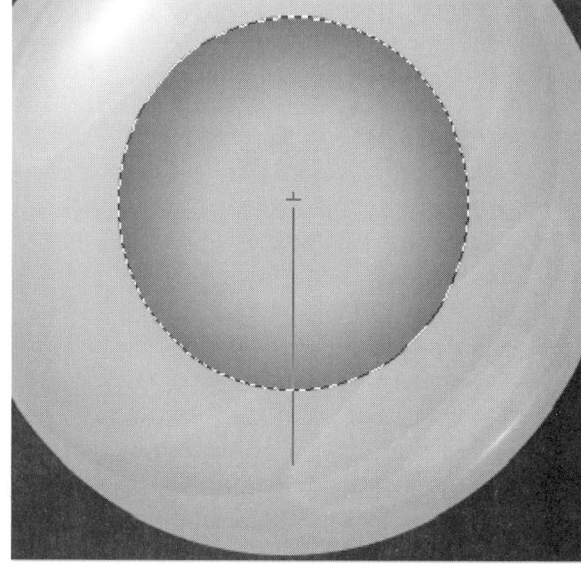

2.27

STEP 5: APPLY THE LENS

- Create a new layer above the iris layer.
- Again, create an elliptical selection with the settings used in the last step. Center this selection in the middle of the iris. The size should be about half that of the iris.
- Fill the selection with black.
- Create a new layer above the newly created lens.
- Select white as the foreground color. You may do this by pressing **D** (resetting the default colors) and pressing **X**. Doing so puts white in the foreground color box and black in the background.
- In the Toolbox, select the **Paintbrush** tool.
- In the Options bar, use the following settings:
  - **Soft Round Brush**
  - Brush Size = **35 pixels**
  - Mode = **Normal**
  - Opacity = **76%**
- Paint a few white areas over the lens. While painting, use semicircular, short strokes or simple spots of white, as shown in **Figure 2.28**. This step forms the basis of the reflections on the lens.
- Choose **Filter ➢ Blur ➢ Gaussian Blur**. Apply a blur setting of **7.8** pixels.
- Select the lens layer. In the Filter menu, choose **Artistic ➢ Plastic Wrap**. Enter the following settings:
  - Highlight Strength = **20**
  - Detail = **15**
  - Smoothness = **4**
- Click **OK**.

STEP 6: STREAK THE IRIS

- Create a new layer beneath the lens layer.
- Click the foreground color in the Toolbox. Enter a color value of **#18048E**, or R = **24**, G = **4**, and B = **142**.

2.28

- Check that you still have an active selection the same dimension as the lens. If not, ⌘/**Ctrl**+click the lens layer to make an active selection. You do not want to select the lens layer, however. Click the new layer beneath the lens layer.
- Choose **Edit ➢ Stroke**. Use these settings:
  - Width = **4 pixels**
  - Color = **Foreground** (this will be displayed automatically)
  - Location = **Center**
  - Mode = **Normal**
  - Opacity = **100%**
  - Preserve Transparency = **Unchecked**
- Click **OK**. Deselect.
- Choose **Filter ➢ Noise ➢ Add Noise**. Apply the following settings:
  - Amount = **180**
  - Distribution = **Uniform**
  - Monochromatic = **Checked**
- Now add some streaks. Choose **Filter ➢ Blur ➢ Radial Blur** and apply the following:
  - Amount = **100**
  - Blur Method = **Zoom**
  - Quality = **Best**

■ Apply the **Radial Blur** one more time, just as in the step above. Your image should now resemble **Figure 2.29**.

STEP 7: ADD COLOR AND HIGHLIGHTS

Staring at computer monitors for any given length of time inevitably causes eyestrain. It is a fact of this author's life, so add a bit of color reflecting that malady.

■ Select the gradient fill layer that you created in Step 3. Click the **Create a New Layer** icon on the bottom of the Layers palette.

■ ⌘/**Ctrl**+click the original sphere layer to generate a selection encompassing the entire eye. Check that your new layer is still active.

■ Click the foreground color box. In the Color Picker, select a dark red hue. In this example the color number is **#A20109**, or R = **162**, G = **1**, and B = **9**.

■ Select the **Brush** tool in the Toolbox. Set the following settings for the brush in the Options bar:
  ■ Brush Type = **Feathered, circular**
  ■ Brush Size = **100 pixels**
  ■ Mode = **Normal**
  ■ Opacity = **76%**

■ Spray around the perimeter of your selection so that the brush is bisected by the marching ants of the selection. Work your way around to form a red halo around the entire eye, as shown in **Figure 2.30**.

■ In the Layers palette, set the blending mode to **Overlay**. Change the opacity to **40%**.

■ Select the Sphere layer. Now that you've added a bit of reddish hue, the eye needs lightening. Choose **Enhance ➢ Quick Fix**.

■ In the Quick Fix dialog box, click **Brightness** in the Select Adjustment Category column.

■ In the Select Adjustment column, click **Brightness/Contrast**.

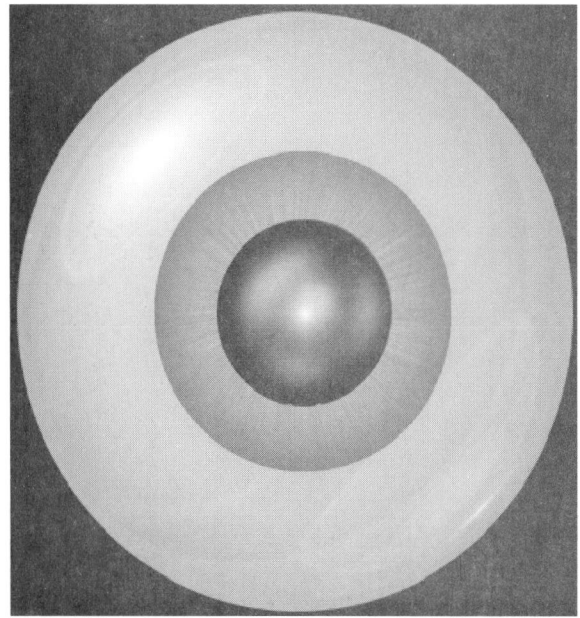

2.29

2.30

- In the Apply Brightness/Contrast column, set the brightness to **+40** and the contrast to **+10**. **Figure 2.31** shows the Quick Fix dialog box.
- Now, work on the iris. ⌘/**Ctrl**+click the iris layer to generate an iris-sized selection.
- Create a new layer above the iris layer.
- Select a dark blue foreground color. Any hue works, as long as it is darker than the gradient colors you originally used to fill the iris.
- Choose **Edit** ➢ **Stroke** and enter the following settings in the Stroke dialog box:
  - Stroke Width = **2**
  - Location = **Inside**
  - Blending Mode = **Normal**
  - Opacity = **100**
  - Preserve Transparency = **Unchecked**
- Click **OK**.
- Choose **Filter** ➢ **Blur** ➢ **Gaussian Blur**. Enter a blur radius of **2** pixels and click **OK**.

STEP 8: ADD CAPILLARIES

I mentioned eyestrain before, and there is no better indicator of such than an eye streaked with capillaries. For this last step, I show how to apply capillaries to the eye, adding to the realism.

- Set your foreground color to poignant red. For this example the color reference is **#FD0511**, or R = **253**, G = **5**, and B = **17**.
- Create a new layer at the top of the layer stack. Place this layer just above the lens highlights layer.
- Select the **Paintbrush** tool. In the Options bar, apply the following settings:
  - Brush = **Feathered, round**
  - Size = **40 pixels**
  - Mode = **Normal**
  - Opacity = **76%**
- Along the left and right halves of the sphere, paint a few warped, branching lines as shown in **Figure 2.32**.

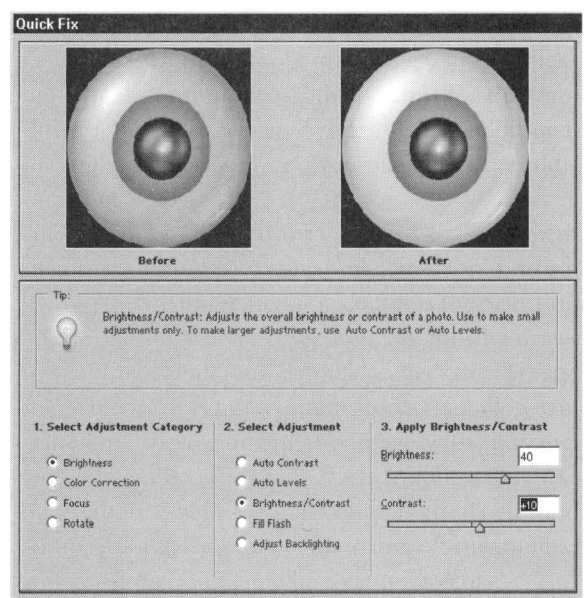

2.31

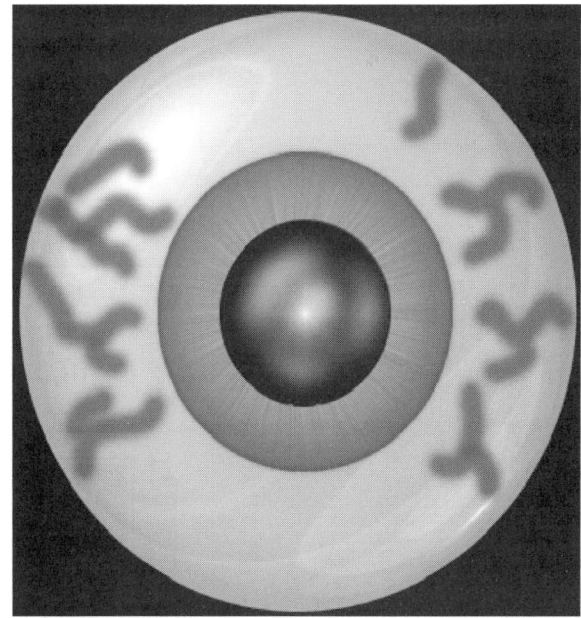

2.32

■ Select the **Burn** tool. In the Options bar, use the following settings:
  ■ Brush = **Feathered, round**
  ■ Size = **23 pixels**
  ■ Range = **Highlights**
  ■ Exposure = **50%**

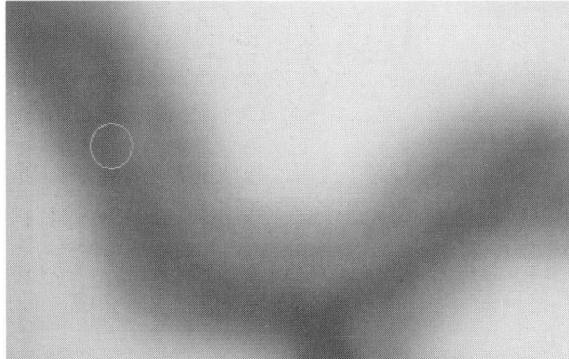

2.33

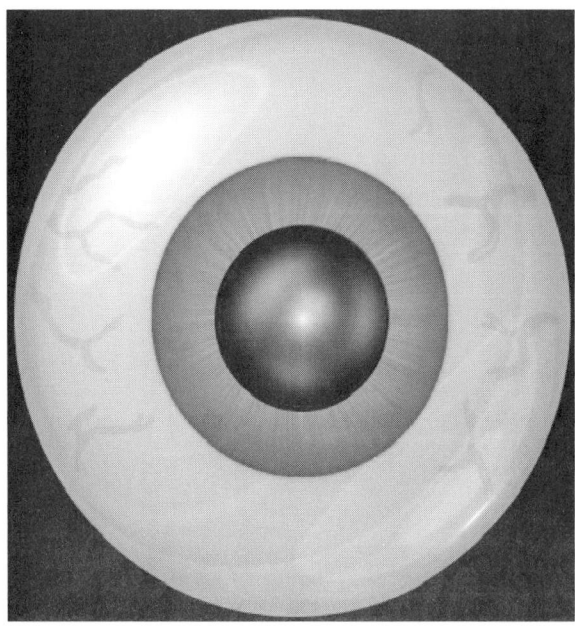

2.34

■ Select the **Zoom** tool and increase the view to **300%**.
■ Using the **Burn** tool, start tracing within the veins. Do not cover the entire swath of paint but rather trace trails through the red streaks (see **Figure 2.33**). You can view the other streaks by switching to the Move tool; click and drag the image. Trace trails through all of the paint swaths.
■ Select the **Magic Wand**. Holding down the **Shift** key, click the burned areas in all the veins to select them.
■ Choose **Select ➢ Inverse** and press the **Delete** key.
■ In the Layers palette, set the blending mode to **Color Burn** and the opacity of the layer to **10%**. See **Figure 2.34**.

STEP 9: FINISH UP

The eye is almost done. This last step brightens things up a bit and adds just a bit more realism.

■ ⌘/**Ctrl**+click the iris layer to bring up a selection.
■ Create a new layer just above the iris.
■ Choose **Select ➢ Feather** and feather the selection by **4** pixels.
■ Select a dark-blue background color and a light, almost turquoise color for the foreground color.
■ Select the **Gradient** tool. Set the Gradient Style to Radial. All other settings remain as they were in previous gradient applications in this tutorial.
■ Again, draw the gradient from the center of the selection to just outside the selection border, much as you did in Step 4.
■ In the Layers palette, set the blending mode to **Overlay**.

Figure 2.35 (CP4) shows the finished eye.

Though the process was a bit different in the beginning from the first tutorial, you were still able to create a glossy sphere with dimension. There is a lesson in this: there is no set way to achieve an end. With Elements, similar results can be achieved even if the approaches come from two starkly different directions.

You now have an understanding of spheres, so now try creating angular objects.

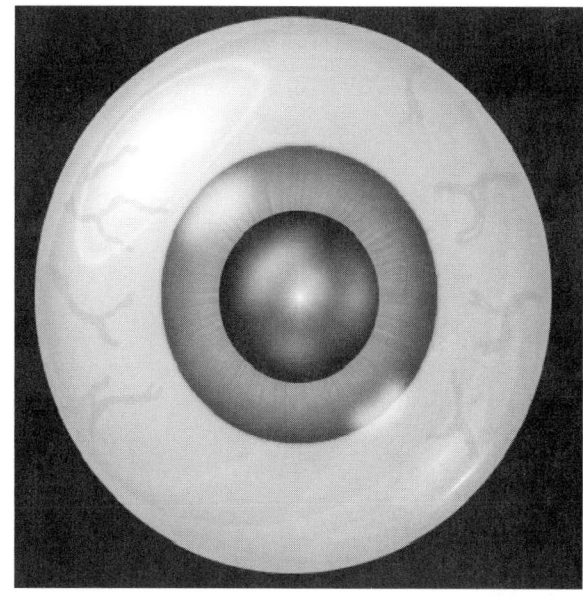

2.35 (CP4)

CREATING CUBES

D imension is more than an exercise in shape, shading, and light. Objects with distinct angles require a bit more than gradient application. This tutorial demonstrates that by applying perspective changes to shapes, piecing those shapes together, and adding shading, lighting, and texturing Elements can transform simple squares into three-dimensional cubes.

STEP 1: CREATE THE SIDES OF A BOX

- Create a new image. Use the following settings:
  - Name = **Cube**
  - Width = **9 inches**
  - Height = **6 inches**
  - Resolution = **100 pixels/inch**
  - Mode = **RGB Color**
  - Background = **White**
- On the Layers palette, click the **Create a New Layer** icon.
- Select the **Rectangular Marquee** tool. In the Options bar, enter the following settings:
  - Selection type = **New Selection**
  - Feather = **0** (zero)
  - Style = **Fixed Size**
  - Width = **3 inches**
  - Height = **3 inches**

When you click the image, a new selection appears with the dimensions set above. Note that the point where you click will represent the upper-left corner of the selection.

- Click to create your selection.
- Select your foreground color. For this example, I use a dark gray, with the color reference number **#616161**, or RGB values set to R = **97**, G = **97**, and B = **97**.

■ Choose **Edit** ➢ **Fill** and fill the selection with the foreground color.

■ Choose **Edit** ➢ **Deselect**.

■ Choose **Image** ➢ **Transform** ➢ **Skew**.

■ Click the top-left anchor point of the transform box that appears around the square. Move it vertically about a half to 1 inch. Repeat this step with the bottom-left anchor point. When you are done, both the W (width) and H (height) in the Options bar should read **100%**. See **Figure 2.36**.

■ In the Options bar, change the W (width) setting to **80%**.

■ Rename this layer **Side 1**.

■ Make a copy of the Side 1 layer and rename it **Side 2**.

■ With Side 2 active, choose **Image** ➢ **Rotate** ➢ **Flip Layer Horizontal**.

■ Select the **Move** tool.

■ To aid in keeping the two layers even horizontally, move Side 2 to the right using the arrow keys. Holding **Shift** while you move the layer increases the amount of movement per keystroke to 5 pixels. Move the layer so that both sides join to form a corner of the cube by holding down the **Shift** key and dragging with the **Move** tool. See **Figure 2.37**.

■ Create a new layer at the top of the stack. Name this layer **Top**.

■ Again, select the **Rectangular Marquee** tool.

■ You are going to create a top that is a lighter shade than the sides, just to help keep track of placement. Click the foreground color on the Toolbox to open the Color Picker. The color used in this example is **#C1C1C0**, or RGB values of R = **193**, G = **193**, and B = **192**.

2.36

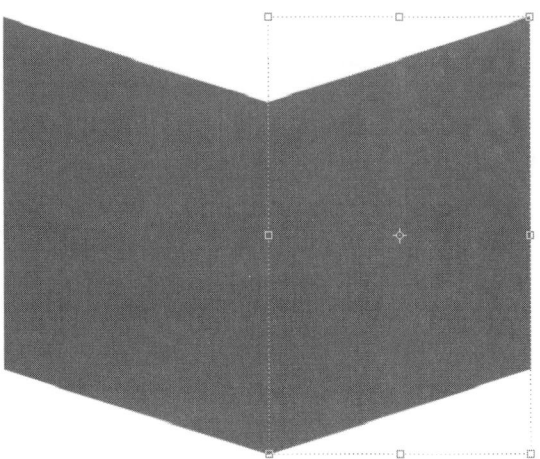

2.37

- Select the **Rectangular Marquee** tool. Maintain the settings used in the previous tutorial and create a new rectangular setting in the Top layer.
- Fill the selection with the foreground color. Your image should now resemble **Figure 2.38**.
- Choose **Image** ➢ **Rotate** ➢ **Free Transform Selection**. In the Angle box on the Options bar, enter **45**. The layer rotates so that the corners are pointing up, down, left, and right.
- Choose **Image** ➢ **Transform** ➢ **Distort**. Move the top and bottom points closer together, until the bottom point meets the junction of the top where the two sides come together. Move the left and right points outward so that they meet the top outside corners of each side.
- When aligned as in **Figure 2.39**, click **OK**.

After you are satisfied with the dimensions of your cube, save the file in .psd format, retaining the layers. The following steps show how to apply texture to the sides of the cube, and saving a copy of the cube will save a lot of time if you have need to develop more later.

STEP 2: TEXTURE THE CUBE

Now that you have a cube, what can you use it for? Several things, actually. Photographs can be fitted to each side, creating a photo cube. With a bit of texturing, the cube can take on a cardboard appearance. For this tutorial, I take my inspiration from another source. On occasion, I shut down my graphics programs and open a guilty pleasure — Unreal Tournament. If you are familiar with the game, then you have seen the 3D world the character interacts with. Using a seamless wood texture I've created, you can make a crate that appears as though it exists in that world.

2.38

2.39

- Open **Crate_Texture.jpg**, found on the CD-ROM. See **Figure 2.40**.
- Press ⌘/**Ctrl+A** to generate a selection of the entire texture.
- Press ⌘/**Ctrl+C** to copy the texture.
- Minimize the texture document and go back to the cube image.

- Create a new layer at the top of the layer stack.
- Press ⌘/**Ctrl+V** to paste the copied texture into the new layer (see **Figure 2.41**).
- Following the steps done previously to create the first side of the box, use the transform tools to shape the texture to match the dimensions of the first side. Use the Side 1 layer as a guide and overlay Side 1 with the texture. See **Figure 2.42**.
- Follow the cube creation steps to finish texturing Side 2 and the top.

The concept here is similar to the idea 3D modelers use: First, a structure is created and then a skin is applied to the shell. Because you saved the original cube, learning to use that model as a guide to applying textures saves a lot of time, should you decide to create cubes with other skins.

STEP 3: TRIM THE CRATE

The texture applied to the crate needs a bit of work to make it fit into the 3D world. The next step is to add contours to the distinct edges.

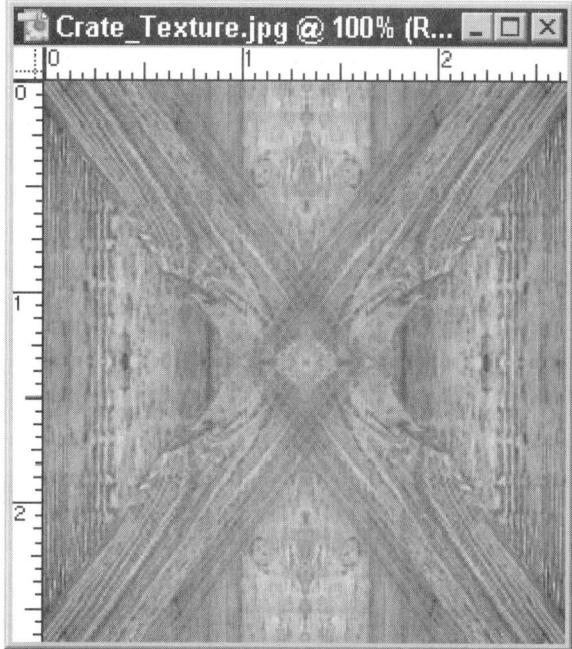

2.40

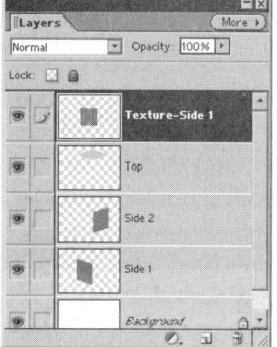

2.41

2.42

■ Select the background layer. Fill the background with black. Choose **Edit** ➢ **Fill** ➢ **Black**, with opacity set to **100%**.

■ Press **L** to select the **Polygonal Lasso** tool.

Take notice of the crossbeams on the crate sides. As they appear now, the edges don't display a third dimension. The texture appears as though it is wallpaper thin. To fix that, some trimming needs be done around the perimeter of the box where the slats stand out from the rest of the wood.

■ In the Options bar, set the selection type to **New Selection**, Feather Radius to **0** (zero), and check **Anti-alias**.

■ Starting with the left side of the crate, select a narrow portion of the edge between the crossbeams, as shown in Figure **2.43**.

■ Delete the selection from the corresponding texture layer.

■ You may also delete the selection from the Side 1 layer. However, you may just want to click the small eye next to the Side 1 layer in the palette, rendering the layer invisible. Then, if you need to rework the project later, the original cube will still be present.

■ Repeat the above step around the perimeter of the crate.

When you have completed the trimming process, the difference will be subtle but in this case subtle is good. The little adjustments such as this add a dimension of realism often overlooked by new designers. See **Figure 2.44**.

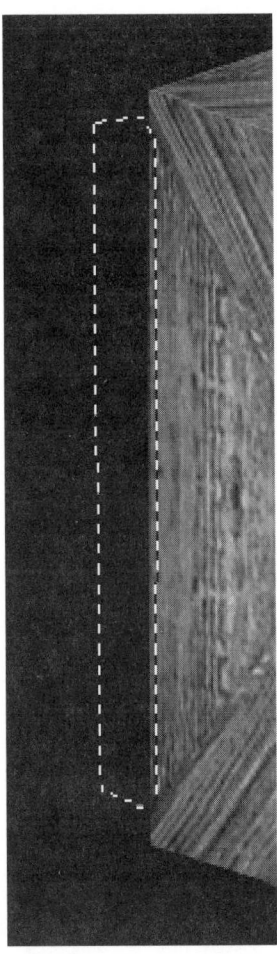

2.43

2.44

STEP 4: BURN DETAILS AND HIGHLIGHTS

- Select the **Burn** tool from the Toolbox.
- Use the following settings for the Burn tool in the Options bar:
  - Brush Type = **Feathered, round**
  - Brush Size = **13 pixels** (this will be adjusted as needed)
  - Range = **Highlights**
  - Exposure = **40%**
- Select the topmost texture layer.
- Press ⌘/**Ctrl+Shift+R** to merge it with the right-side texture layer beneath it. Repeat this step to merge with the left-side texture. All three texture layers should now be combined into a single layer, while the original cube side layers are untouched.
- Name the newly merged layer All Sides Merged, Crate, or something similar to distinguish it from the rest of the layers.

- Select the crate layer.
- Click and drag the mouse over any area where shadows should appear, or where you feel darker spots should appear opposite where light hits the crate. The edges of the cross beams should be darkened, as should areas where pieces of the crate fit together. **Figure 2.45** gives an example of areas where the Burn tool should be applied. You may need to increase or decrease the size of the brush as you burn to fit all the nooks, crannies, and edges.

When done, you can choose **Image ➢ Transform ➢ Distort** to shrink the height, dress up the image with a background, or apply text to the side, as shown in **Figure 2.46 (CP5)**.

If you want to see the completed .psd file for this project, including the layers, you can find it on the CD-ROM.

2.45

2.46 (CP5)

FASHIONING TUBES

T hus far you have seen Elements create spheres and cubes, but what about cylinders? This tutorial walks you through one way to create an object with both rectangular and round attributes.

STEP 1: TUBES TAKING SHAPE

- Create a new image named **Tubes**. Set the dimensions as follows:
    - Width = **9 inches**
    - Height = **6 inches**
    - Resolution = **100 dpi**
    - Color Mode = **RGB**
    - Contents = **Transparent**
- Select a color for the background. I prefer not to use white (personal taste), so I set the background color on this example to a light gray, **#C2C1C0**, or RGB values of R = **194**, G = **193**, and B = **192**.
- Fill the background with the color.
- Create a new layer by clicking the **Create a New Layer** icon on the bottom of the Layers palette.

■ Select the **Rectangular Marquee** tool in the Toolbox. Set the following options for the tool in the Options bar:

- ■ Selection Type = **New Selection**
- ■ Feather = **0 pixels**
- ■ Style = **Normal**

2.47

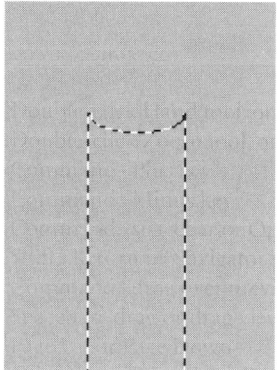

2.48

■ Draw a rectangular selection that is about 1 x 5 inches. The bottom edge of the selection should rest on the bottom of the image boundary, as shown in **Figure 2.47**.

■ Select the **Circular Marquee** tool. In the Options bar, click the **Subtract from Selection** icon.

■ At the top of the rectangular selection, make a small oval selection that overlaps the top of the rectangular selection. This subtracts a portion of the tube, which helps with the illusion that the tube is round when you fill it with a gradient. See **Figure 2.48**.

■ Click the **Gradient** tool. In the Options bar, click the **Gradient Picker** arrow. From the Gradient menu, load the **Tubes-Metal** gradient set from the CD-ROM. From this set, select the **Tube Gradient**.

■ In the Options bar, enter the following settings:

- ■ Gradient Type = **Linear Gradient**
- ■ Mode = **Normal**
- ■ Opacity = **100%**

■ Starting from the left of the selection to the right, fill the selection with the Tubes gradient. See **Figure 2.49**.

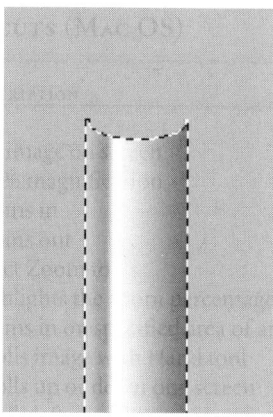

2.49

- Select the **Elliptical Marquee** tool again, changing the style to **New Selection**.
- Draw a selection at the top of the tube. Make it the same size as the previous elliptical selection. See **Figure 2.50**.
- Select a dark gray foreground color.
- Choose **Edit ➤ Stroke**. Apply a stroke to the selection, 2 pixels wide, centered.
- Click **OK**.
- Select the **Gradient** tool again. Click the first gradient in the Tubes-Metal set. Set the Gradient options as follows:
    - Gradient Style = **Linear Gradient**
    - Mode = **Normal**
    - Opacity = **100%**
- Starting from the left side of the selection to the right, fill with the gradient. See **Figure 2.51**.
- Choose **Select ➤ Deselect (⌘/Ctrl+D)**.

STEP 2: REALISM VIA GRADIENT ADJUSTMENTS

- ⌘/**Ctrl**+click the tube layer to make an active selection of the tube.
- On the bottom of the Layers palette, click the **Create a New Fill or Adjustment Layer** icon.
- Choose **Gradient** from the menu.
- When the Gradient Fill dialog box appears, open the **Gradient** menu (the small arrow to the right of the gradient viewer) and choose **Reset Gradients** from the menu.
- In the Gradient picker, click the **Copper Gradient**. Adjust the settings as follows: (see **Figure 2.52**)
    - Style = **Linear**
    - Angle = **0**
    - Reverse = **Unchecked**
    - Dither = **Unchecked**
    - Align with Layer = **Checked**

- Click **OK**.
- Choose **Select ➤ Deselect**.

Now you have a copper tube, complete with metallic reflection. You may duplicate the tube layer and move the copy but be sure to duplicate the gradient fill layer also and move it to overlay the new tube.

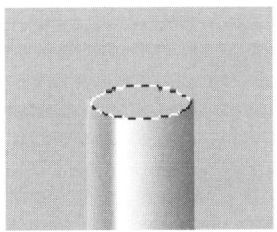

2.50

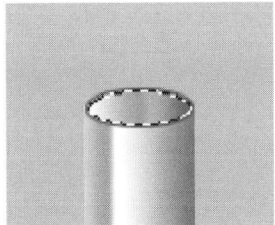

2.51

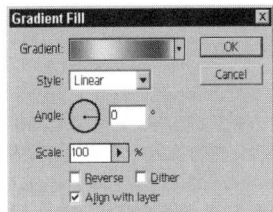

2.52

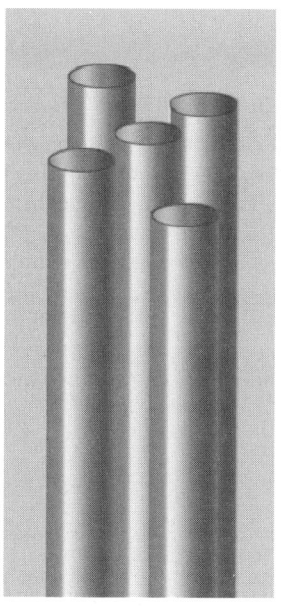

2.53

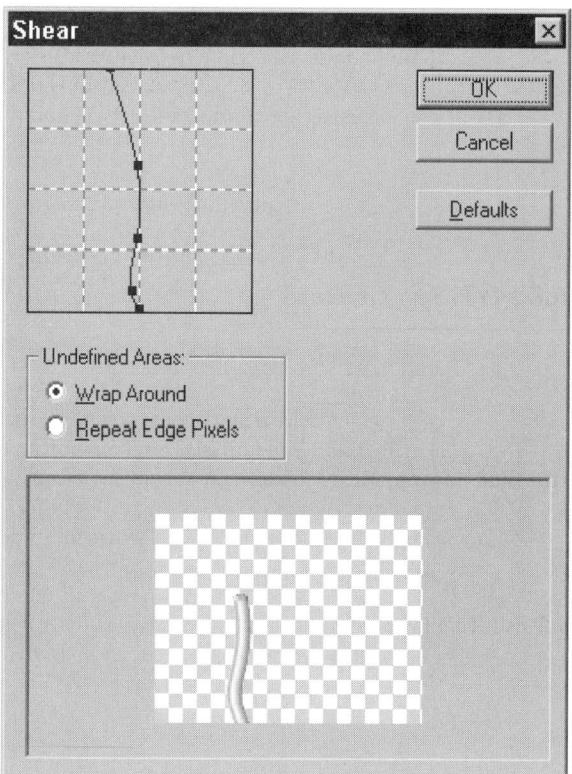

2.54

Figure 2.53 shows several copies of the tube placed at varying heights.

STEP 3: WARP A TUBE

For this last step, I demonstrate one way to warp a tube, giving it a slight curve to stand out from its peers.

- Select the tube layer you would like to warp. I am selecting one of the foreground tubes in this example.
- Choose **Filter ➢ Distort ➢ Wave**.
- Select **Shear** from the Wave menu.
- In the Shear dialog box, add a couple points to the vertical editor, moving the points slightly off center, as shown in **Figure 2.54**. Do not move the bottommost point. Observe the Preview window. It shows how much warp is being applied to the tube. When satisfied, click **OK**.

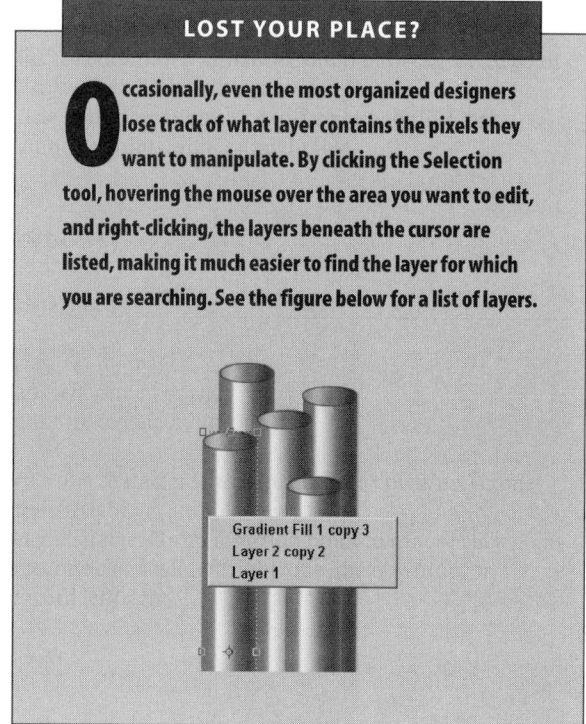

LOST YOUR PLACE?

Occasionally, even the most organized designers lose track of what layer contains the pixels they want to manipulate. By clicking the Selection tool, hovering the mouse over the area you want to edit, and right-clicking, the layers beneath the cursor are listed, making it much easier to find the layer for which you are searching. See the figure below for a list of layers.

- Select the **Gradient Fill** layer that directly overlays the tube you warped.
- Choose **Filter** ➢ **Distort** ➢ **Wave** ➢ **Shear**.
The same settings you just applied are still active,
so click **OK**. You may also press ⌘/**Ctrl+F** to
re-apply the previous filter settings to the
selected layer.

You may now apply a drop shadow to the tubes, add
a background, and so forth. See **Figure 2.55**.

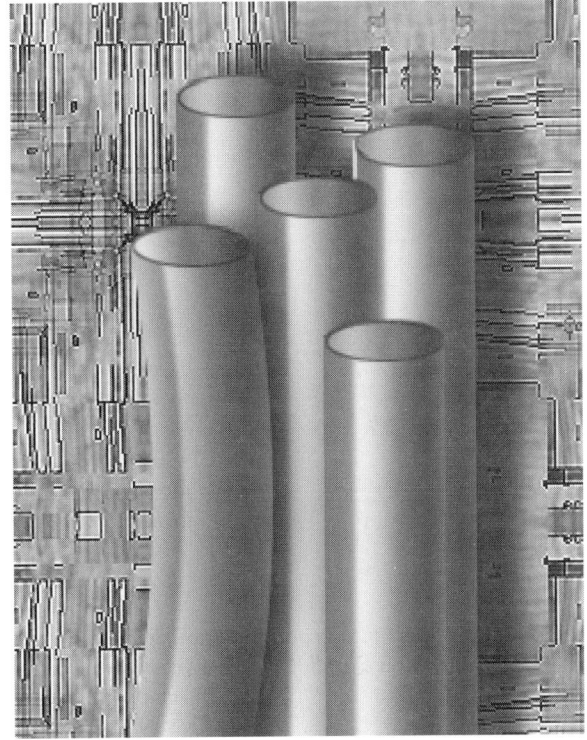

2.55

BUILDING A PYRAMID

The construction of the pyramid demonstrated in this tutorial is similar to the cube-crate built in Tutorial 3. The primary difference is the approach used. In the cube tutorial, I approached the creation of the initial squares using a fixed-sized selection. In this tutorial, I demonstrate using a shape.

In this tutorial you get hands-on experience using the Shape tool. Though a bit different from filling selections (shapes use vector rather than raster data), the result can be similarly dynamic. A bit of practice is all you need, so jump right in.

STEP 1: CONSTRUCT THE SIDES

- Create a new image with the following settings:
  - Name the image **Pyramid**
  - Width = **9 inches**
  - Height = **6 inches**
  - Resolution = **100 dpi**
  - Mode = **RGB**
  - Contents = **Transparent**
- Click the **Create a New Layer** icon on the bottom of the Layers palette. Name this layer **Side 1**.

- Click the **Shape** tool in the Toolbox.
- In the Options bar, enter the following settings:
  - Shape tool type = **Polygon** tool
  - Sides = **3**
  - **Create New Shape Layer** icon selected
  - Layer Style = **None**
  - Color = **Foreground or dark gray**
- To help lay out the sides of the pyramid, choose **View ➢ Grid**.

- Using the visible grid as a guide, draw and rotate a large triangle so that the base is flat against a gridline. See **Figure 2.56**.
- Choose **Image ➢ Transform ➢ Distort**.

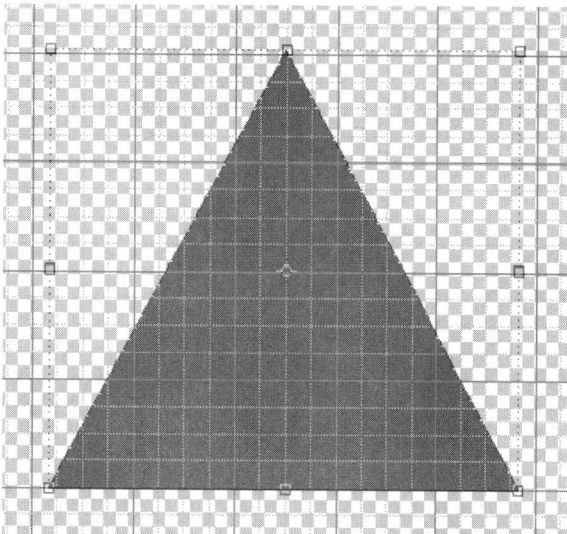

2.56

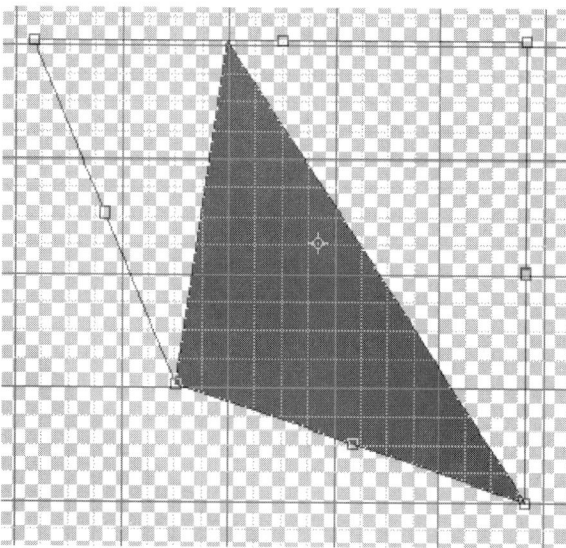

2.57

- Click and drag the lower-right corner of the triangle up one grid division and toward the center, as shown in **Figure 2.57**.
- Click and drag the top-center anchor point and drag to the right until the right side is vertical, as demonstrated in **Figure 2.58**. Click the **Apply Change** icon.
- Duplicate the Side 1 layer. Name this layer **Side 2**.
- Choose **Image ➢ Rotate ➢ Flip Layer Horizontal**.
- Click the **Move** tool. Slide Side 2 into place, so that the two shape layers meet along their vertical sides. See **Figure 2.59**.

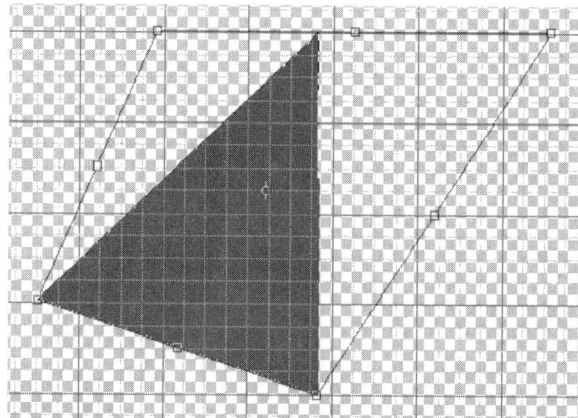

2.58

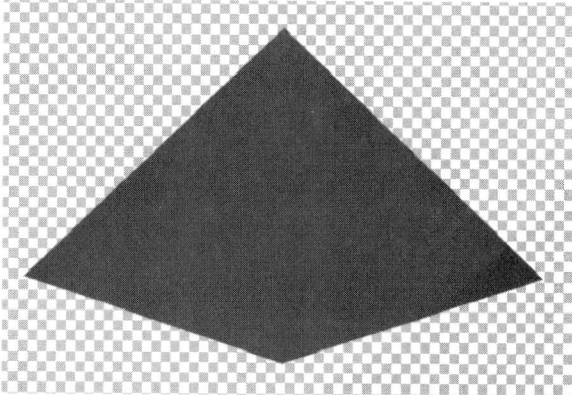

2.59

I recommend that, as with the cube, you save this image as a .psd file now. You may then texture it later, or use it as a model for other pyramid designs.

STEP 2: APPLY A STONE TEXTURE

■ Open the image **Stone_Texture-1.jpg**, found on the CD-ROM.

■ Press ⌘/**Ctrl+A** to select the texture image.

■ Press ⌘/**Ctrl+C** to copy the image. See **Figure 2.60**.

■ Minimize the texture image and go back to the pyramid.

■ Press ⌘/**Ctrl+V** to paste the texture into a new layer.

■ Select **Image** ➢ **Transform** ➢ **Distort** to reshape the triangle and fit the texture to Side 1 of the pyramid.

■ Repeat the process for Side 2 by copying the texture layer, flipping it, and moving it into place over the second side. See **Figure 2.61**.

■ Due to the transform process, the pixels appear stretched on the lower portion of the pyramid sides. This is an excellent example of when to use the Clone tool. Select the **Clone** tool.

■ Sample the stone pattern close to the top of the pyramid. To collect a sample, Alt+click the area you want to copy.

■ In the Options bar, make sure that Aligned is unchecked.

■ ⌘/**Ctrl**+click the first texture side to select it. Stamp the sampled pattern into the selection, covering the blurred areas.

■ Repeat the process for the texture covering Side 2.

■ If you need to, select the **Polygonal Lasso** and make a small triangular point at the top of the pyramid. In a new layer, fill this selection with the sampled pattern. See **Figure 2.62**.

■ Almost done! Select the first texture layer. Choose **Enhance** ➢ **Adjust Brightness/Contrast** ➢ **Brightness** ➢ **Contrast.** Set the Brightness to **−30** and the contrast to **+30**.

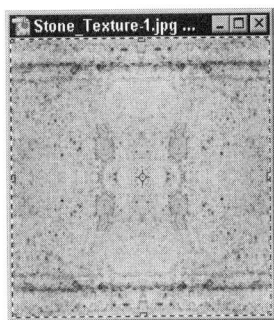

2.60

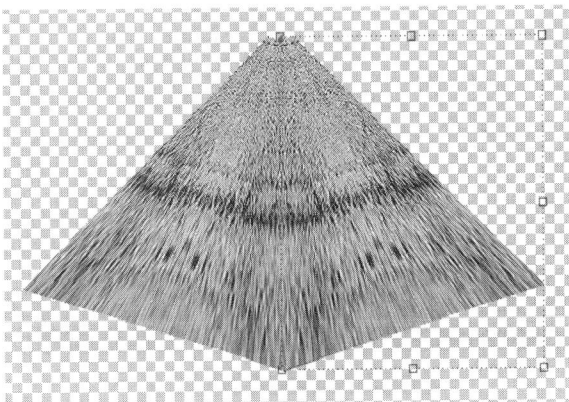

2.61

2.62

2.63

You now have a stylish sandstone pyramid. Try embedding text into the sides for a logo or even placing it in your own desert. See **Figure 2.63**.

You now have some basics on shaping objects in Elements. Some of the techniques are quick and easy and some a bit more in depth, but the approaches are designed to get you used to working with a variety of tools and to not be intimidated by experimentation. You started with the analogy of a toolbox and knowing the tools. I hope that above all else you are getting to know your way around the tools in Elements. A firm grasp of tools and settings will serve you well through the rest of the book and beyond.

CHAPTER 3

UNNATURALLY NATURAL ELEMENTS

I f Chapter 2 is an exercise in manipulating shapes, Chapter 3 is an exercise in creating textures to apply to shapes. You are not, however, done with using shapes. Now that you have a few ideas on how to create objects with more than two dimensions, I can focus on how to actually create textures. The tutorials continue to give hands-on experience on creating objects, texturing objects, lighting, shadowing, and more.

Adobe Elements enables you to manipulate color pixels in such a way as to have the appearance of wood, water, or stone. Chapter 3 demonstrates a few approaches to creating natural-looking images.

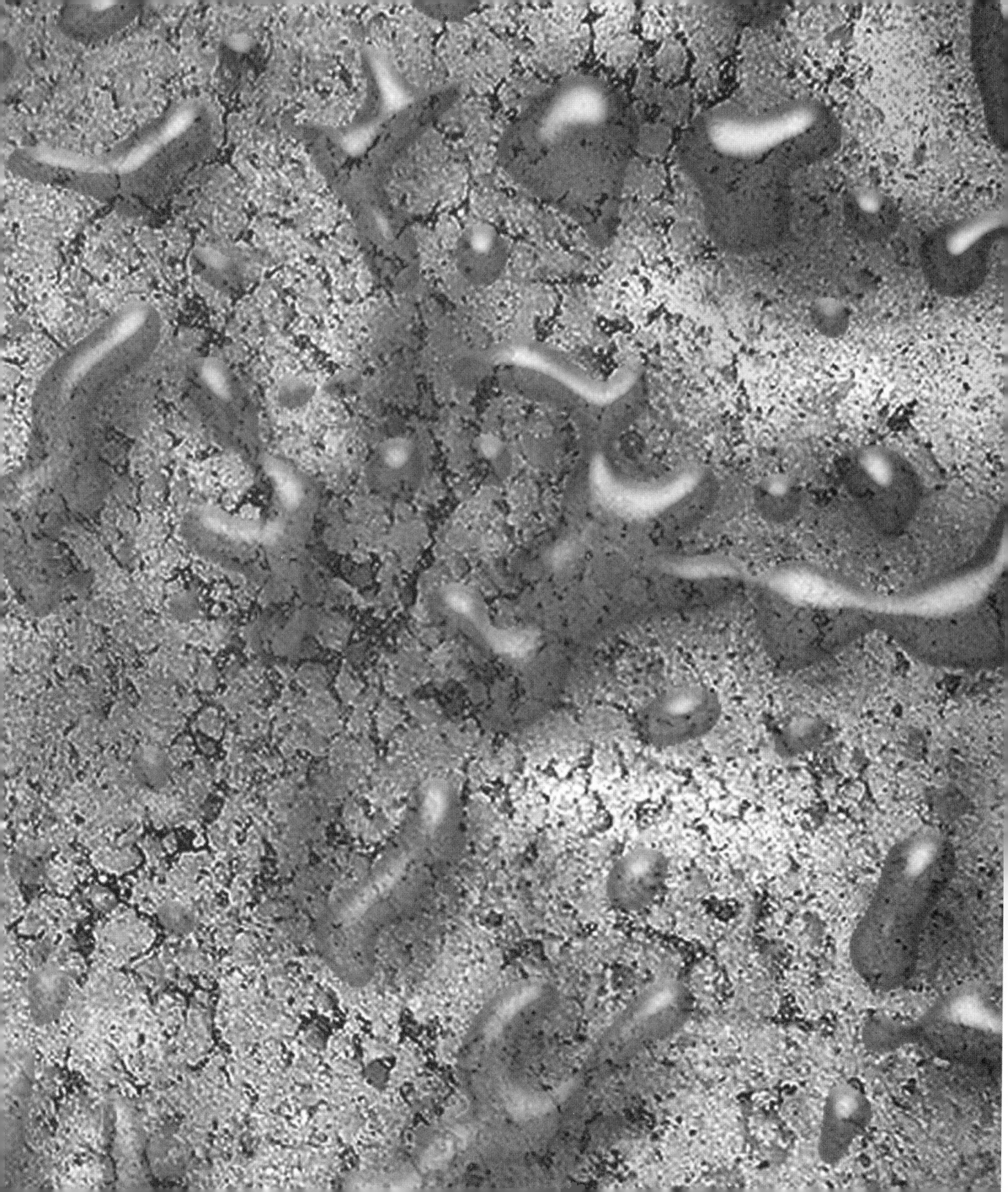

6

PHOTO-REALISTIC WATER DROPS

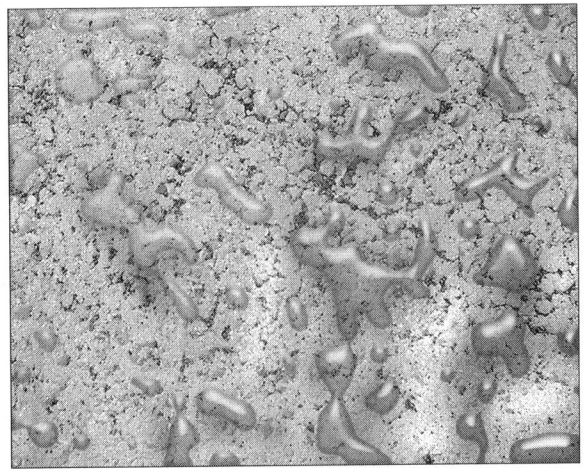

T his tutorial requires the following from the CD-ROM:

- Concrete-01.jpg
- AFXBevels-1.asl layer styles set

This style set must be loaded into Elements prior to starting this tutorial. Please refer to Appendix B for layer style set installation instructions.

STEP 1: SET UP THE IMAGE

- Open image **Concrete-01.jpg** (see **Figure 3.1**) from the CD-ROM.
- Click the **Create a New Layer** icon on the bottom of the Layers palette.

STEP 2: ISOLATE DROPS

- Select **Edit** ➢ **Fill**. The Fill dialog box opens. Fill the new layer with white at **100%** opacity.
- Choose **Filter** ➢ **Noise** ➢ **Add Noise**. Select the following settings:
    - Amount = **400%**
    - Distribution = **Gaussian**
    - Monochromatic = **Checked**
- Click **OK**.

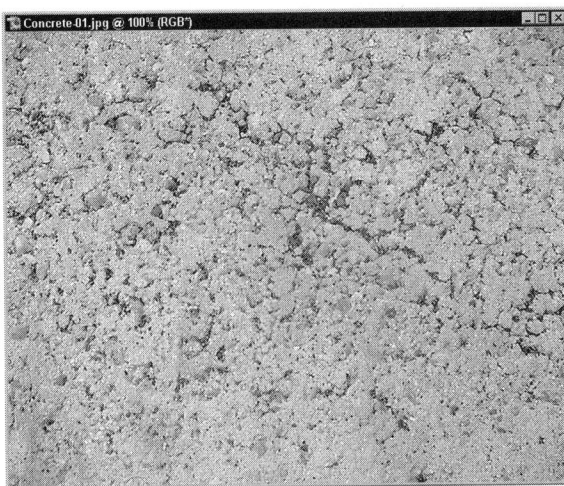

3.1

- Choose **Filter** ➤ **Blur** ➤ **Gaussian Blur**. Enter a blur radius of **3** pixels.
- Choose **Image** ➤ **Adjustments** ➤ **Threshold**. In the Threshold dialog box, move the **Threshold Level** slider to the right until a black-and-white Holstein pattern forms in the layer. See **Figure 3.2**.
- Click **OK**.
- Press ⌘**/Ctrl+F** to reapply the Gaussian Blur filter.
- Again, choose **Image** ➤ **Adjustments** ➤ **Threshold**. Again, move the slider until a black-and-white Holstein pattern appears. The white areas should be larger this time.
- Click **OK**. See **Figure 3.3**.
- Select the **Magic Wand** tool. In the Options bar, make sure that Contiguous is unchecked.
- The majority of the layer should be black, with large white spots scattered about. Select the black areas with the **Magic Wand**.
- Press **Delete**.
- Choose **Select** ➤ **Inverse** (**Shift+⌘/Ctrl+I**) to select the white spots.
- Again, press **Delete**.

- You now have several rounded selections across the entire layer.
- Press **D** to reset the foreground/background colors. Change the white background color to black.
- Select the **Gradient** tool from the Toolbox.
- In the Options bar, click in the Gradient Picker window to open the Gradient Editor.
- Select the **Foreground to Background Gradient** from the Gradient Picker in the upper window of the Gradient dialog box.
- Click the **Opacity Stop** on the left side of the Gradient Editor. Set the opacity to **70%**.
- Click the **Opacity Stop** on the right side of the Gradient Editor. Set the opacity to **25%**.
- Click **OK**.
- Check the **Reverse** checkbox in the Gradient Options bar.
- Starting in the upper-left corner, draw the gradient across the entire image to the lower-right corner. All of the selected areas now contain gradual color information, giving the appearance of **Figure 3.4**.

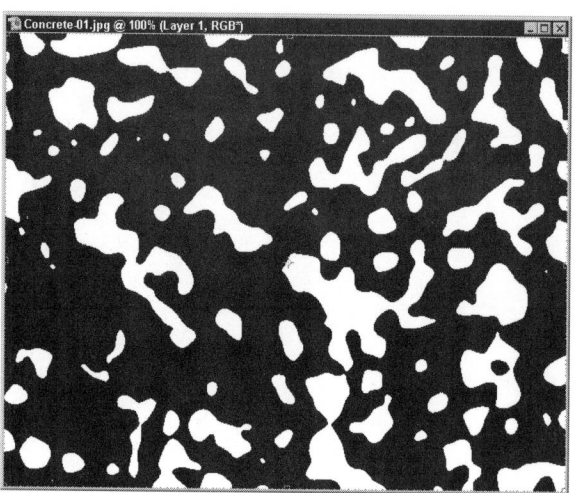

3.2

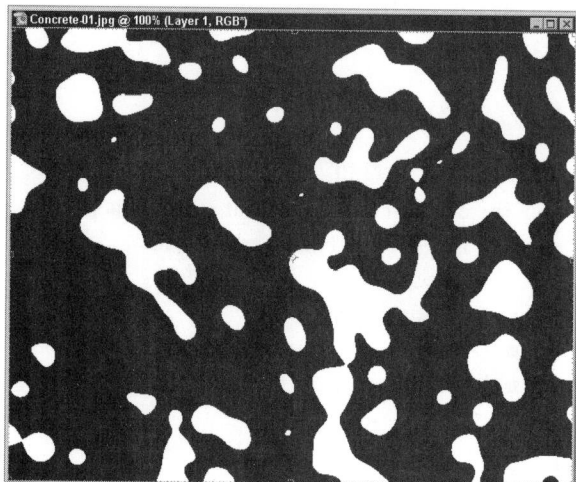

3.3

STEP 3: ADD BEVELING AND LIGHTING

■ If you followed the process of loading Layer Styles into Elements as directed, then the layer style set AFXBevels-1 should be in your Layer Styles palette menu. Click the **Layer Styles** palette tab. Click the drop-down arrow at the top, next to the active style viewer window. From the menu, select **AFXBevels-1**. Doing this loads the style set into the Styles palette.

■ Click the **Style 4** icon.

■ Click the **Create a New Layer** icon on the bottom of the Layers palette.

■ With the selection still active, select the new layer. Set black as the foreground color (**D**). Choose **Edit ➤ Stroke** and enter the following settings in the Stroke dialog box:

- ■ Width = **4 pixels**
- ■ Color = **Black**
- ■ Location = **Inside**
- ■ Blending Mode = **Normal**
- ■ Opacity = **60%**
- ■ Preserve Transparency = **Unchecked**

■ Click **OK**. See **Figure 3.5**.

■ Create a new layer.

■ Choose **Edit ➤ Fill**. Enter the following in the Fill dialog box:

- ■ Fill Type = **Color**
- ■ Fill Color = **White**
- ■ Opacity = **100%**

■ Click **OK**. See **Figure 3.6**.

■ Set the layer blending mode to **Soft Light** in the Layers palette.

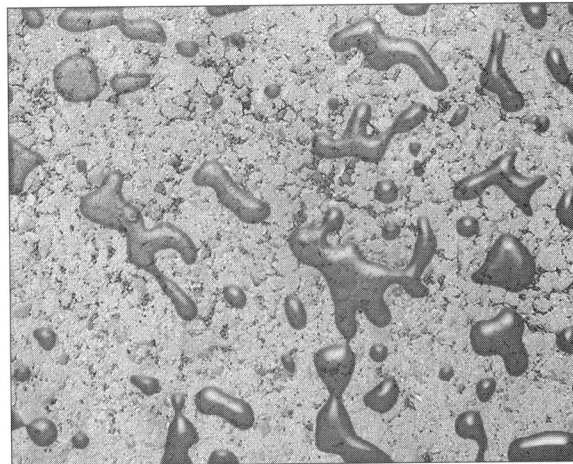

3.5

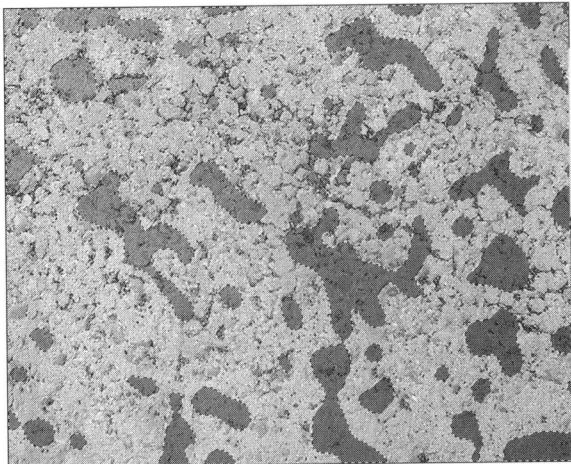

3.4

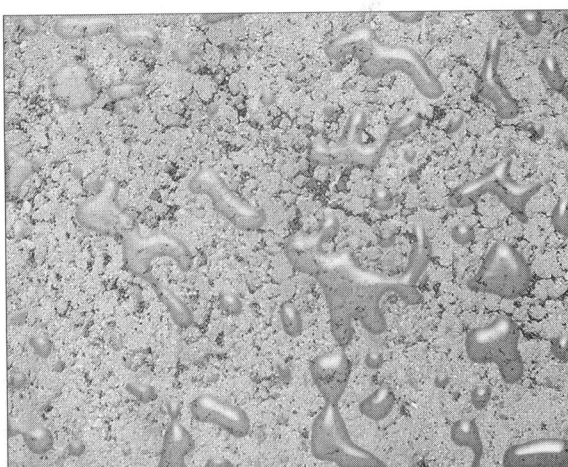

3.6

STEP 4: FURTHER ENHANCEMENTS: DAMPENING AND SHADING

■ Click the original layer containing the concrete photo.

■ Select the **Dodge** tool from the Toolbox. Set the options as follows:

- ■ Brush set = **Default Brushes**
- ■ Brush type = **Round, Soft**
- ■ Size = **65**
- ■ Range = **Highlights**
- ■ Exposure = **50%**

■ Apply the **Dodge** tool to the areas between the spots, as shown in **Figure 3.7**. Do not stray too close to the spots but lighten the areas halfway between a few of the water areas. Use this tool sparingly — just a few lightened areas will do.

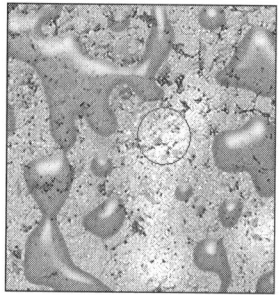

3.7

■ Click the **Burn** tool in the Toolbox. Set the following attributes for the tool in the Options bar:

- ■ Brush type = **Round, Soft**
- ■ Size = **47**
- ■ Range = **Highlights**
- ■ Exposure = **40%**

■ Apply the **Burn** tool to the areas beneath and around the edges of the water spots. Doing so gives the concrete the appearance of being damp. See **Figure 3.8**.

Someone had best get a mop!

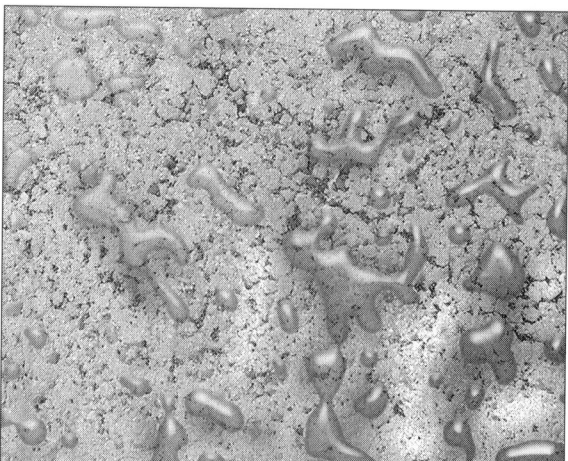

3.8

LIQUID TYPE

T his tutorial requires the following from the CD-ROM:

- Concrete-02.jpg
- Water-Seamless-1.jpg
- AFXBevels-1 layer styles set
- Ripple-map.psd

This style set must be loaded into Elements prior to starting this tutorial. Please refer to Appendix B for layer style set installation instructions.

This tutorial is an offshoot — with a twist — of the previous one. Not only can you use Elements to produce realistic water drops splattered on a surface, but you can also force that water to spell out messages.

STEP 1: SET UP THE IMAGE

- Find and open the image **Concrete-02.jpg**. See **Figure 3.9**.
- Click the **Create a New Layer** icon on the bottom of the Layers palette.

3.9

STEP 2: ENTER TYPE AND ADD SPOTS

- Select the **Type Mask** tool from the Toolbox. Enter the following settings in the Options bar:
  - Font Style = **Bold**
  - Font = **Times New Roman** (or any other font)
  - Size = **250 points**
  - Anti-aliased = **on**
  - Justify = **Center**
- Type your text in the new layer.
- Choose **Edit ➤ Fill**. Choose black as your fill color set at **100%**.
- Click **OK**.
- Choose **Select ➤ Deselect** (⌘**/Ctrl+D**).
- Select the **Paintbrush** tool from the Toolbox. Enter the following settings in the Options bar:
  - Brush Type = **Round, Hard**
  - Brush Size = **24 pixels**
  - Mode = **Normal**
  - Opacity = **100%**
  - Airbrush = **Selected**
- Press **D** to set black as the foreground color.
- Paint a few spots around the text, as shown in **Figure 3.10**.

STEP 3: ADD WATER COLOR

- Minimize the current image.
- Open **Water-Seamless-1.jpg**, found on the CD-ROM.
- Next, ⌘**/Ctrl**+click the image in the Layers palette to select the entire image as in **Figure 3.11**.
- Choose **Edit ➤ Define Pattern**.
- When the Pattern Name dialog box opens, click **OK**.
- Go back to the image with your text.
- Next, ⌘**/Ctrl**+click the type layer to create a selection. Make sure that the type layer is selected.
- Choose **Edit ➤ Fill** and choose **Pattern** as the fill type. Click the pattern you just defined and then click **OK**. See **Figure 3.12**.
- Create a new layer.
- Change your foreground color to a blue-gray. For this example, the color settings are **#6D95A6**, or R = **109**, G = **149**, and B = **166**.
- Stroke the selection twice. First, choose **Edit ➤ Stroke**.
  - Width = **4 pixels**
  - Location = **Center**
  - Mode = **Normal**
  - Opacity = **60%**

3.10

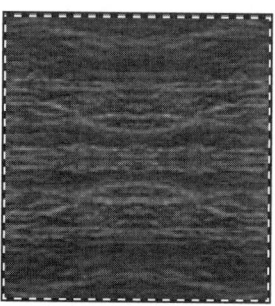

3.11

- Click **OK**.
- Now apply a second stroke with the following settings:
    - Width = **4 pixels**
    - Location = **Inside**
    - Mode = **Normal**
    - Opacity = **100%**
- Click **OK**.
- With the selection still active, choose **Filter ➤ Blur ➤ Gaussian Blur**. Enter a blur radius of **3** to **4** pixels and click **OK**.
- In the Layers palette, set the blending mode for the stroked layer to **Color Dodge** at **100%** opacity.
- Create a new layer.
- Choose **Select ➤ Modify ➤ Contract** and enter a value of **10**.
- You should still have the same blue-gray color in the foreground. Choose **Edit ➤ Fill ➤ Foreground Color** with opacity set to **100%**.

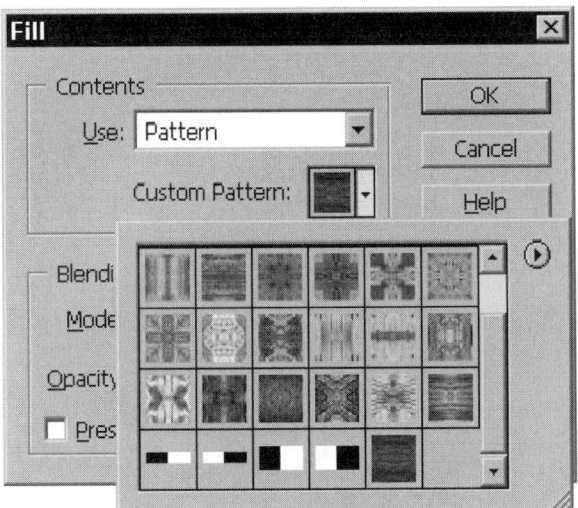

3.12

- Click **OK**.
- Choose **Select ➤ Deselect (⌘/Ctrl+D)**.
- Choose **Filter ➤ Blur ➤ Gaussian Blur**. Enter a blur radius of **8** to **9** pixels.
- Click **OK**.
- Set the blending mode for this layer to **Screen**. See **Figure 3.13**.

STEP 4: APPLY DEPTH, BEVEL, AND WARP

- Select the original text layer.
- If you followed the process of loading layer styles into Elements as directed, then the layer style set AFXBevels-1 should be in your Layer Styles palette menu. Click the **Layer Styles** palette tab. Click the drop-down arrow at the top, next to the active style viewer window. From the menu, select **AFXBevels-1** to load the style set into the Styles palette.
- Click the icon for **Style 5**.
- ⌘/**Ctrl**+click the layer in the palette to generate a selection of the type.

3.13

- Choose **Filter ➤ Blur ➤ Gaussian Blur**. Enter a blur radius of **2.5**. See **Figure 3.14**.
- Click **OK**.

STEP 5: FROM GLASSY TYPE TO WATERY TYPE

- Choose **Filter ➤ Distort ➤ Displace**. Enter the following settings in the Distort dialog box:
    - Horizontal Scale = **5**
    - Vertical Scale = **5**
    - Displacement Map/Undefined Areas = **Settings do not matter**
- Click **OK**.
- The Choose a Displacement Map dialog box now appears. Select **ripple-map.psd**, which is on the CD-ROM.
- Click **Open**.
- Select the **Stroke** layer.
- Press ⌘/**Ctrl+F** to apply the same displacement to this layer.
- Click **OK**.
- Repeat the process for the top layer, which is filled with the blurred color fill.
- Click **OK**.

The watery type is progressing nicely, but one major problem exists. There is too much color to give a realistic rendering of water on a sidewalk. Vibrant hues,

such as in **Figure 3.15**, just do not occur in the real world, not splattered on concrete, anyway. The color and shading can use a bit more tweaking.

- Select the original type layer.
- Click the **Layer Styles** tab to open the Styles palette.
- In the Styles menu, select **Inner Shadows**. This set is one of the default sets that are installed with Elements 2.
- Click the **High** icon.
- In the Styles menu, select **Drop Shadows**.
- Click the **Soft Edge** style.
- Choose **Enhance ➤ Color ➤ Hue/Saturation** (⌘/**Ctrl+U**).
- Change the saturation setting to **–70**.
- Click **OK**.
- In the Layers palette, change the opacity of the type layer to **50%**.
- Select the stroke layer. Change the blending mode to **Multiply** and set the opacity to **60%**. See **Figure 3.16**.

STEP 6: FINAL DETAILS

- Select the background layer.
- Select the **Burn** tool in the Toolbox. Enter the following settings in the Options bar:

3.14

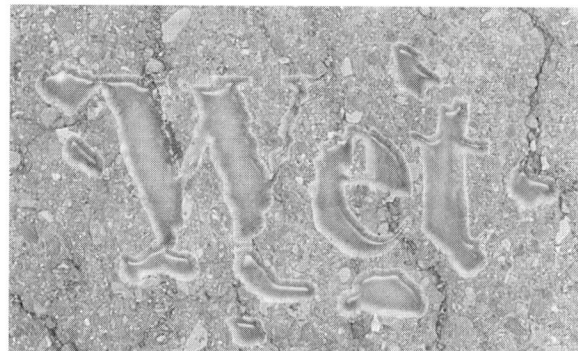

3.15

- Brush type = **Rounded, Feathered**
- Size = **80 to 100 pixels**
- Range = **Highlights**
- Exposure = **26%**
- As with the Water Drops tutorial, paint with the **Burn** tool beneath and around the edges of the water spots. Apply just enough to give the hint that the sidewalk is darker here due to the water. See **Figures 3.17** and **3.18**.
- Select the **Background** layer. Click the **Create a New Layer** icon on the bottom of the Layers palette.
- Select the text layer. Press ⌘/**Ctrl+E** to merge the text layer with the new layer.

When a layer with layer styles applied is merged with a blank layer beneath it, the style settings are applied to the layer permanently and can no longer be adjusted. Why would Elements do such a thing? Because now the layer can have filters applied to it that will also affect the applied style. If a filter is applied to a layer with the layer style uncollapsed, then the filter will only affect the layer information and not the style applied to it.

- Choose **Filter ➢ Artistic ➢ Plastic Wrap.** Enter the following settings in the Plastic Wrap dialog box:
    - Highlight Strength = **10**
    - Detail = **10**
    - Smoothness = **10** (see **Figure 3.19**)

3.16

- Select the topmost layer. Make sure that the blending mode is set to **Screen**; if not, do that now.
- Choose **Enhance ➢ Brightness/Contrast ➢ Adjust Brightness/Contrast.** Increase the brightness setting to +85 and click **OK**.
- Select the **Stroke** layer. Change the blending mode to **Hard Light** at **100%** opacity.

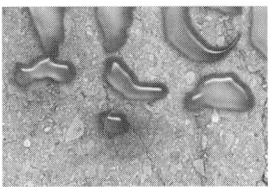

3.17

3.18

3.19

3.20

3.21 (CP8)

■ Select the **Type** layer. With the blending mode set to normal, change the opacity setting to **72%**. See **Figure 3.20**.

■ You may leave the image as it now appears, or you can experiment with one more blending mode. Select the type layer, and change the blending mode to **Vivid Light** set opacity to **72%**. See **Figure 3.21 (CP8)**.

There you go . . . messages splattered on a sidewalk!

POND RIPPLES AND SURFACE DISTURBANCES

Creating water drops is cool, but as you've seen, a lot of steps are required to generate the desired effect. Adobe Elements has filters that, when applied to images in a certain way, can generate water effects quickly and with very satisfying results.

This tutorial is fairly quick but rates high on the cool-o-meter. This tutorial demonstrates how to create realistic water ripples, as though a stone or raindrop hit the surface of a pond.

STEP 1: SET UP THE IMAGE

- Create a new image. Set the image attributes in the **New Image** dialog box as follows:
    - Preset Size = **1024 x 768 pixels**
    - Resolution = **72 dpi**
    - Color Mode = **RGB**
    - Background contents = **Transparent**
- Select the **Gradient** tool in the Toolbox.
- Press **D** to reset the default colors.
- Set up the Gradient options as follows:
    - Gradient Picker = **Foreground to Background gradient (Black to White)**
    - Gradient Type = **Linear Gradient**
    - Mode = **Normal**
    - Opacity = **100%**
    - Reverse = **Checked**
    - Dither = **Checked**
    - Transparency = **Checked**

3.22

- Starting at the top of the image, draw the gradient to the bottom edge, as shown in **Figure 3.22**.
- Rename this layer **Gradient Background**.

3.23

3.24

STEP 2: PAINT HIGHLIGHTS

- Duplicate the layer.
- Choose **Filter ➢ Distort ➢ Wave**. Enter the following settings in the Wave dialog box:
    - Number of Generators = **5**
    - Type = **Sine**
    - Wavelength: Minimum = **10**, Maximum = **120**
    - Amplitude: Minimum = **5**, Maximum = **35**
    - Scale: Vertical = **100%**, Horizontal = **100%**
    - Repeat Edge Pixels = **Checked**
- Click **OK**. See **Figure 3.23**.
- Press ⌘/**Ctrl+U** to bring up the Hue/Saturation dialog box. Enter the following settings:
    - Colorize = **Checked**
    - Hue = **205**
    - Saturation = **30**
    - Lightness = **0**
- Click **OK**. See **Figure 3.24**.
- Press **X** to place white in the foreground color box.
- Click the **Paintbrush** tool in the Toolbox. In the Options bar, set the following attributes for the brush:
    - Brush Type = **Rounded, Soft Edge**
    - Brush Size = **35 pixels**
    - Mode = **Normal**
    - Opacity = **50%**
    - Airbrush = **Selected**

- Paint several streaks across the face of the layer, as shown in **Figure 3.25**.
- Click the foreground color in the Toolbox.
- In the Color Picker, select a color for additional highlights. For this example, I'm using color **#32f7f4**, or R = **50**, G = **247**, and B = **244**.
- Click **OK**.
- Select the **Paintbrush** again. Do not change the settings but increase the Brush Size to **65** pixels.
- Paint spots of color onto the image. Stay off to the side of the white streaks, because the effect will be more realistic when the two shades do not overlap. See **Figure 3.26**.

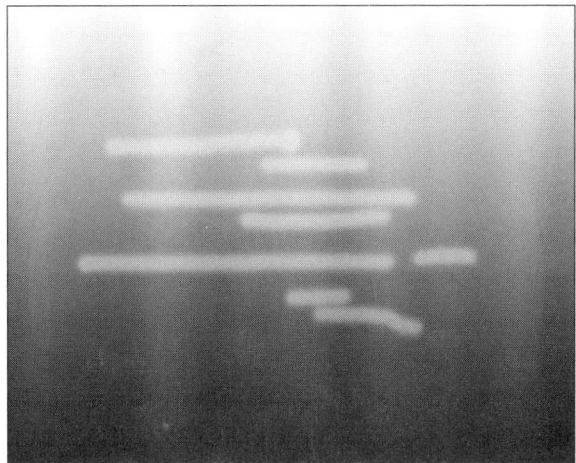

3.25

STEP 3: MAKE WAVES

- Choose **Filter ➢ Distort ➢ Twirl**.
- In the Twirl dialog box, set the angle to **–300**.
- Click **OK**.
- Choose **Filter ➢ Distort ➢ ZigZag**. Enter the following settings:
  - Amount = **60%**
  - Ridges = **7**
  - Style = Pond Ripples

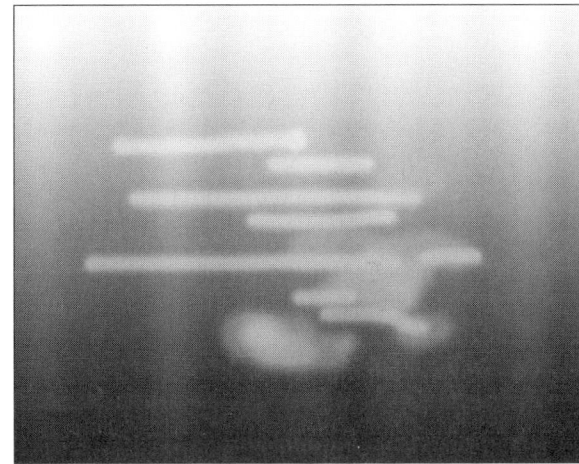

3.26

3.27

3.28

- Click **OK**. See **Figure 3.27**.
- You can increase the ripples and vary them somewhat by applying another type of **ZigZag** filter. Choose **Filter ➤ Distort ➤ ZigZag** and enter the following settings:
  - Amount = **60%**
  - Ridges = **16**
  - Style = Out From Center
- Click **OK**. See **Figure 3.28**.
- Try applying this same technique to a photograph, as shown in **Figure 3.29 (CP6)**.

Time to break out the fishing gear!

3.29 (CP6)

WOOD TEXTURES

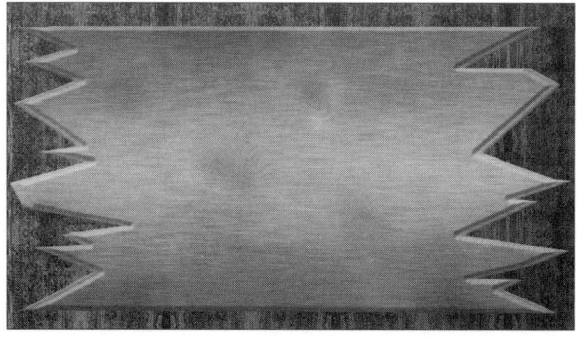

Okay, you've become a master at manipulating water and liquid. Now let's delve into material that is a bit drier, albeit with a few splinters. Break out the chainsaw, and let's have fun with wood.

STEP 1: CREATE THE PLANK

- Create a new image with the following attributes:
    - Name = **Wood Texture**
    - Preset Size = **800 x 600 pixels**
    - Resolution = **72 dpi**
    - Mode = **RGB**
    - **Transparent**
- Click **OK**.
- Click the foreground color. Set the color to **#DOA26B**, or R = **208**, G = **162**, and B = **107**. Click **OK**.
- Click the background color. Set the color to **#9A5F21**, or R = **154**, G = **95**, and B = **33**. Click **OK**.
- Select the **Polygonal Lasso** tool.
- Using the **Polygonal Lasso**, make a selection with jagged sides and a straight top and bottom edge. The shape resembles a piece of broken plank. See **Figure 3.30**.

3.30

- Select the **Gradient** tool. Enter the following attributes in the Options bar:
  - **Foreground to Background gradient**
  - Gradient Style = **Reflected**
  - Mode = **Normal**
  - Opacity = **100%**
  - Reverse = **Unchecked**
- Click the **Create a New Layer** icon on the bottom of the **Layers** palette.
- Starting at the center of the selection, draw the gradient down to the bottom edge of the selection to fill with the gradient. See **Figure 3.31**.
- Duplicate the **Gradient** layer.

3.31

3.32

STEP 2: ADD GRAIN

- With the selection still active, choose **Filter ➢ Noise ➢ Add Noise**. Use the following settings in the Add Noise dialog box:
  - Amount = **15**
  - Distribution = **Gaussian**
  - Monochromatic = **Checked**
- Click **OK**.
- Now choose **Filter ➢ Blur ➢ Motion Blur**. Set the Angle to **0** (zero) and the Distance to **22** pixels.
- Click **OK**.

The result is seen in **Figure 3.32**.

STEP 3: CREATE KNOTS AND DISTORTIONS

- Select the **Elliptical Marquee** tool. In the Options bar, enter the following settings:
  - Selection Type = **Add To Selection**
  - Feather = **10 pixels**
  - Anti-aliased = **Checked**
  - Style = **Normal**
- Make two overlapping selections, similar to those shown in **Figure 3.33**.
- Choose **Filter ➢ Distort ➢ Twirl**. Enter a twirl setting of **95** degrees and press **Return/Enter**.

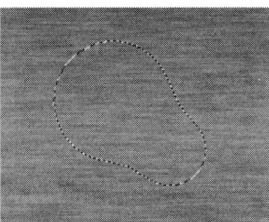

3.33

■ Select the **Burn** tool from the Toolbox. Set the following attributes for the Burn tool in the Options bar:

- ■ Brush Type = **Rounded, Feathered**
- ■ Size = The size depends on the size of your selection. For this example, the Brush Size is set to **93**.
- ■ Range = **Highlights**
- ■ Exposure = **26%**

■ Darken areas within the selection. Do not burn it too much; just give it a hint of being darker than the area outside the selection, as in **Figure 3.34**.

■ Repeat the process for creating knots two or three more times in different areas around the board and at different sizes. You may also lightly apply the **Dodge** tool in a couple of your knots and change the settings on the **Twirl** filter for variations. See **Figure 3.35**.

■ Deselect everything (**Select ➢ Deselect**).

■ Click the **Layer Styles** tab. In the Styles menu, select **Bevels**. This effect is one of the default style sets that installed with Elements. Click the **Simple Sharp Inner** icon.

■ Click the first layer (with the original gradient fill). Apply the same layer style. The image should now look like **Figure 3.36**.

Figure 3.37 gives an example of a wood plank with a background inserted.

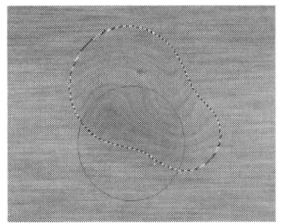
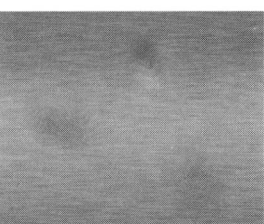

3.34   3.35

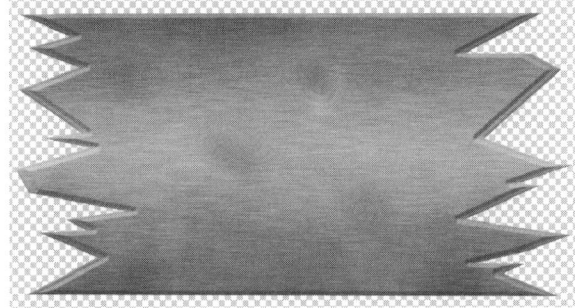

3.36

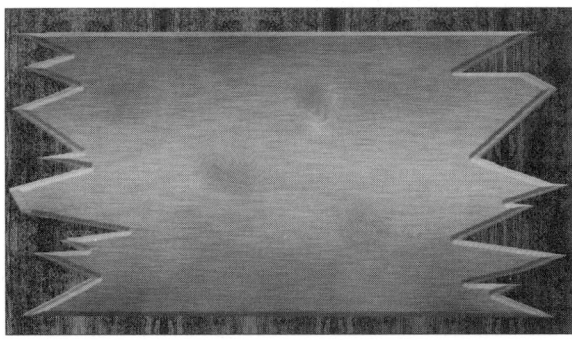

3.37

CARVING TYPE

A s the Webmaster of a site on Photoshop techniques and training, I'm constantly (daily) receiving e-mails requesting information on how to perform certain tasks. Etching or carving type into a surface is one of the more prevalent questions that I receive. In truth, an etching effect is actually an easy effect to achieve, with a veritable potpourri of methods in which to go from clean surface to carved message.

Elements, having inherited most of the traits of its big brother, can also be used to generate some pretty cool carving effects. This tutorial demonstrates one method for the most popular form of high school vandalism — etching in a wood surface.

This tutorial requires the following from the CD-ROM:

- Woodgrain-1.jpg
- jul02-88-woods.asl layer style set
- jul02-86-woods.asl layer style set

STEP 1: PREPARE THE SURFACE

- Open the image **Woodgrain-1.jpg**, found on the CD-ROM. **Figure 3.38** gives an example of the texture used for this tutorial, although any would do just fine.

3.38

STEP 2: GENERATE TEXTURED TYPE

■ Click the **Type Mask** tool in the Toolbox. Enter the following attributes:

■ Font Style = **Regular**

■ Font = **your choice**; Times New Roman is used in this example

■ Font Size = **200 points**

■ **Center Justified**

■ Click in the center of the image to set the starting point for your type. Type your word.

■ When the word is typed using the **Mask** tool, a rubylith color appears over the layer with what appears to be your type cut out, indicating the areas to be selected (the type) and not selected (the red-hued areas), as shown in **Figure 3.39**.

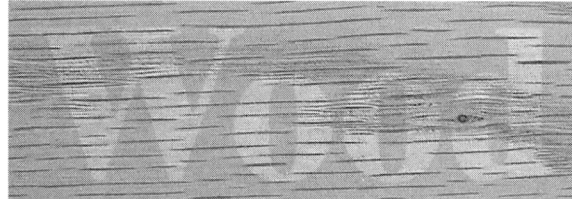

3.39

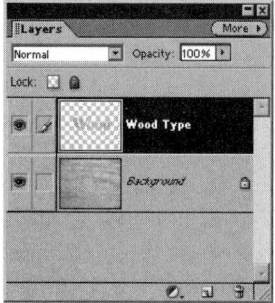

3.40

■ The area is not yet selected. Click the layer to bring up the marching ants or type selection.

■ A type selection on the original background layer now appears. Choose **Layer ➤ New ➤ Layer via Copy**; this takes a snapshot of your selection and pastes it into a new layer that you can manipulate free of the background. In effect, this copies the wood pattern in the shape of your type and pastes it into a new layer (see **Figure 3.40**).

STEP 3: ADD DEPTH AND BEVELS

■ Make sure that the new wood type layer is selected in the Layers palette.

■ Click the **Layer Styles** palette. In the Styles menu, select **Bevels**. This set is installed with Elements 2.

■ Click the **Simple Outer** layer style icon to apply this style to the type. **Figure 3.41** demonstrates the effect of applying this style to the pattern type.

■ As it appears now, the type stands out from the background as though it is raised. The style settings can be altered to give the type a recessed appearance. Choose **Layer ➤ Layer Style ➤ Scale Style Settings**.

3.41

- In the Scale Style Settings dialog box, change the scale to **50%**.
- Click **OK**.
- Choose **Layer** ➤ **Layer Style** ➤ **Style Settings** (or double-click the **F** key in the Layers palette). In the dialog box, enter the settings as follows:
  - Lighting Angle = **125**
  - Use Global Light = **Unchecked**
  - Bevel Size = **3 pixels**
  - Bevel Direction = **Down**
- Click **OK**.
- ⌘/**Ctrl**+click the type layer to bring up a selection in the shape of the text.
- Click the **Create a New Layer** icon on the bottom of the **Layers** palette.
- Click the Foreground color in the Toolbox to activate the Color Picker. Enter a color value of **#784B1B**, or R = **120**, G = **75**, and B = **27**.
- Click **OK**.
- Ensure the new empty layer is selected. Choose **Edit** ➤ **Stroke**. Enter the following settings:
  - Width = **6 pixels**
  - Location = **Inside**
  - Blending Mode = **Normal**
  - Opacity = **100%**
  - Preserve Transparency = **Unchecked**
- Click **OK**. Your image should now resemble **Figure 3.42**.

- Choose **Filter** ➤ **Blur** ➤ **Gaussian Blur**. Enter a blur radius of **7** pixels.
- Click **OK**.
- Choose **Select** ➤ **Deselect**. The type should look like **Figure 3.43**.
- Again, ⌘/**Ctrl**+click the type layer to bring up the text selection. Click the stroked layer.
- Choose **Filter** ➤ **Noise** ➤ **Add Noise**.
- Enter the following settings:
  - Amount = **20%**
  - Distribution = **Gaussian**
  - Monochromatic = **Checked**
- Click **OK**. The noise applied to the blur adds just a hint of texture, as shown in **Figure 3.44**.

3.43

3.42

3.44

STEP 4: DEFAULT LAYER STYLES VARIATION

As I stated at the beginning of this tutorial, you can achieve a wide variety of carving effects in Elements. Here are a couple variations that you can apply to the image you created.

- Select the type layer.
- Select the **Layer Styles** palette. Bevels should still be loaded. Click the **Inner Ridge** icon. Look at **Figure 3.45**. Instead of having a recessed type effect, the text now appears to have a ridge around it.
- Now click the **Scalloped Edge** layer style icon.
- Choose **Layer** ➢ **Layer Style** ➢ **Style Settings**. Change the Bevel size to **18** and click **OK**.
- Go back to the **Layer Styles** palette. Select **Drop Shadows** from the drop-down menu.
- Click the **High** layer style icon. Note in **Figure 3.46 (CP9)** the effect these settings have on your text.

STEP 5: ADDITIONAL LAYER STYLES VARIATIONS

The CD-ROM includes several layer style sets that can be applied to a layer, generating wooden effects. Take a look at a couple of these styles. If you haven't done so already, follow the instructions for loading new style sets into Elements found in Appendix B. You will be required to close Elements to enact the change, so please save anything you have open that you want to work with later. You will need to save your image as a .psd file first to keep the layer structure. If the styles are loaded, then continue the tutorial.

- Click the **Layer Styles** palette tab.
- In the drop-down menu, select **jul02-88-woods**, as shown in **Figure 3.47**.
- Click the small eye to the left of the stroked layer in the Layers palette. Turning off the eye renders this layer invisible, enabling you to see the effect in the following step better.
- Click **Style 12**. **Figure 3.48** gives an example of this style applied to the text layer.

3.45

3.46 (CP9)

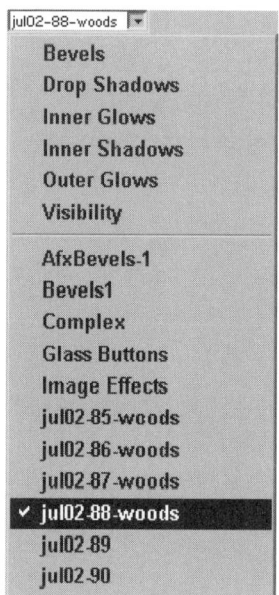

3.47

■ Now, alter the scale of the applied style. Choose **Layer ➤ Layer Style ➤ Scale Layer Effects**. Change the scale setting to **250%**. **Figure 3.49** demonstrates the expanded style setting.

■ Try another variation. Click the **Layer Styles** tab again. Select **jul02-86-woods** from the drop-down menu.

■ Click the **Style 4** icon. See **Figure 3.50** for an example of the effect.

As you can see, Elements has much to offer when working with textured type. These same effects work for interface design, button creation, and so forth. Now you can move on to another natural element, stone.

3.48

3.49

3.50

CHISELING STONE

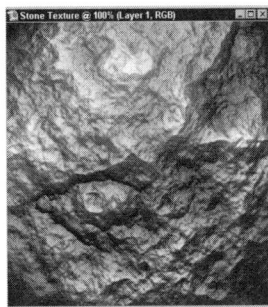

T he following technique is by far the easiest way to generate realistic stone from scratch. The process is nearly identical to that used in Adobe Photoshop, because the filters used are resident in both Photoshop and Elements.

STEP 1: PREPARE THE IMAGE

- Create a new image with the following attributes:
  - Name = **Stone Texture**
  - Width = **400 pixels**
  - Height = **400 pixels**
  - Resolution = **100 pixels per inch**
  - Mode = **RGB**
  - Contents = **White**
- Press **D** to reset the default colors.

STEP 2: GENERATE THE STONE PATTERN

- Choose **Filter ➤ Render ➤ Difference Clouds**.
- Press ⌘**/Ctrl+F** five times to reapply the filter. Applying the filter multiple times increases the contrast between the light and dark areas. Also, holding the **Shift** key while running the filter increases the amount of contrast. This is optional, and depends on the amount of variation in depth and texture you desire. The heavier the filter application, the deeper the texture in the end result. After you have applied the filter several times, you should have a black-and-white pattern similar to (but not exactly like) **Figure 3.51**.

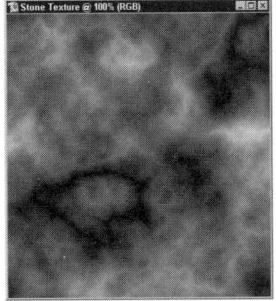

3.51

- Choose **Filter** ➢ **Render** ➢ **Lighting Effects**.
- In the Lighting Effects dialog box, click the lighting color to the right of the **Intensity** slider. The Color Picker appears. Enter a color value of **#AO8D7A**, or R = **160**, G = **141**, and B = **122**.
- Click **OK**.
- For the rest of the settings (seen in **Figure 3.52**), set the following attributes:
    - Style = **Default**
    - Light Type = **Spotlight**

- Intensity = **35**
- Focus = **69**
- Gloss = **32**
- Material = **–90**
- Exposure = **0**
- Ambience = **6**
- Texture Channel = **Red**
- White is High = **Checked**
- Height = **100**
- Click **OK**.

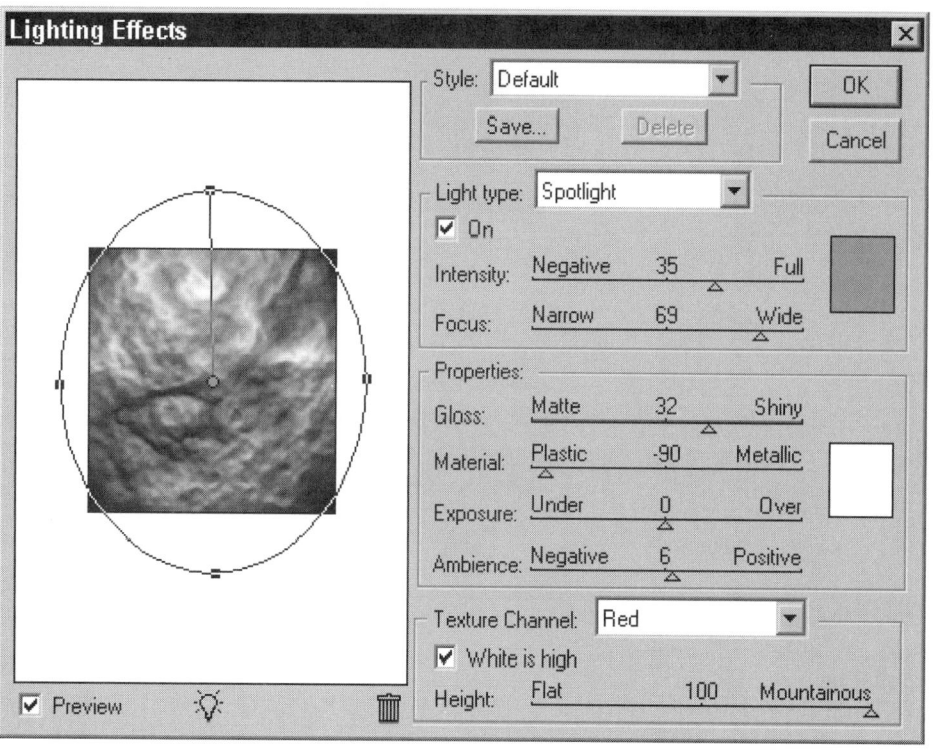

3.52

Figure 3.53 demonstrates the result the lighting effects have on the image.

- Click the **Create a New Layer** icon on the bottom of the **Layers** palette.
- Click the **Gradient** tool in the Toolbox.
- In the Options bar, click in the Gradient field to bring up the Gradient Editor dialog box.
- Click the **Copper Gradient** (in the default gradient set).
- Change the hue of the two lightest color stops to a light gray.
- Click **OK**.
- In the Gradient Options bar, select the **Linear** gradient.
- Starting in the upper-left corner, draw the gradient to the lower-right corner.
- Choose **Filter ➢ Noise ➢ Add Noise**. In the Add Noise dialog box, enter the following settings:
  - Amount = **15**
  - Distribution = **Gaussian**
  - Monochromatic = **Checked**

- Click **OK**.
- In the Layers palette, set the blending mode of the Gradient layer to **Soft Light**. **Figure 3.54 (CP7)** gives an example of the stone with the grain added.

There you have it . . . the fastest stone texture known to man!

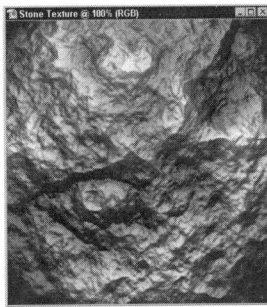 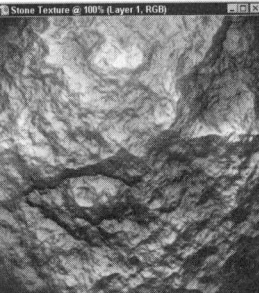

3.53 3.54 **(CP7)**

STONE TYPE

I n the previous tutorial, you created a stone effect from scratch. You can also apply the technique to a type selection to generate homemade stone type rather than a background. In this tutorial, I demonstrate one method for chiseling stone letters from an image of a rock face.

This tutorial requires the following from the CD-ROM:

- Stone-1.jpg
- stone-map.psd

STEP 1: OPEN THE IMAGE AND CAPTURE TEXT

- Open the image **Stone-1.jpg**, found on the CD-ROM. **Figure 3.55** shows the photo in question.
- Click the **Type Mask** tool in the Toolbox. In the Options bar, enter the following settings:
  - Font Style = **Regular**
  - Font = **Times New Roman** (any font will do)
  - Size = **200 pts**
  - Anti-aliased = **Selected**
- Type your text on the image. Click the layer in the palette to activate the selection. The reason for clicking the layer is that the selection must be active (marching ants visible) before a copy can be made in the next step.
- Choose **Layer ➢ New ➢ Layer via Copy**.
- Name the newly copied layer **Stone Type**.
- ⌘/**Ctrl**+click the **Stone Type** layer in the Layers palette to bring up the selection again.

3.55

- Select the background layer and click the **Create a New Layer** icon on the bottom of the Layers palette. You want to create a new layer beneath the Stone Type layer.
- Name the new layer **Black Type**. Fill the type selection with black.
- Click the small eye next to the Stone Type layer in the Layers palette. Doing this turns off the layer, making it invisible. Your image should now resemble **Figure 3.56**.

3.56

3.57

3.58

STEP 2: CARVE THE TEXT

- Select the black type layer. Choose **Filter ➢ Distort ➢ Displace**. Enter the following settings:
  - Horizontal Scale = **5**
  - Vertical Scale = **5**
- Click **OK**.
- When the Choose a Displacement Map dialog box appears, you will be directed to find an image to use as the displacement map. Find **stone-map.psd** on the CD-ROM.
- Click **OK**. **Figure 3.57** gives an example of the distortion applied to the type.
- Choose the **Layer Styles** palette. Select **Bevels** from the styles list to load that set into the palette.
- Click the **Simple Sharp Outer** icon to apply that style to the black type layer.
- Choose **Layer ➢ Layer Style ➢ Scale Effects**.
- Set the scale to **150%**.
- Click **OK**. This applies a chiseled effect, as shown in **Figure 3.58**.
- Select the **Stone Type** layer. Doing this makes it visible again.
- Press ⌘/**Ctrl+F** to apply the displace filter to this layer also. Both text layers should now have a distortion applied, as shown in **Figure 3.59**.

STEP 3: SHADE THE TYPE

- ⌘/**Ctrl**+click either type layer to make an active selection.

3.59

- Click the **Create a New Layer** icon on the bottom of the layers palette. Name the new layer **Shading.**
- Click the **Eyedropper** tool. Take a sample of a dark-brown section of the rock face. This places the tone in the foreground color.
- Choose **Edit ➤ Stroke**. Enter the following settings:
  - Width = **8 pixels**
  - Location = **Inside**
  - Blending Mode = **Normal**
  - Opacity = **100%**
  - Preserve Transparency = **off**
- With the arrow keys, move the selection down five pixels and to the right five pixels. Press the **Delete** key.
- In the Layers palette, set the blending mode for the Shading layer to **Multiply**. Set the layer opacity to **75%**.
- Deselect.
- Choose **Filter ➤ Blur ➤ Gaussian Blur**. Enter a blur radius of **2.5** pixels.
- Click **OK**. **Figure 3.60** shows the effect of the blurred shadow.
- Select the **Stone Type** layer.
- Click the **Layer Styles** tab. Bevels should still be loaded into the palette. Click the **Simple Outer** layer style icon. Although you are applying an outer bevel, when used in conjunction with the Sharp Outer bevel setting on the layer beneath, the combination of the two bevels deepens the appearance of the chiseling. See **Figure 3.61 (CP10)**.

This concludes the chapter on natural elements. Hopefully, you now see that working with natural elements in Elements (pardon the pun) is a fairly easy process. Now you can explore the realm of refined materials, as we delve into the realm of metalwork.

3.60

3.61 (CP10)

CHAPTER 4

GETTING TECHNICAL: INDUSTRIAL EFFECTS

T he combination of texture, lighting, shading, and color gradation are the primary ingredient to generating faux realism. You've seen this in previous chapters, and industrial effects are no different. In Chapter 3, you took a crack at reproducing and manipulating natural elements. In this chapter, you find out how to generate refined elements, such as steel and glass.

True, you won't be melting anything here. The key similarity between forging steel and manipulating pixels is that both involve a process of many steps to meet a desired result. I can't make a steel bar. I don't have the tools, the manpower, or the understanding of the process required for such a feat. I could certainly learn had I the interest and time. However, I'm a digital guy and have focused on creating metal-appearing images rather than smelting ore. I have a computer, the tool (Elements), and the knowledge required to generate steel in the digital realm. You are about to as well.

SHEET METAL

T ime to fire up the smelter and begin refining!

STEP 1: PREPARE THE IMAGE

- Create a new image with the following attributes.
    - Preset Size = **640 x 480 pixels**
    - Resolution = **72 dpi**
    - Mode = **RGB**
    - Contents = **White**
- Click **OK**.
- Select the **Gradient** tool in the Toolbox.
- The default gradients are required for this step. In the Options bar, click the drop-down arrow next to the Gradient Picker. If the default set is loaded, you should have a gradient called Copper visible. If so, click this gradient to select it. If not, open the Gradient menu (click the small arrow in the upper-right of the Gradient Picker). From the menu that appears, click **Reset Gradients** and then click the **Copper** gradient.
- In the Options bar, set the following attributes for the gradient:
    - Gradient Type = **Linear**
    - Mode = **Normal**
    - Opacity = **100%**
- Starting in the upper-left corner of the image. Draw the gradient down to the lower-right corner, as shown in **Figure 4.1**.

4.1

■ Choose **Enhance ➢ Adjust Color ➢ Remove Color (Shift+⌘/Ctrl+U)**. When the color is removed, you are left with a metal-hued gradient, as shown in **Figure 4.2**.

STEP 2: REFINE THE METAL SHEET

■ Duplicate the background layer.
■ Choose **Filter ➢ Noise ➢ Add Noise** and enter the following settings in the Add Noise dialog box:
  ■ Amount = **8%**
  ■ Distribution = **Gaussian**
  ■ Monochromatic = **Checked**
■ Click **OK**.
■ Choose **Filter ➢ Blur ➢ Motion Blur**. Enter the following settings:
  ■ Angle = **0** (zero)
  ■ Distance = **24 pixels**
■ Click **OK**.

STEP 3: ADD COLOR

■ On the bottom of the Layers palette, click the **Add an Adjustment Layer** icon.
■ Select **Solid Color** from the drop-down menu.
■ The Color Picker appears. Enter a color with the following number or values: **#8A8BAA**, or R = **138**, G = **139**, and B = **170**.
■ Click **OK**.
■ Set the layer mode for the adjustment layer to **Overlay** and the opacity to **50%**. **Figure 4.3** shows your new sheet metal.

Granted, that effect is rather quick, but it is very popular in Web site design and creating graphics for print media. Try running this tutorial using a text selection or an interface shape!

4.2

4.3

RUST AND TARNISH

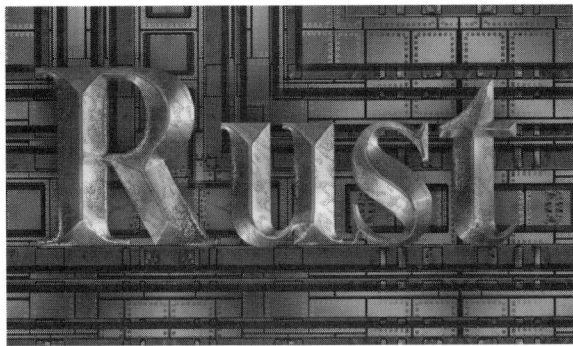

This tutorial requires you to have loaded the layer style set AFX-HardMetals1.asl and Bevels1.asl into Elements. If you need help doing this, refer to Appendix B, "Loading and Changing the CD Layer Styles," prior to proceeding.

This tutorial requires the following from the CD-ROM:

- AFX-Metals-1.pat
- AFX-HardMetals1.asl
- Bevels1.asl

STEP 1: PREPARE THE IMAGE

Many cool effects look even better with a fancy background. Here's how to create one for this effect.

- Create a new image with the following attributes.
    - Name = **Rust**
    - Preset Size = **640 x 480 pixels**
    - Resolution = **72 dpi**
    - Mode = **RGB**
    - Contents = **White**

- Click **OK**.
- Choose **Edit ➢ Fill**.
- Select **Pattern** as the fill type. In the Patterns menu, select **Replace Patterns**. Find AFX-Metals-1.pat on the CD-ROM and load it into the Patterns palette.
- Click **metals58.jpg**.

- Set the mode to **Normal**.
- Set opacity to **100%**.
- Click **OK**. **Figure 4.4** represents the new background.

STEP 2: CREATE THE TYPE

- Create a new layer.
- Fill the layer with black, Mode = **Normal**, and opacity set to **40%**.
- Click **OK**.

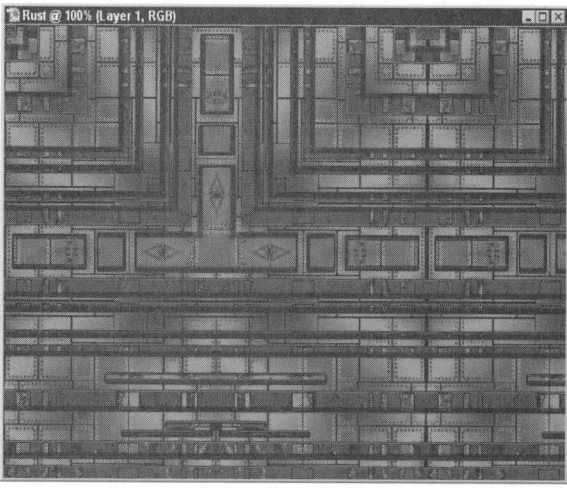

4.4

4.5

- Press **D** to reset the default foreground and background colors.
- Click the **Type** tool. In the Options bar, set the following attributes:
  - Font Style = **Regular**
  - Font = **Times New Roman** (any font will do)
  - Size = **200 points**
  - Anti-aliased = **Selected**
  - Justified = **Center**
  - Color = **Black**
- Click in the center of the image and enter your type, as shown in **Figure 4.5**.

STEP 3: TRANSFORM TEXT TO METAL

- Click the **Layer Styles** tab. Load **AFX-HardMetals1.asl** into the Layer Styles palette.
- Click the **AFX-High Metal** icon to apply that style to the text layer. **Figure 4.6** shows the effects applied.
- ⌘/**Ctrl**+click the type layer in the Layers palette to generate a selection.
- Create a new layer above the type layer.
- Select the **Paintbrush** tool.
- Click the foreground color to bring up the Color Picker. Enter a color with the following numbers or values: **#C29A32**, or R = **194**, G = **138**, and B = **50**.
- Click **OK**.

4.6

STEP 4: TARNISH METAL

■ In the Paintbrush options, set the following attributes:

- ■ Brush Type = **Rounded, Feathered**
- ■ Brush Size = **40 pixels**
- ■ Mode = **Normal**
- ■ Opacity = **50%**
- ■ Airbrush = **Selected**

■ Paint several spots of color within the type selection. Do not completely fill the type; just spray in a few areas. Also, do not hold the mouse down too long while applying the paint. **Figure 4.7** gives a good example of what the spot-painted image should look like.

■ Choose **Filter ➤ Noise ➤ Add Noise**. Set the following attributes for the filter:

- ■ Amount = **55**
- ■ Distribution = **Gaussian**
- ■ Monochromatic = **Checked**

■ Click **OK**.

■ Choose **Select ➤ Deselect** (⌘/**Ctrl+D**).

■ Choose the **Layer Styles** palette. Load **Bevels1.asl** into the palette.

■ Click the **Style 10** icon in the Layer Styles palette to apply this style to the painted layer. You now have a rough tarnish applied to the metal type, as shown in **Figure 4.8**.

■ ⌘/**Ctrl**+click the painted layer in the Layers palette. Doing this brings up a feathered selection.

■ Click the foreground color to activate the Color Picker. Enter a color with the following number or values: **#44B03F**, or R = **68**, G = **176**, and B = **63** as shown in **Figure 4.9**.

■ Click **OK**.

■ Choose **Edit ➤ Stroke**. Enter the following settings:

- ■ Width = **2 pixels**
- ■ Color = **Foreground** (don't change the setting, because it is already set)
- ■ Location = **Outside**
- ■ Mode = **Normal**
- ■ Opacity = **40%**

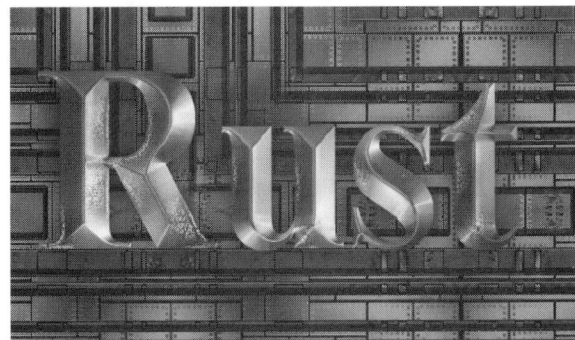

4.8

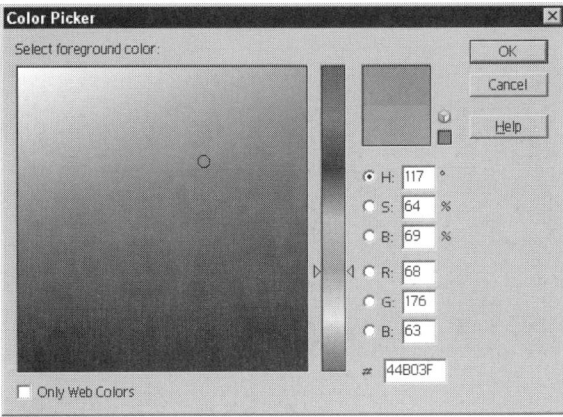

4.7

4.9

- Click **OK**. **Figure 4.10** shows the effect of the stroke on the selection.
- ⌘/**Ctrl**+click the type layer to create a selection.
- Click the foreground color to activate the Color Picker. Enter a color with the following number or values: **#5F4232**, or R = **95**, G = **66**, and B = **50**.
- Click the **Add a Layer** icon to create a new layer.
- Choose **Edit** ➢ **Stroke**. Enter the following settings in the Stroke dialog box:
  - Width = **8 pixels**
  - Color = **Foreground**
  - Location = **Inside**
  - Mode = **Normal**
  - Opacity = **80%**
- Click **OK**.

4.10

4.11

- Choose **Filter** ➢ **Distort** ➢ **Ripple**. Enter the following settings in the Ripple dialog box:
  - Amount = **999%**
  - Size = **Medium**
- Click **OK**.
- Choose **Filter** ➢ **Noise** ➢ **Add Noise**. Enter the following settings:
  - Amount = **8%**
  - Distribution = **Gaussian**
  - Monochromatic = **Checked**
- Click **OK**.
- Click the **Layers Palette** tab. Load the layer style set **Bevels**.
- Click the style **Simple Pillow Emboss**.
- Choose **Layer** ➢ **Layer Style** ➢ **Scale Effects**. Change the scale of the bevel to **1%**.
- Click **OK**. Your image should now look like **Figure 4.11**.
- Change the blending mode for the layer to **Multiply** and set the opacity to **35%**.
- Choose **Enhance** ➢ **Brightness/Contrast** ➢ **Brightness/Contrast** and increase the contrast setting to **+100**.

The finished image (**Figure 4.12**) shows two separate layers of tarnish in varying degrees on the same metal type.

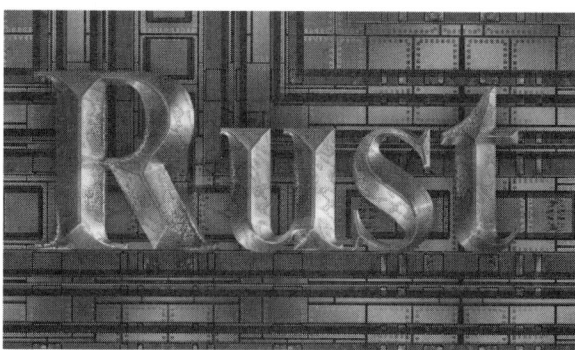

4.12

15

METAL SPHERES

I n Chapter 2, you found out how to create sphere images. This tutorial is an offshoot of the tutorials in that chapter, but it focuses on giving the sphere a metallic surface, similar to a steely marble or a ball bearing.

This tutorial requires the following from the CD-ROM:

- AFX-Metals-1.pat

STEP 1: GENERATE A BACKGROUND

- Create a new image with the following attributes.
  - Name = **Metal Spheres**
  - Preset Size = **640 x 480 pixels**
  - Resolution = **72 dpi**
  - Mode = **RGB**
  - Contents = **White**
- As with the previous tutorial, give this image a stylish background. Choose **Edit ➢ Fill**. Select **Pattern** as the fill type.
- If AFX-Metals-1.pat is not loaded, do so now by opening the Patterns menu and selecting **Replace Patterns**. Find AFX-Metals-1.pat on the CD-ROM and click **OK**.
- Select **metalplates** from the Pattern set and click **OK**. The image should look like **Figure 4.13**.

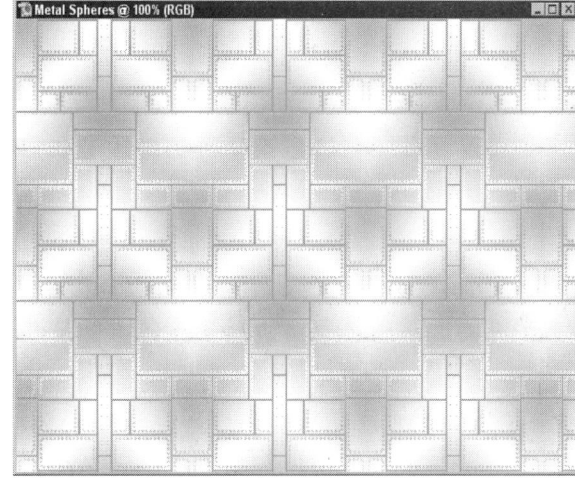

4.13

97

STEP 2: CREATE A SPHERE

- Select the **Elliptical Marquee** tool in the Toolbox.
- In the Options bar, choose the following settings for the Marquee tool:
  - **New Selection**
  - Feather = **0 pixels**
  - Anti-aliased = **Checked**
  - Style = **Fixed Aspect Ratio**
  - Width = **1**
  - Height = **1**
- Create a new layer and name it **Sphere**.
- Make a large circular selection on the new layer, as shown in **Figure 4.14**.
- Click the **Gradient** tool.

- Load the **Metals** gradient set found in the Adobe Elements 2 Presets/Gradients folder.
- Select the **Silver** gradient. When loaded, click in the Gradient window to bring up the Gradient Editor.
- Click the first Color stop (on the bottom left of the gradient editor bar). Change the color to white. You may want to save the gradient for later use, so name it something such as **Sphere Gradient**, click the **New** button, and then click **OK**.
- Click the **Radial Gradient** icon in the Options bar.
- Starting in the upper-left quadrant of the selection, draw the gradient down and to the right until you reach the selection edge, as shown in **Figure 4.15**. **Figure 4.16** shows the filled selection.

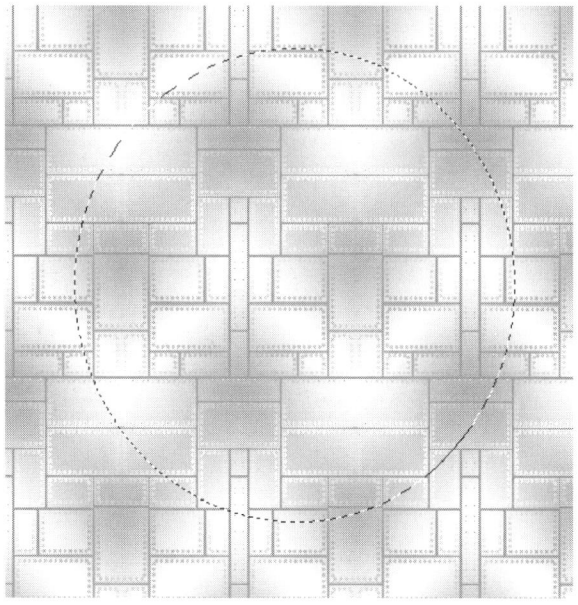

4.14

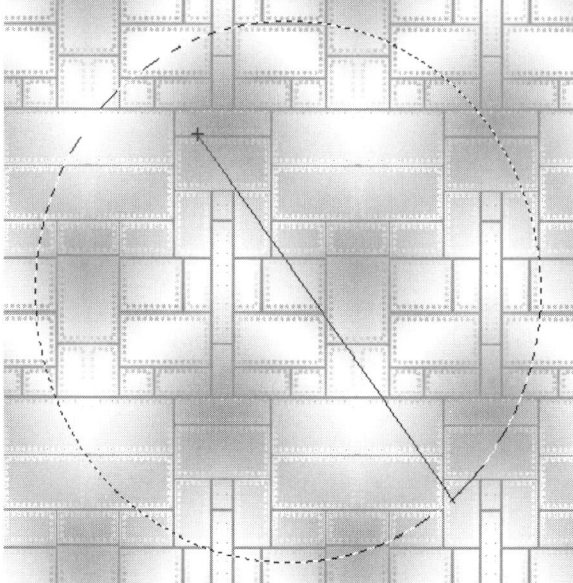

4.15

STEP 3: ENHANCE THE METALLIC EFFECT

■ Choose **Enhance ➤ Brightness/Contrast/ Brightness/Contrast**. Reduce the Brightness to **–16** and the Contrast to **–13**.

■ ⌘/**Ctrl**+click the Sphere layer to generate a selection.

■ Click the **Add an Adjustment Layer** icon on the bottom of the Layers palette.

■ Fill this layer with the gradient also. Set the layer mode to **Darken** and the opacity for the adjustment layer to **65%**.

■ Choose **Filter ➤ Distort ➤ Spherize**. Set the Amount to **100%**, Mode to **Normal**, and click **OK**.

■ Select the Sphere layer. Click the **Create a New Layer** icon so that a new layer appears above the Sphere layer but below the adjustment layer.

■ Click the **Gradient** tool again. This time, open the Gradient menu and select **Reset Gradients** to load the default set.

■ Select a light blue or turquoise for the foreground color.

■ In the Gradient Picker, select the **Foreground to Transparent Gradient**. In the Options bar, check **Reverse**. The radial gradient should still be selected.

■ Starting in the same area as the original gradient fill, draw this gradient to the lower right also. **Figure 4.17** shows the effect on the sphere.

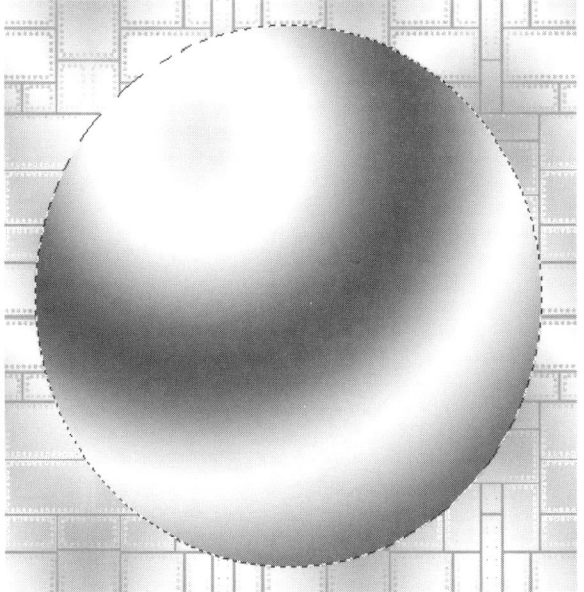

4.16

4.17

■ Set the blending mode for this layer to **Overlay** and the opacity to **60%**. **Figure 4.18** shows how the metal sphere is shaping up.

■ Select the topmost layer. Merge down (press **⌘/Ctrl+E**) until all layers are merged into one, with the exception of the background layer.

■ The newly merged layer looks a bit different from the premerged image, but that's okay. **Figure 4.19** shows the new sphere.

STEP 4: ADD DETAILS

In just a few steps we can take our steel ball and apply chrome-like qualities to the overall hues and reflections.

■ Create a new layer above the background. Fill this layer with **20%** black and click **OK**.

■ Copy the Sphere layer.

■ Choose **Image ➤ Adjustments ➤ Invert** (**⌘/Ctrl+I**).

■ Set the blending mode of the inverted layer to **Soft Light**.

■ **⌘/Ctrl**+click the Sphere layer to generate a selection.

■ Create a new layer beneath the inverted top layer.

■ Click the **Gradient** tool. Select the Chrome gradient and fill the new layer with the gradient, using the same method as the other two gradient applications.

■ Choose **Filter ➤ Blur ➤ Gaussian Blur**. Enter a blur radius of **3** to **5** pixels.

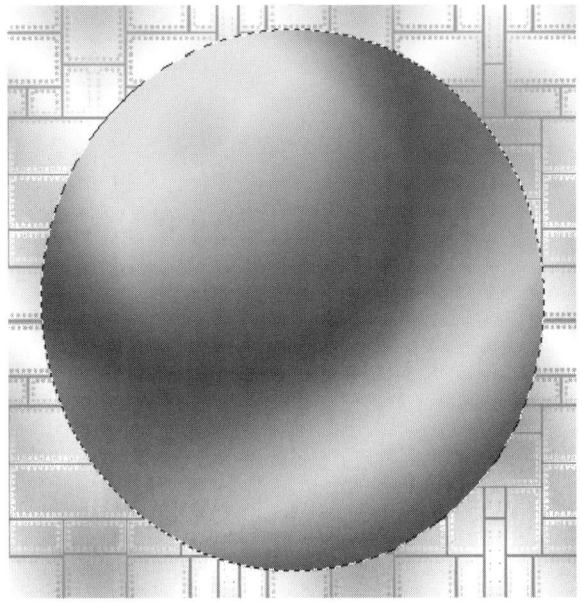

4.18

4.19

- Click **OK**.
- Set the layer blending mode to **Pin Light**. The sphere should resemble **Figure 4.20**.
- Select **Filter**> ➤ **Render**> ➤ **3D Transform**.
- In the 3D Transform dialog box, select the **Sphere** tool and draw a circle around the gradient fill.

- With the **Trackball** tool, rotate the selection up and to the right, as seen in **Figure 4.21**.
- Click **OK**. See **Figure 4.22**.

It is now a simple matter to place the sphere in worlds and backgrounds of your own choosing, as I've done in **Figure 4.23**.

4.20

4.22

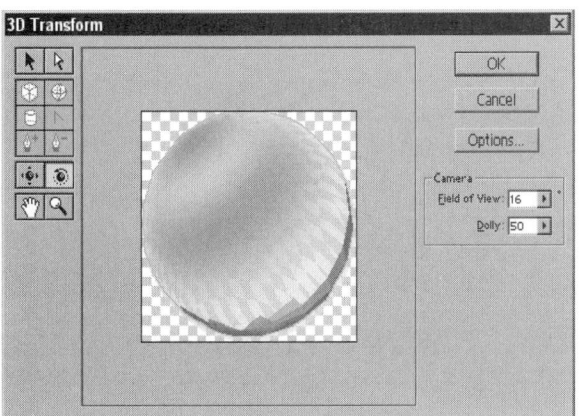

4.21

4.23

PIPES

T his tutorial requires the following from the CD-ROM:

- ActionFx-PipesGradient.grd

Pipes are a very popular effect on the Web, although most are created by following techniques similar to those in the tubing tutorial found in Chapter 2. This tutorial raises the bar a bit by creating incredibly realistic metal pipe, such as you would see in household plumbing. The tutorial is a bit more difficult than those previous, but the results are fantastic.

STEP 1: PREPARE THE IMAGE

- Choose **File ➤ New**.
- In the New Image dialog box that appears, set the following attributes (shown in **Figure 4.24**):
  - Name = **Pipes**
  - Preset Size = **800 x 600 pixels**
  - Resolution = **72 dpi**
  - Mode = **RGB**
  - Contents = **White**
- Choose **Edit ➤ Fill**. Fill the background with black.
- Create a new layer by clicking the **Add a Layer** icon on the bottom of the Layers palette.

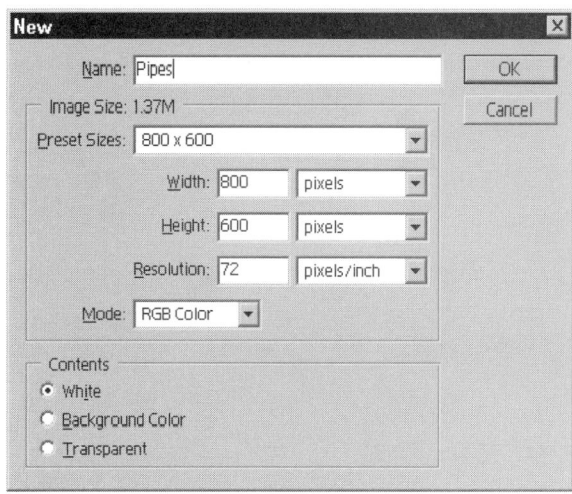

4.24

STEP 2: CREATE PIPE SEGMENTS

- Select the **Rectangular Marquee** tool.
- In the Options bar, set the following attributes for the selection:
    - Type = **New Selection**
    - Feather = **0**
    - Mode = **Normal**
- Make a selection that appears to the eye to be about 2 inches high and 3½ to 4 inches wide. Make your selection on the left side of the image.
- Select the **Gradient** tool.
- In the Options bar, open the Gradient palette by clicking the small arrow to the right of the Gradient Viewer window.
- Open the Gradient menu by clicking the small arrow in the upper-right corner of the Gradient palette. Select **Load Gradient** from the menu.
- Find and load **ActionFx-PipesGradient.grd**, found on the CD-ROM.
- Select **ActionFx-PipesGradient.grd** in the Gradient palette so that it becomes the active gradient, as shown in **Figure 4.25**.
- Set the following options for the gradient in the Options bar:
    - Type = **Linear Gradient**
    - Mode = **Normal**
    - Opacity = **100%**
    - Reverse, Dither, Transparency = **All Checked**
- Fill the entire selection with the gradient, starting at the top straight down to the bottom. **Figure 4.26** shows the filled selection.
- Rename the layer **Segment 1**.
- Duplicate the pipe layer. Name the duplicate layer **Segment 2**.
- Click the **Move** tool. With the arrow keys, move the new segment horizontally to the other side of the image as shown in **Figure 4.27**.

STEP 3: MAKE A PIPE JOINT

- Duplicate the Segment 2 layer. Rename this layer **Joint Section**.

> **NOTE**
>
> Holding the **Shift** key while using the arrow keys to move a layer increases the distance moved with each click from 1 to 5 pixels.

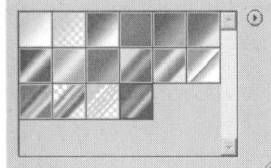

4.25

4.26

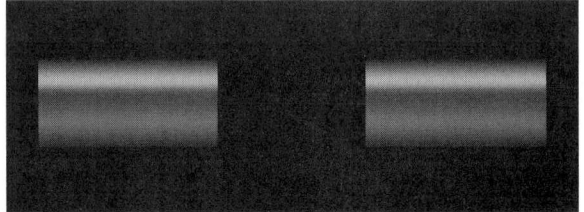

4.27

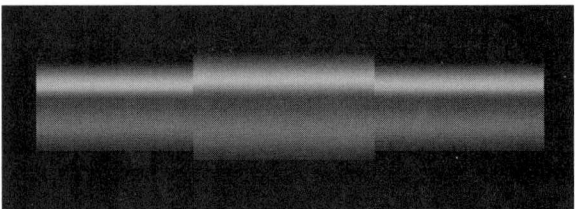

4.28

- Hold down the **Shift** key and move the Joint layer horizontally with the arrow keys so that it overlaps both Segment 1 and Segment 2.
- Choose **Image** ➢ **Transform** ➢ **Distort**.
- In the Options bar, change the Height to **120%**. **Figure 4.28** shows the state of the image this far.
- Click the eye next to the background layer in the Layers palette to render the layer invisible.
- ⌘/**Ctrl**+click the Joint Section layer to generate a selection.
- Click the **Rectangular Marquee** tool. Set the selection type to **Subtract from Selection**. Draw

the selection over the majority of the selection, leaving only a small vertical selection along the left side, as shown in **Figure 4.29**.

- Choose **Layer** ➢ **New** ➢ **Layer via Cut**.
- Choose **Image** ➢ **Transform** ➢ **Perspective**.
- Select the point on the top left of the crop selection. Move it down so that it meets the top of Segment 1. Note that the Perspective Transform also moves the bottom point the same distance to meet the bottom of Segment 1. See **Figure 4.30**.
- Change the name of this layer to **Joint Bevel**.
- Duplicate the Joint Bevel layer. Rename this layer **Joint Bevel 2**.
- Choose **Image** ➢ **Rotate** ➢ **Flip Layer Horizontal**.

4.29

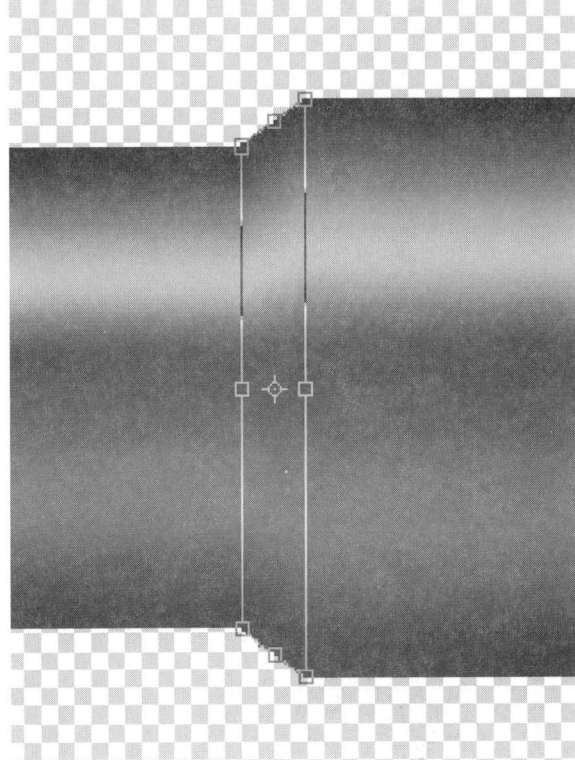

4.30

- With the **Shift+right arrow** key combination, move Joint Bevel 2 to the right side of the joint segment. Your pipe should appear joined, as shown in **Figure 4.31**.

STEP 4: BEND PIPE

These next steps will require a bit of finesse, but I'm sure you are up to the task!

- Duplicate the Segment 1 layer again. Name the new layer **Bend**.
- Move the Bend layer to just below the Segment 1 layer.

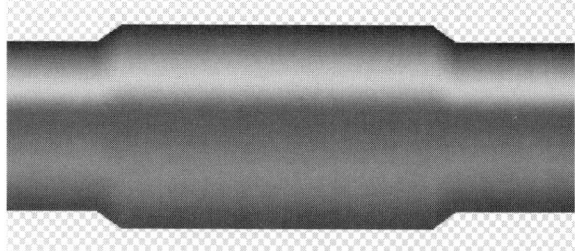

4.31

4.32

- Select the top layer in the Layers palette. The top layer should be Joint Bevel 2. Merge the layers down until you have three layers — Segment 1, Bend, and Background.
- Click the eye next to the Segment 1 layer to render the layer invisible.
- Click the **Move** tool. Center the Bend segment horizontally on the image so that there is equal space on either side of the segment. Then move it vertically so the bottom edge is in about the center of the image.
- Choose **Image ➢ Transform ➢ Distort**. In the Options bar, change both the Height and Width percentages to **200%**. Figure **4.32** shows the expanded segment with all other layers invisible.
- Click the **Polygonal Lasso** tool.
- In the Options bar, click the **Add to Selection** button.
- Starting at the top-left corner of the segment, select a triangular portion of the pipe, drawing the lasso down and to the right until it is beyond the bottom edge of the segment. Complete the selection by adding one more point outside of the segment and then by drawing the lasso back to the starting point. Repeat the process on the right side of the segment. These two selections need to be nearly identical for this to work in further steps, as shown in **Figure 4.33**. After you select both sections, press the **Delete** key.

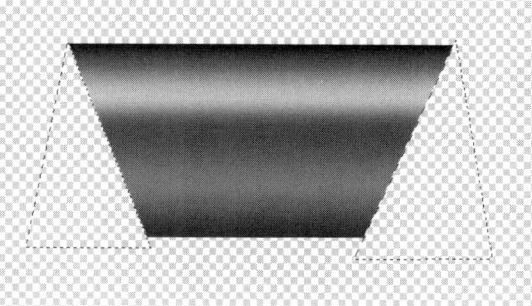

4.33

■ Press ⌘/Ctrl+D to deselect.

■ Choose **Filter ➢ Distort ➢ Polar Coordinates**. Select the **Rectangular to Polar** option and click **OK**. The segment now appears distorted (see **Figure 4.34**); don't worry, because that is a good thing.

■ Choose **Layer ➢ Transform ➢ Distort**.

■ In the Options bar, change the Width percentage to **80%**.

STEP 5: JOIN THE PIECES

■ Click the Segment Layer 1 layer.

■ Move the segment so that it is halfway off the screen in the lower-left quadrant of the image. See **Figure 4.35**.

■ Select the Bend layer.

■ Choose **Image ➢ Rotate ➢ Free Rotate Layer**.

■ Rotate the Bend layer so that the edges and reflections on the pipe sections match. When in Free Rotate you can also move the section into place by clicking the center point of the transform selection and moving it into place with the mouse as in **Figure 4.36**.

■ Use the **Rectangular Marquee** tool to select the portion of the Bend layer that protrudes above the edge of Segment 1 and press **Delete**.

4.35

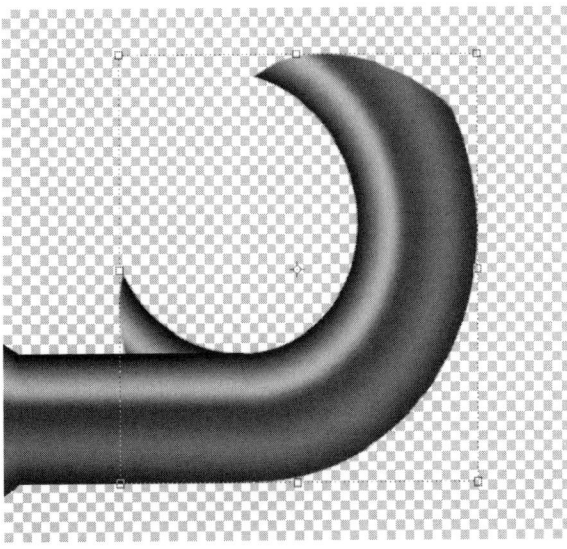

4.36

4.34

■ Duplicate the Bend layer. Move it to match the other bend section as shown in **Figure 4.37**.

■ Duplicate the Segment 1 layer.

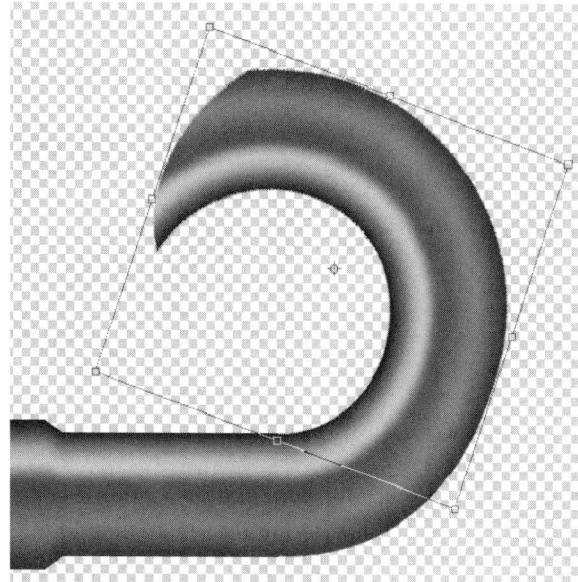

4.37

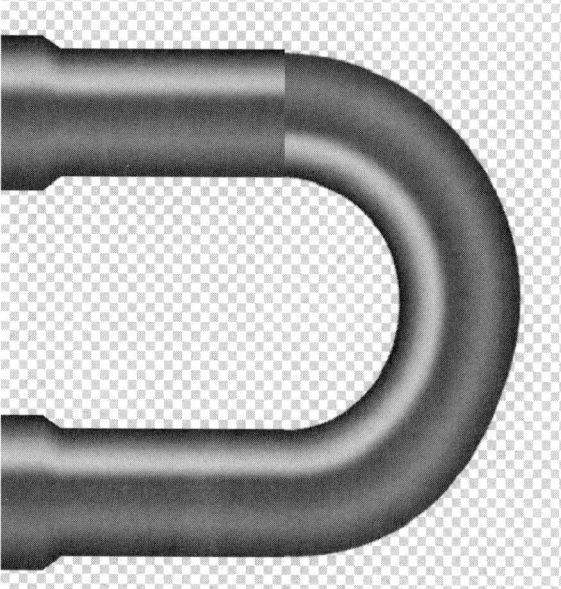

4.38

■ Move the duplicate layer into place to meet the top portion of the bent pipe.

■ Select the **Rectangular Marquee** tool.

■ Draw a selection around the protruding edges along the bar. This needs a bit of finesse, because only a few pixels of the depth need be deleted. Use the **Zoom** tool to get a close shot of the offending pixels, make your selection so that the bar edge is flush, and then press the **Delete** key. See **Figure 4.38**.

■ Merge the segment layers together.

STEP 6: FIX HIGHLIGHTS AND SHADOWS

■ Select the **Rectangular Marquee** tool in the Toolbox. Set the attributes in the Options bar as follows:

   ■ Selection Type = **New Selection**
   ■ Feather = **6 pixels**
   ■ Style = **Normal**

■ Select the area where the two mismatched pieces come together. Do not extend your selection beyond the pipe edges. See **Figure 4.39**.

■ Choose **Filter ➢ Blur ➢ Gaussian Blur**. Enter a blur radius of **2.5** pixels.

■ Click **OK**.

■ Click the **Selection Brush** tool. Set the options as follows:

   ■ Brush Size = **45 pixels**
   ■ Mode = **Selection**
   ■ Hardness = **0**

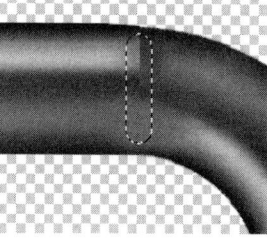

4.39

- Paint a selection where the highlights/reflection on the straight segment meet the dark shadow of the curved pipe section as shown in **Figure 4.40**.
- Click the **Eyedropper** tool. Take a sample of the highlight/reflection color to place it in the foreground.
- Select the **Paintbrush** tool. Enter the following option settings:
  - Size = **45 pixels**
  - Mode = **Normal**
  - Opacity = **32%**
  - Airbrush = **Selected**
- Lightly paint in the selected area as shown in **Figure 4.41**.
- Click the **Dodge** tool. With a large brush, run the tool over the highlighted/reflected areas of the pipe. See **Figure 4.42**.
- Click the **Burn** tool in the Toolbox. Set the following attributes in the Options bar:
  - Brush Type = **Rounded, Feathered**
  - Size = **32 pixels**
  - Range = **Highlights**
  - Exposure = **60%**
- Run the **Burn** tool over the shadow areas. Again, just lightly will suffice.

- Duplicate the Pipe layer.
- Select the duplicate layer. Choose **Image ➢ Adjustments ➢ Invert**.
- Set the blending mode of the layer to **Overlay** and the opacity to **65%**.
- Click the background layer to make it visible again. **Figure 4.43** shows the result.

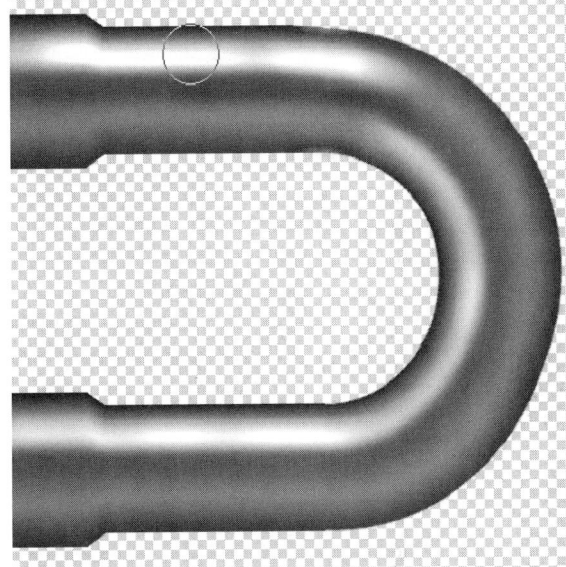

4.42

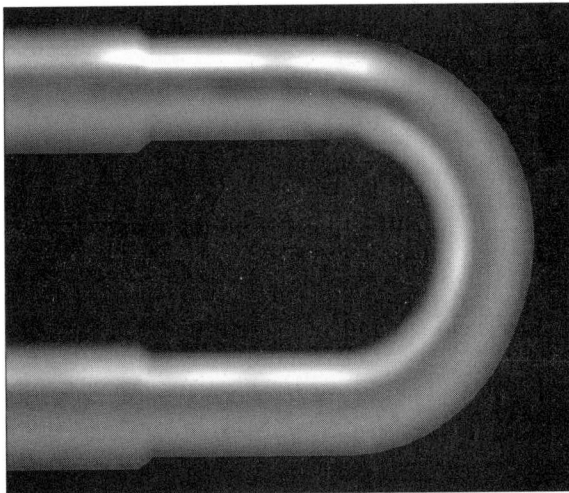

4.43

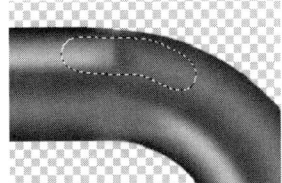

4.40

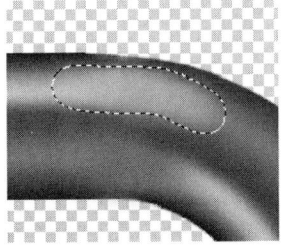

4.41

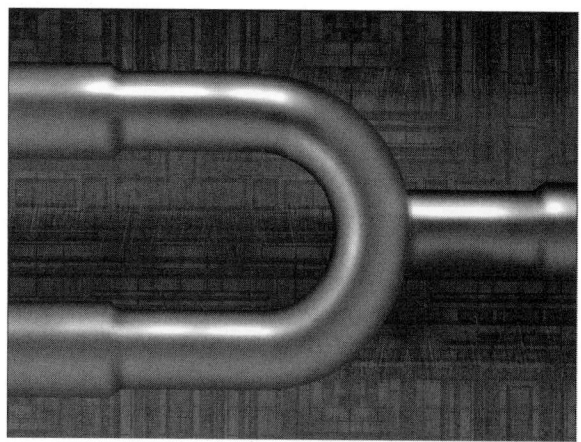

4.44

Following the process of segment creation and join-ing, I've added another section in **Figure 4.44**. Not bad for a cost-effective software package!

BOLTS

T his tutorial requires the following from the CD-ROM:

- AFX-ScrewHead.grd

STEP 1: CREATE A NEW IMAGE

- Choose **File ➢ New**. Set the attributes in the New Image dialog box as follows:
    - Name = **Bolt**
    - Preset Size = **800 x 600 pixels**
    - Resolution = **72 dpi**
    - Mode = **RGB**
    - Background = **White**
- Click **OK**.
- Click the **Create a New Layer** icon on the bottom of the Layers palette.

STEP 2: WORK WITH SELECTIONS AND GRADIENTS

- Select the **Elliptical Marquee** tool. Set the following attributes in the Options bar:
    - Type = **New Selection**
    - Feather = **0**
    - Anti-aliased = **Checked**
    - Style = **Normal**
- Draw a circular selection near the top of the layer. Make is fairly large — about 2 inches in diameter or so.

- Select the **Rectangular Marquee** tool. Keep most of the settings but change the selection type to **Subtract from Selection**. Select the lower two-thirds of the circle so that only a third of the original selection is still active, as shown in **Figure 4.45**.

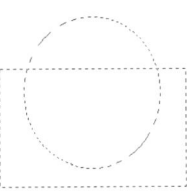

4.45

■ Make another rectangular selection in the top of the remaining porting, as though taking a square out of the top center of the selection, as shown in **Figure 4.46**.

■ Select the **Gradient** tool. Load **AFX-ScrewHead.grd** into the Gradient palette. Set the gradient options as follows:

   ■ Type = **Linear Gradient**
   ■ Mode = **Normal**
   ■ Opacity = **100%**

■ Fill the selection with the gradient. Start outside the upper left of the selection, drawing down and to the right through the selection, as shown in **Figure 4.47**.

■ Name the layer **Bolt Head**.

4.46

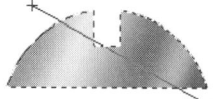

4.47

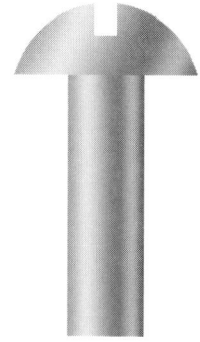

4.48

■ Create a new layer beneath the Bolt Head layer. Name this layer **Bolt Shaft**.

■ Click the **Rectangular Marquee** tool. Set the following attributes in the Options bar:

   ■ Type = **New Selection**
   ■ Feather = **0**
   ■ Style = **Normal**

■ Make a vertical selection coming out of the bottom of the bolt head. Fill the selection from left to right with the Bolt Head gradient, as shown in **Figure 4.48**.

STEP 3: ADD THREADS

■ Create a new layer beneath the Bolt Head layer and above the Bolt Shaft layer.

■ Zoom in the image so that the view is at **500%**. Pressing ⌘/Ctrl+ increases the zoom by 100% per click.

■ Make a small rectangular selection, as shown in **Figure 4.49**. Select the **Pencil** tool and fill a quarter of the selection with black, a third with white, and the bottom remainder with gray.

■ Choose **Edit ➢ Define Pattern**. Name the pattern in the dialog box and click **OK**.

■ Press the **Delete** key to clear the selection.

■ Choose **Select ➢ Deselect**.

■ ⌘/Ctrl+click the Bolt Shaft layer to bring up a selection but stay in the now empty layer where the pattern was created and deleted.

4.49

■ Choose **Edit ➢ Fill**. Select **Pattern** as the fill type and choose the pattern you just defined. Click **OK**. **Figure 4.50** shows the image with the filled selection.

■ Click the **Magic Wand**. Zoom in on the shaft and, holding down the ⌘/**Ctrl** key, select the white lines along the shaft. As soon as all the white areas are selected, press **Delete**.

■ Select the Bolt Shaft layer. ⌘/**Ctrl**+click the layer to create a selection.

■ Choose **Select ➢ Modify ➢ Contract**. Enter a contract setting of **2** and click **OK**.

■ Choose **Select ➢ Inverse**. Press the **Delete** key. The bolt now appears to have threads that protrude from the shaft, as in **Figure 4.51**.

■ Click the thread layer and rename it **Threads**.

■ Choose **Image ➢ Transform ➢ Distort**.

■ Select the top-right transform-point and move it vertically a few pixels with the mouse.

■ Select the bottom-right transform-point and move it vertically a few pixels, the same amount as the top point. These two steps angle the threads as shown in **Figure 4.52**.

■ Click the Bolt Shaft layer.

■ Select the **Polygonal Lasso** tool. Click the **Add to Selection** icon in the Options bar and make sure that the feather is set to **0** (zero).

■ Make a small selection of the bottom-left corner of the bolt. Do the same on the bottom-right corner and press **Delete**. Doing this adds the beveled look seen on a real bolt. See **Figure 4.53**.

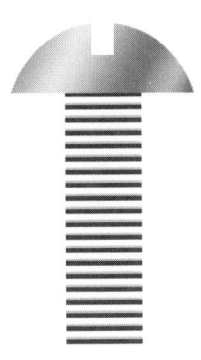

4.50

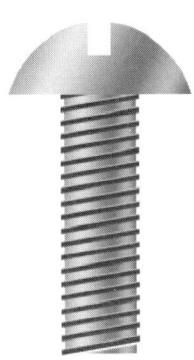

4.52

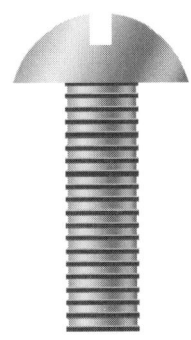

4.51

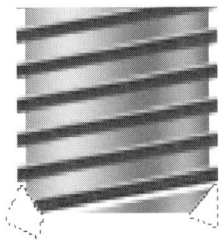

4.53

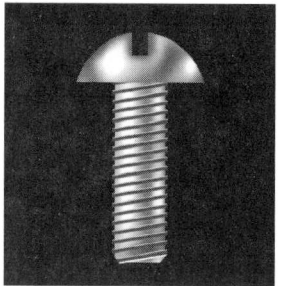

4.54

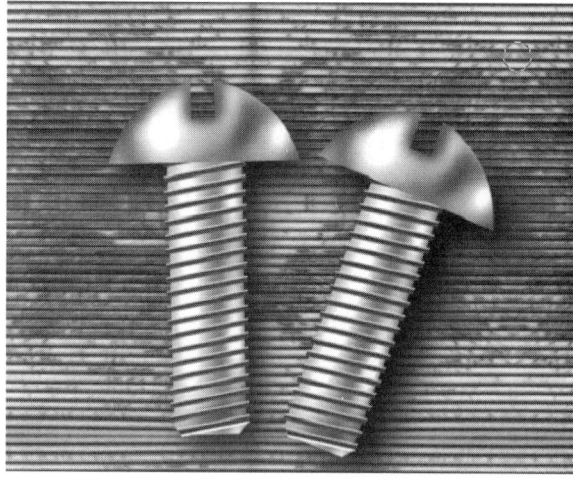

4.55

■ To increase the reflection and shadow, lightly go over the layers with the **Dodge** and **Burn** tools, as in the Pipes tutorial. **Figure 4.54** shows the new bolt with a black background to show the contrast.

When you lay metal on a texture, remember to change the tone to reflect the background colors. **Figure 4.55** shows the bolt and a friend on a textured background.

SCREWS

N ow that you have created the shaft of the bolt down, this tutorial is a quick walk-through to create the top of the bolt from a different perspective.

This tutorial requires the following from the CD-ROM:

- WoodGrain-2.jpg

STEP 1: PREPARE THE IMAGE

- Open the file **WoodGrain-2.jpg**, found on the CD-ROM. This image is seen in **Figure 4.56**.
- Create a new layer.

STEP 2: MOLD THE SCREWHEAD

- Click the **Elliptical Marquee** tool. Set the following options in the Options bar:
    - Type = **New Selection**
    - Feather = **0**
    - Style = **Fixed Aspect Ratio**
    - Width = **1**
    - Height = **1**

4.56

- Make a selection somewhere on the image. For this example, the bevel in the wood serves as a nice starting point.
- Choose **Edit ➢ Fill**. Use the following settings in the Fill dialog box:
  - Contents = **Black**
  - Mode = **Normal**
  - Opacity = **40%**
- Click **OK**.
- Create a new layer above the filled layer.
- Change the foreground color to a light gray and the background to a darker shade of gray. The number values aren't important at this point, so long as both hues are in the black to white spectrum.
- Click the **Gradient** tool in the Toolbox. In the Options bar, set the following attributes:
  - Gradient Type = **Foreground to Background**
  - Style = **Radial Gradient**
  - Mode = **Normal**
  - Opacity = **100%**
  - Reverse = **Unchecked**
- ⌘/**Ctrl**+click the filled layer to bring up a selection if it isn't still active.

- Select the new, empty layer.
- Choose **Select ➢ Modify ➢ Contract** and contract the selection by two pixels.
- Click **OK**.
- Starting in the upper-left quadrant of the selection, draw the gradient down and to the right so that the mouse stops on the selection edge in the lower-right quadrant. When filled the image should look like **Figure 4.57**.

STEP 3: GET THE GROOVE

- Press ⌘/**Ctrl+D** to deselect.
- Select the **Rectangular Marquee** tool. Make a small square selection overlapping the top of the filled circle. Select the gradient filled layer and press **Delete**. See **Figure 4.58**.
- Move the selection with the down arrow and delete a selection on the bottom of the gradient filled layer also.
- Create a new layer at the top of the layer stack.
- With the **Rectangular Marquee** tool, make a vertical selection across the face of the gradient, starting at the bottom edge of the topmost-deleted section and proceeding to the topmost edge of the bottom-deleted section. See **Figure 4.59**.

4·57

4·58

- Choose **Edit** ➤ **Fill** ➤ **Black**.
- Click **OK**.
- Select a very light gray foreground color.
- Select the **Pencil** tool from the Toolbox.
- Set the pencil size to **10** pixels or so. Holding down the **Shift** key to generate a straight line, fill one-half of the selection with gray. The fill needs to be either on the left or right of the selection, and not top/bottom. See **Figure 4.60**.

STEP 4: BEVEL THE WOOD

- Select the original black filled layer.
- Click the **Layer Styles** tab to open the palette. Select **Bevels** from the drop-down menu.
- Click **Simple Sharp Pillow Emboss** to apply this style to the black filled layer.

- You may increase or decrease the bevel settings by choosing **Layer** ➤ **Layer Style** ➤ **Style Settings** and increasing or decreasing the size percentage.

STEP 5: SHINE THINGS UP

- Click the **Burn** tool. Set the following attributes for the tool in the Options bar:
  - Brush Type = **Round, Feathered**
  - Brush Size = **22 pixels**
  - Range = **Highlights**
  - Exposure = **60%**
- Run the **Burn** tool over the outside edges of the gradient fill. Also, apply a burn to the area alongside the thread groove as in **Figure 4.61**.
- Select the **Dodge** tool. With the same settings as the Burn tool, apply the **Dodge** tool to highlight areas where reflections might be. See **Figure 4.62**.

4.59

4.60

4.61

4.62

4.63

For the final example (**Figure 4.63**), duplicates were made of the finished screwhead and placed around the image. The Burn tool was applied to the background layer to give the appearance of water stains over time.

CHROME

O ur minds are trained from birth to distinguish between things natural and those made by man. You would not expect to see wires in a tree limb, or insects with metallic limbs. Images containing aspects of both nature and mechanized objects are a bit surreal, but are also very eye-catching. This tutorial shows how to create a robotic bug, blending the two worlds, natural and industrial, together.

This tutorial requires the following from the CD-ROM:

- AFX-Woods-1.pat
- AFX-grids.pat
- AFX-HardMetals1.asl

STEP 1: PREPARE THE IMAGE

- Create a new image by choosing **File ➤ New**. Enter the following attributes in the New Image dialog box:
    - Name = **Chrome Critter**
    - Preset Size = **800 x 600 pixels**
    - Resolution = **72 dpi**
    - Mode = **RGB**
    - Contents = **White**
- Click **OK**.
- Create a new layer.

STEP 2: MAKE A BUG

- Select the **Elliptical Marquee** from the Toolbox. Set the following attributes for the tool in the Options bar:
    - Selection Type = **New Selection**
    - Feather = **0 (zero)**
    - Anti-aliased = **Checked**
    - Style = **Normal**
- Make a large oval selection in the center of the new document, as shown in **Figure 4.64**.
- Set the foreground color to light gray and the background to dark gray.
- Click the **Gradient** tool. In the Options bar, select the foreground to background linear gradient.
- Find the middle point in the selection. Go up about an inch, click and drag the mouse to an inch outside the lowest edge at the bottom of the selection. This fills the selection with the gradient, as shown in **Figure 4.65**.

- Select the **Dodge** tool. Set the following attributes in the Options bar:
    - Brush Type = **Round, Feathered**
    - Size = **50 pixels**
    - Range = **Highlights**
    - Exposure = **25 to 30%**
- Use the **Dodge** tool to create a few highlights on the face of the gradient, as shown in **Figure 4.66**. Keep in mind that this is a curved surface, so the reflections should have some curve to them as well.
- Continue making highlights along the both the top and bottom edges. As the curve gets sharper along the edges, decrease the size of the brush used with the **Dodge** tool to narrow the area reflected. **Figure 4.67** gives an example of this.

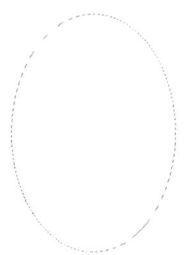

4.64

4.66

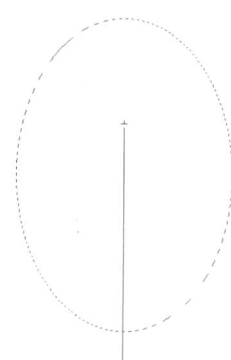

4.65

4.67

- Again, select the **Elliptical Marquee** tool.
- Create a new layer.
- In the new layer, create another oval. Make it larger than the first, covering the entire oval just created. Doing this serves as an outer shell for the bug. See **Figure 4.68** for an example.
- Select the **Gradient** tool again. Fill this layer as you did the one previous.
- Choose **Select ➢ Deselect** (⌘/Ctrl+D).
- Select the **Rectangular Marquee** tool from the Toolbox.
- Make a narrow selection, top to bottom, through the newly filled gradient layer.
- Press **Delete**. **Figure 4.69** shows the image thus far.
- Press ⌘/Ctrl+D to deselect.
- ⌘/Ctrl+click the split oval layer to generate a selection of the two pieces or wings.
- Select the **Dodge** tool again. With the same settings as before, create highlights on this layer as well. When satisfied with the reflections, select the **Burn** tool and trace the perimeter of the selections to darken them a bit. See **Figure 4.70**.
- Duplicate the wing layer.
- Choose **Image ➢ Adjustments ➢ Invert** (⌘/Ctrl+I).
- Set the blending mode for the new layer to **Overlay**. Doing this adds a bit of metallic sheen to the bug.
- ⌘/Ctrl+click the wings layer again to generate the selection.
- Create a new layer at the top of the layer stack.
- Select the **Gradient** tool. In the Options bar, select the **Chrome Gradient** in the default gradient set. Set the attributes for the Gradient tool as follows in the Options bar:
  - Gradient Type = **Linear Gradient**
  - Mode = **Normal**
  - Opacity = **100%**
  - Reverse = **Unchecked**

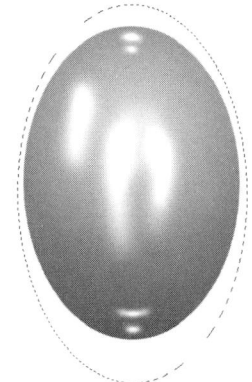

4.68

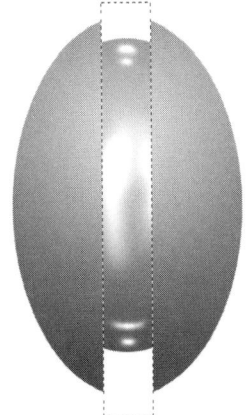

4.69

4.70

- Starting at the top of the selection and moving down to about one-third from the bottom of the selection, fill the bug with the Chrome gradient. See **Figure 4.71**.
- Choose **Filter ➤ Blur ➤ Gaussian Blur**. Enter a blur radius of **30** pixels.
- Click **OK**.
- Press ⌘/Ctrl+D to deselect.
- Click the background layer. Choose **Edit ➤ Fill** and fill the layer with black, **100%** opacity.
- Click **OK**.

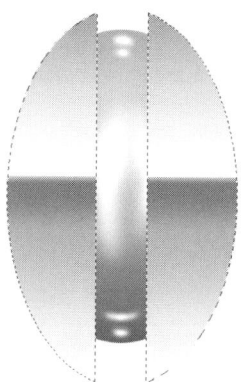

4.71

- ⌘/**Ctrl**+click the wings layer again to generate the selection or just choose **Select ➤ Reselect**. See **Figure 4.72**.
- Create a new layer above the chrome gradient filled layer.
- Press **D** to reset the default colors (Black = foreground, White = background).
- Choose **Edit ➤ Stroke**. Enter stroke values as follows:
    - Width = **1**
    - Color = **Black**
    - Location = **Inside**
    - Mode = **Normal**
    - Opacity = **80%**
- Click **OK**.
- ⌘/**Ctrl**+click the Chrome Fill layer. Doing this brings up an irregular, feathered selection.
- Create a new layer just above the chrome filled layer.
- Choose **Edit ➤ Fill**. In the Fill dialog box, select **Pattern** as the fill type. Click the small arrow next to the pattern viewer and open the pattern menu. Load **AFX-Woods-1.pat** found on the CD-ROM. Select any of the wood patterns. The one used here is the second from the right, top row. Set the opacity of the fill to **20%**.
- Click **OK**. See **Figure 4.73** for the result.

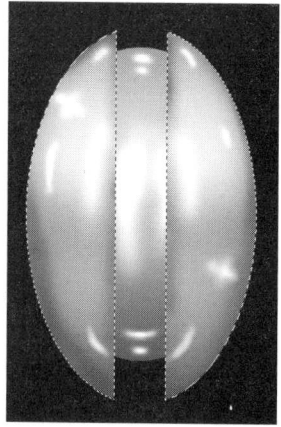

4.72

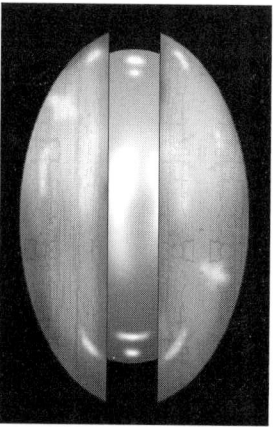

4.73

STEP 3: MAKE LEGS (CREEPERS)

- Create a new layer above the background layer.
- Select the **Polygonal Lasso** tool.
- Make a pointed selection extending from beneath the bug out in the upper-left quadrant. See **Figure 4.74**.
- Choose **Edit ➢ Fill**. Fill the selection with 100% black.
- Click **OK**.
- Click the **Layer Styles** tab. Load **AFX-HardMetals1.asl** into the Layer Styles palette.
- Click **Style 5** to apply it to the bug leg. See **Figure 4.75**.

- You can create another selection overlaying the leg on the same layer and fill it with black as well to create more character on the leg. Duplicate this layer five times and place the legs around the perimeter of the bug as shown in **Figure 4.76**.

STEP 4: BUG EYES

- Create a new layer just above the original oval and below the wings.
- ⌘/**Ctrl**+click the original oval layer to generate a selection.
- Select the **Rectangular Marquee** tool. Set the following attributes in the Options bar:
    - Selection Type = **Subtract from Selection**
    - Feather = **0 (zero)**
    - Style = **Normal**
- Select all but the top portion of the bug to delete the majority of the existing selection, as shown in **Figure 4.77**.

4.74

4.75

4.76

4.77

4.78

4.79 (CP11)

- Press **D** to reset the default colors.
- Select the **Gradient** tool again.
- In the Options bar, leave everything the same (Foreground to Background gradient, and so forth) but check the **Reverse** box.
- Starting in the center of the selection and going to just beyond the bottom edge of the selection, fill with the gradient.
- Choose **Edit ➢ Stroke**. Repeat the settings as before (they are already in place). Click **OK**.
- Add some color to the eyes. Choose **Enhance ➢ Adjust Color ➢ Hue/Saturation (⌘/Ctrl+U)**. Set the following attributes in the Hue/Saturation dialog box:
  - Hue = **0**
  - Saturation = **65**
  - Lightness = **0**
  - Colorize = **Checked**
- Click **OK**.
- Make sure that the eye selection is still active; if not, ⌘/**Ctrl**+click the eye layer.
- Create a new layer above the eye layer.
- Choose **Edit ➢ Fill**. Set the fill type to **Pattern**.
- Load the Pattern set **AFX-grids.pat**, found on the CD-ROM.
- Fill the selection with one of the grid patterns. See **Figure 4.78**.

You may also alter the eye shapes with the Polygonal Lasso or other selection tool by selecting and deleting corners from the eye layer and the grid fill layer. See **Figure 4.79 (CP11)**. I encourage you to experiment, because no two bugs are exactly alike!

BLOWING GLASS

A great way to bring realism into your design is to have the background of the image or elements of the photo become part of the effect itself. In this tutorial you will learn to manipulate a photograph to generate glass.

This tutorial requires the following from the CD-ROM:

- StormClouds-1.jpg

STEP 1: PREPARE THE IMAGE

- Open **StormClouds-1.jpg**, found on the CD-ROM.
- Duplicate the background layer.

STEP 2: CREATE THE SPHERE

- Select the **Elliptical Marquee** tool from the Toolbox. Set the following attributes in the Options bar:
  - Selection Type = **New Selection**
  - Feather = **0**
  - Anti-aliased = **Checked**
  - Style = **Fixed Aspect Ratio**
  - Width = **1**
  - Height = **1**

4.80

4.81

- Make a large selection in the center of the image, as shown in **Figure 4.80**.
- Choose **Filter ➢ Distort ➢ Spherize**.
- In the Spherize dialog box, set the Amount to **100%** and the Mode to **Normal**.
- Click **OK**.
- Choose **Select ➢ Inverse** (⌘/Ctrl+I).
- Press the **Delete** key. **Figure 4.81** shows the image thus far.
- Choose **Select ➢ Reselect**.
- Press ⌘/Ctrl+I to select the inverse. The sphere should now be reselected.
- Duplicate the Sphere layer.
- Choose **Filter ➢ Render ➢ 3D Transform**.
- In the 3D Transform dialog box, click the **Sphere** tool. Draw a spherical selection around the object by clicking the mouse in the upper-left corner and dragging down to the lower-right corner. A green circle is drawn around the sphere object.
- Click the **Trackball** tool. Click the mouse in the center of the sphere and drag to the upper right a few degrees. The clouds distort as though rotating on the face of the sphere (see **Figure 4.82**). Also, some gray harmonics, or excess pixels, appear on the left side of the sphere. They look bad now, but don't worry — these come to good use shortly.

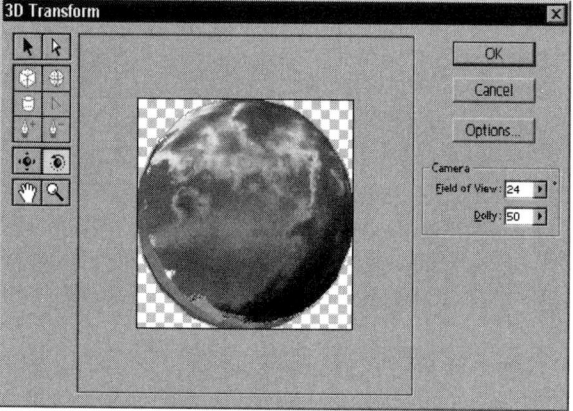

4.82

■ Click **OK**.

■ The sphere selection should still be active: If not, choose **Select ➤ Reselect** or press **Shift+⌘/Ctrl+D**.

■ Click the **Elliptical Marquee** tool. Leave all settings as before, except change the selection type to **Subtract from Selection**.

■ Select all but a sliver of the left side where the gray distortion is as in **Figure 4.83**.

■ Choose **Filter ➤ Blur ➤ Gaussian Blur**. Enter a blur radius of **8** or **9** pixels and click **OK**. **Figure 4.84** shows how the gray area is starting to help create the reflections on the glass surface.

STEP 3: CREATE REFLECTIONS

■ **⌘/Ctrl**+click the Sphere layer to create a round selection.

■ Create a new layer at the top of the layer stack.

■ Press **D** to reset the default colors.

■ Press **X** to swap the foreground and background colors.

■ Click the **Gradient** tool. In the Gradient Options bar, select the **Foreground to Transparent** gradient. Click the **Linear** gradient and set the opacity for the gradient to **80%**.

■ Starting at the top of the selection, click and drag the mouse to the center of the sphere.

■ Choose **Select ➤ Deselect**.

■ Choose **Image ➤ Transform ➤ Perspective**.

■ Select the bottom-left or bottom-right transform point. Move the point toward the center, as shown in **Figure 4.85**.

■ Set the blending mode of the white gradient layer to **Overlay**.

■ **⌘/Ctrl**+click the sphere layer again.

■ Select the **Elliptical Marquee** tool. In the Options bar, click the **Intersect With Selection** button.

4.83

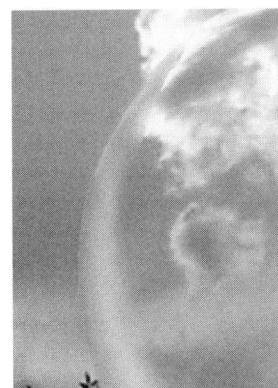

4.84

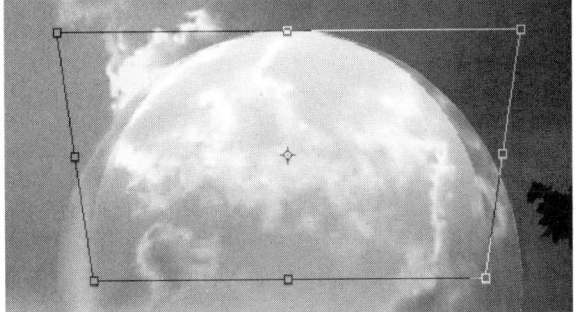

4.85

4.86

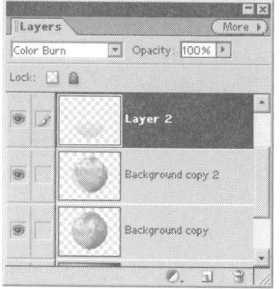

4.87

- Draw an oval over the bottom of the sphere selection, as shown in **Figure 4.86**.
- Create a new layer beneath the white gradient layer.
- Click the **Eyedropper** tool. Take a sample of a brown tone directly from the image. This places that color in the foreground slot.
- Click the **Gradient** tool. Stay with the **Foreground to Transparent** gradient.
- Starting at the bottom of the selection, drag the gradient up to the center of the sphere.
- Change the blending mode for this layer to **Color Burn**. See **Figure 4.87**.
- Choose **Filter ➢ Blur ➢ Gaussian Blur**. Enter a blur radius of **15** pixels.
- Click **OK**.
- Select the Sphere copy layer.
- Choose **Filter ➢ Render ➢ Lens Flare**.
  - Select a point in the upper-left quadrant of the sphere.
  - Set the brightness to **90%**.
  - Select **105mm Prime** as the lens type.
- Click **OK**. See **Figure 4.88**.
- Select the **Dodge** tool. In the Options bar, set the following attributes:
  - Brush Type = **Rounded, Feathered**
  - Size = **44 pixels**
  - Range = **Highlights**
  - Exposure = **25%**

4.88

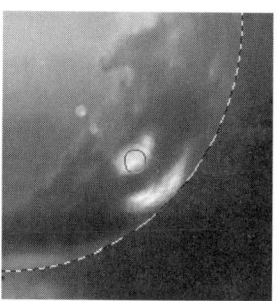

4.89

■ Take a look at where the small light reflections appear in the lower right of the sphere. Apply the **Dodge** tool in line with the lens flare/reflection in a short curved motion to generate inner reflections, as shown in **Figure 4.89**.

■ Select the **Burn** tool. With the same settings as the Dodge tool, trace around the perimeter of the selection on the three quadrants opposite the light source. See **Figure 4.90**.

■ Using both the **Dodge** and **Burn** tools, add more reflections and shadows around the image. Keep in mind that this is a sphere, so the shadows and reflections need to be curved somewhat. When done, you should have a glassy sphere, as shown **Figure 4.91 (CP12)**.

4.90

4.91 (CP12)

QUICK PLASTIC TYPE

Plastic has some qualities of glass, in that both generally have surfaces that reflect light more readily than other materials. Plastic can also share translucent qualities with glass. There are a few subtle differences between the two materials, however, so this tutorial addresses that. You will learn to generate plastic type; see if you can spot the differences in lighting and shading that separate it from the glass tutorial.

STEP 1: PREPARE THE IMAGE

- Create a new image. Set the attributes as follows:
  - Name = **Plastic**
  - Preset Size = **800 x 600 pixels**
  - Resolution = **72 dpi**
  - Mode = **RGB**
  - Contents = **White**
- Fill the background image with a color or gradient. For this example, a light-blue to dark-blue gradient was used.
- Create a new layer.

STEP 2: MAKE SELECTIONS AND APPLY COLOR

- Select the **Type Mask** tool. In the Options bar, set the following attributes:
  - Type = **Regular**
  - Font = **Times New Roman** (any font will do)
  - Size = **200 points**
  - Anti-aliased = **Selected**
  - Justify = **Center**

- Enter your text in the new layer. See **Figure 4.92**.
- Because you used blue as a background, use orange as a fill color. These appear opposite on the color wheel and work well together. Click the Foreground color and enter the following color value in the Color Picker: **#FF8B03**, or R = **255**, G = **139**, and B = **3**.
- Click **OK**.
- Choose **Edit ➢ Fill**. Select **Foreground Color** as the fill type and set the opacity to **100%**.
- Click **OK**.
- Press **X** to swap the foreground and background colors. Set white as the foreground color.

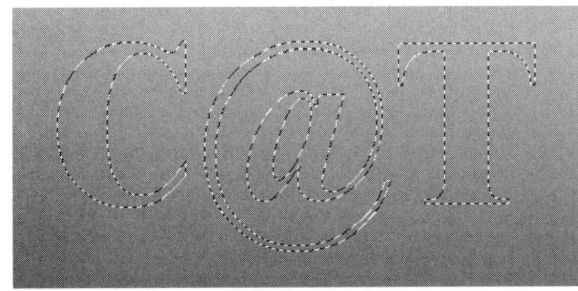

4.92

- Create a new layer.
- Choose **Edit ➢ Fill**. Fill the new layer with white, with the opacity set to **90%**.
- Click **OK**.
- Press **X** to swap the foreground and background colors.
- Choose **Edit ➢ Stroke**. Apply a stroke with the following settings:
  - Width = **8 pixels**
  - Color = **Foreground (orange)**
  - Location = **Inside**
  - Mode = **Normal**
  - Opacity = **100%**
- Click **OK**.
- Choose **Filter ➢ Blur ➢ Gaussian Blur**. Enter a blur radius of **6** pixels.
- Click **OK**. See **Figure 4.93**.
- Click the foreground color. In the Color Picker, enter a color value of **#834700**, or R = **131**, G = **71**, and B = **0**.

- Click **OK**.
- Choose **Edit ➢ Stroke**. Enter the following values in the Stroke dialog box:
  - Width = **4 pixels**
  - Location = **Inside**
  - Mode = **Normal**
  - Opacity = **100%**
- Click **OK**.
- Choose **Filter ➢ Blur ➢ Gaussian Blur**. Enter a blur radius of **2** pixels.
- Click **OK**. See **Figure 4.94**.
- With the arrow keys, move the selection a few pixels to the right. See **Figure 4.95**.
- Create a new layer.
- Choose **Edit ➢ Fill**. Fill the selection with white, **90%** opacity.
- Click **OK**.
- Again, move the selection with the arrow keys a few pixels to the right.
- Press **Delete**. See **Figure 4.96**.

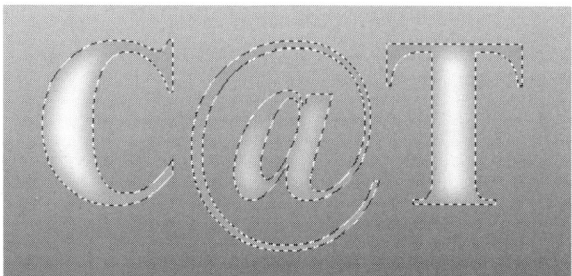

4.93

4.95

4.94

4.96

- ⌘/**Ctrl**+click the original type layer. Stay on the layer that you have been working on. You need a type selection active on the white fill layer.
- Choose **Select** ➤ **Inverse**.
- Press the **Delete** key.
- Choose **Select** ➤ **Inverse** again to make the type selection active.
- Choose **Filter** ➤ **Blur** ➤ **Gaussian Blur**. Enter a blur radius of **1** pixel.
- Click **OK**.
- Set the blending mode of the white fill layer to **Hard Light**. See **Figure 4.97**.
- Select the original Stroke layer, which is just above the type layer.
- Choose **Filter** ➤ **Artistic** ➤ **Plastic Wrap**. Set the following attributes for the filter:
  - Highlight Strength = **10**
  - Detail = **10**
  - Smoothness = **10**
- Click **OK**. See **Figure 4.98**.
- Set the layer blending mode to **Overlay**. Set the opacity to **80%**.
- Press **D** to reset the fore and background colors.
- ⌘/**Ctrl**+click the type layer to generate the type selection.
- Create a new layer.
- Choose **Edit** ➤ **Stroke** and set the following attributes in the Stoke dialog box:
  - Size = **1 pixel**
  - Color = **Black**
- Location = **Center**
- Mode = **Normal**
- Opacity = **100%**
- Click **OK**.

In the final image, the Wave filter was applied to the background and a drop shadow added to the text. See **Figure 4.99**.

I hope you have come to understand a bit about lighting, gradients, and blending modes. This chapter also utilized several additional author-created add-ons. Not only did I do this to make cool designs, but I also wanted to show you are not limited to Elements alone, but a variety of tools that can be "plugged in" depending on your needs or artistic tastes. In Elements, you are only limited by your ability and your eye for design. After you understand the technique basics, the art you create is up to your imagination.

4.98

4.97

4.99

5

SHOCK VALUE:
ELECTRONICS

Following the pattern set by time past, you'll now move on from making metal and simple tools to electronics and the digital age.

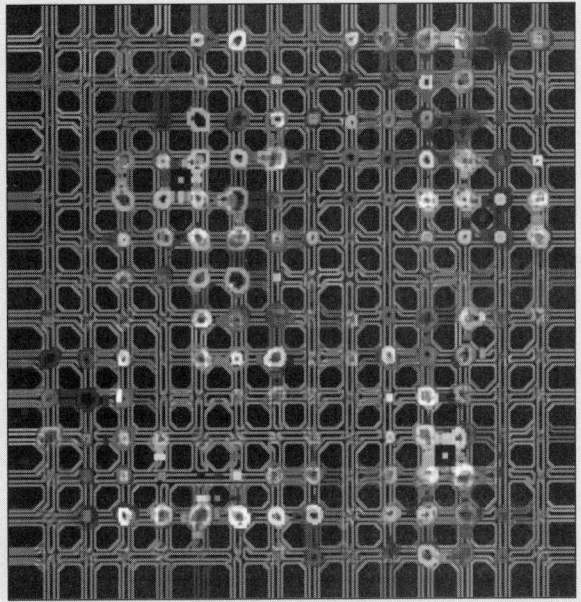

Knowing the Workspace: Tools, Palettes, and Shortcuts

A firm knowledge of the tools at your disposal is essential for effective design and editing. The Sponge tool can saturate the subject of a photo, while taking color away from other areas.

CP1

CP2

3D Objects in a 2D World

Using simple shapes such as squares, circles, and triangles, Elements 2 allows you to create real world objects from a blank image.

CP3

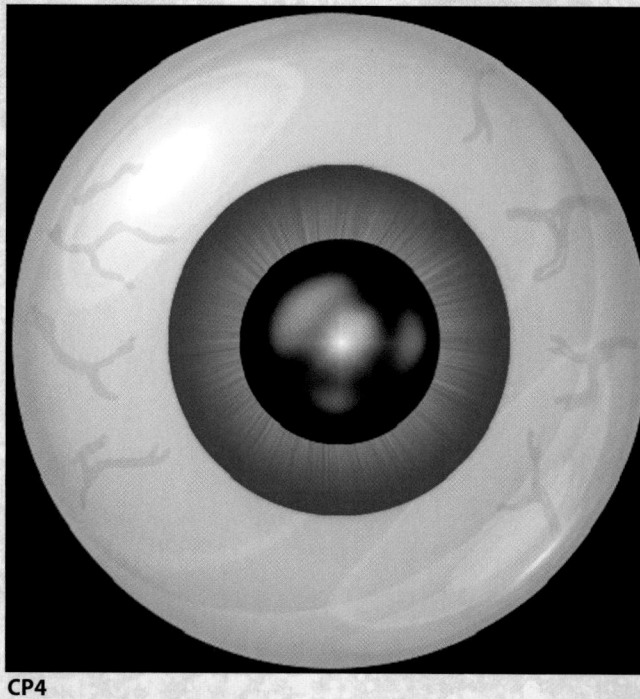

CP4

CP5

Chapter 3
Unnaturally Natural Elements

With Elements 2, you can design materials from nature such as wood, water, and stone.

CP6

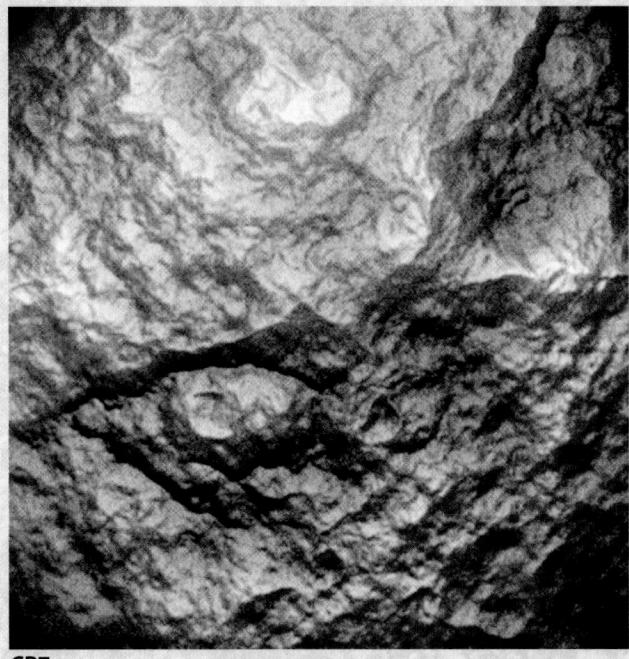

CP7

Unnaturally Natural Elements

With a bit of practice, designers can chisel and carve the materials they create to suit their purposes.

CP8

CP9

CP10

Chapter 4
Getting Technical: Industrial Effects

A firm grasp on lighting and shadows helps create metals and glass. Light is the key ingredient in photo-realism.

CP11

CP12

Chapter 5
Shock Value: Electronics

Certain filters within Elements allow for the creation of wiring and circuitry.

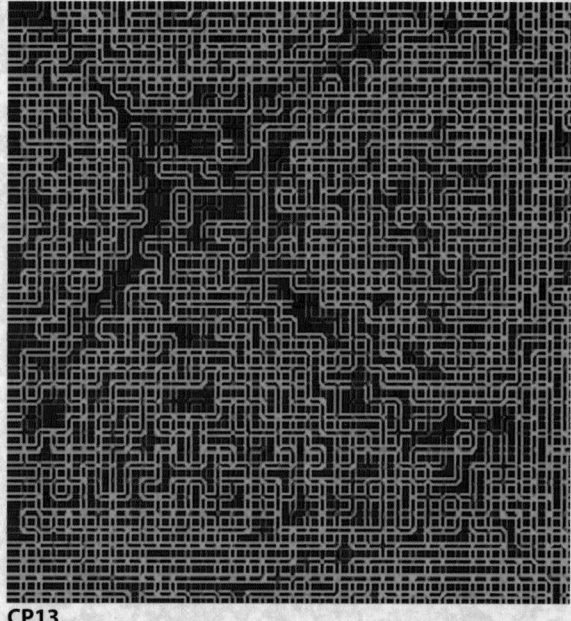

CP13

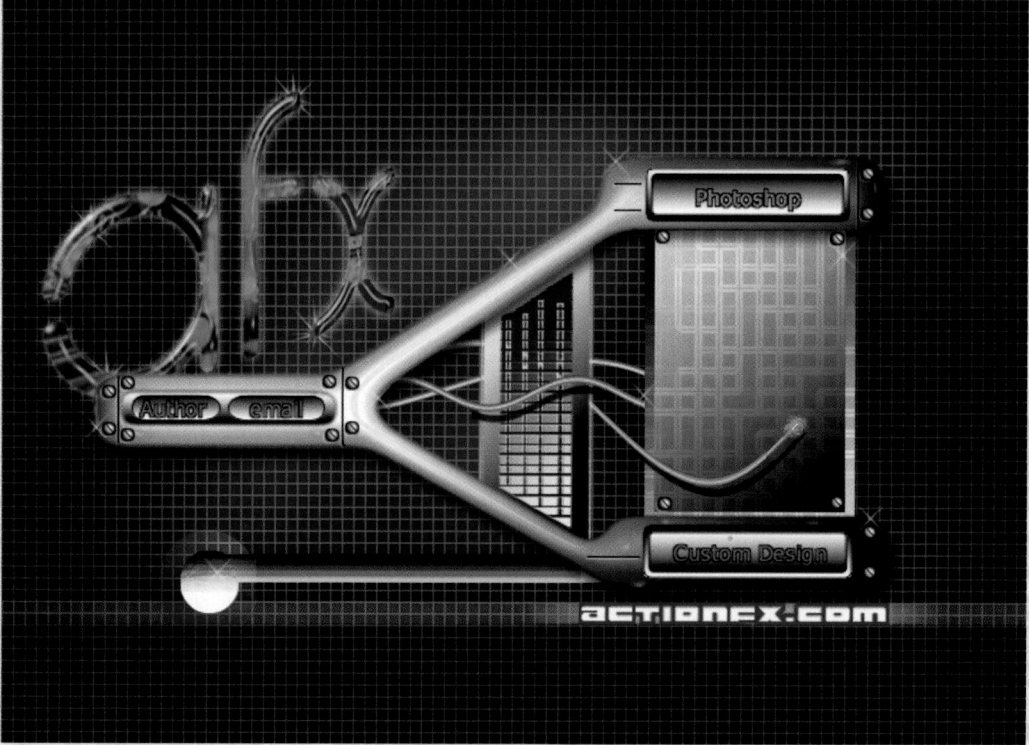

CP14

Chapter 6

Getting a Grasp on Intangibles: Vapors, Rays, and Electricity

Manipulating photos can produce some wild images, such as lightning, ghosts, and x-rays.

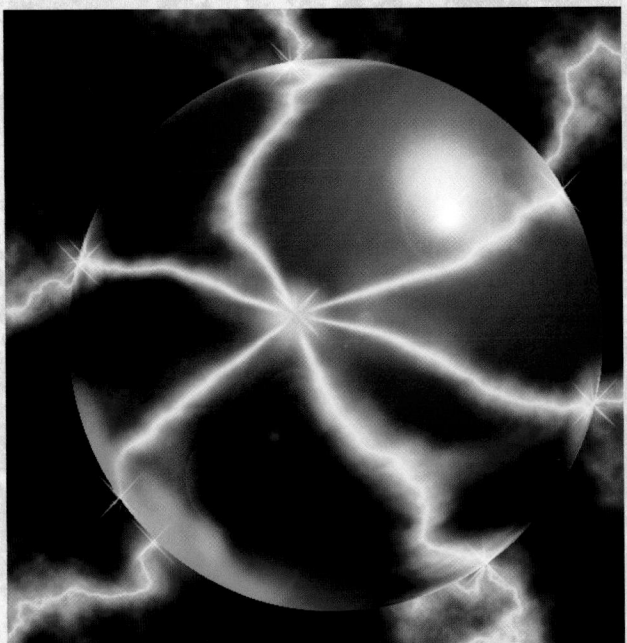

CP15

CP16

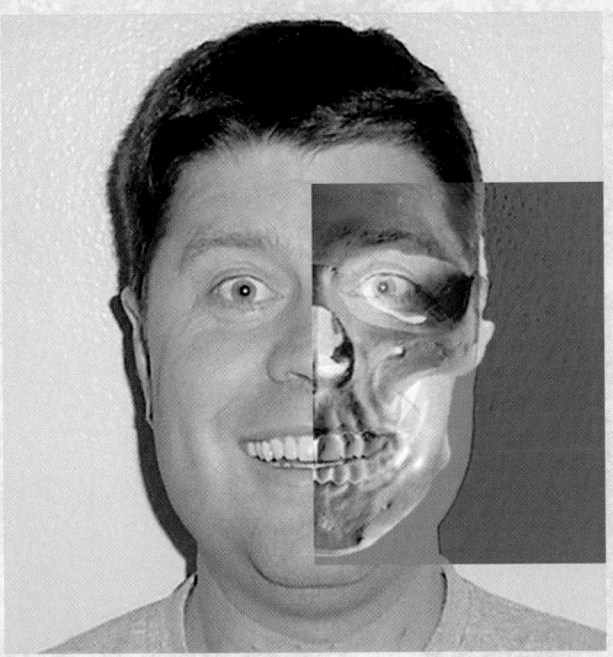

CP17

I Should Have Been a Doctor: Altering Humans and Critters

Elements can combine objects and creatures from different photographs, creating images not likely seen in the real world. A bit of practice and the designer can be a tabloid artist.

CP18

CP19

I Should Have Been a Doctor: Altering Humans and Critters

The Liquify tool can be used to turn family members into other-worldly creatures in just a few steps!

CP20

CP21

CP22

Chapter 8
Interfacing With the Web

Use your knowledge of Elements to interface with the world.
Create Web page layouts and fantastic machines to communicate
your talent to the online community.

CP23

CP24

Chapter 9

How Can You Say That?
Type Treatments

Manipulate type for your banners, headlines, and logos.

CP25

CP26

Example Styles from AFX-EL2-set1

CP27

Example Styles from AFX-FancyType-1.asl

CP28

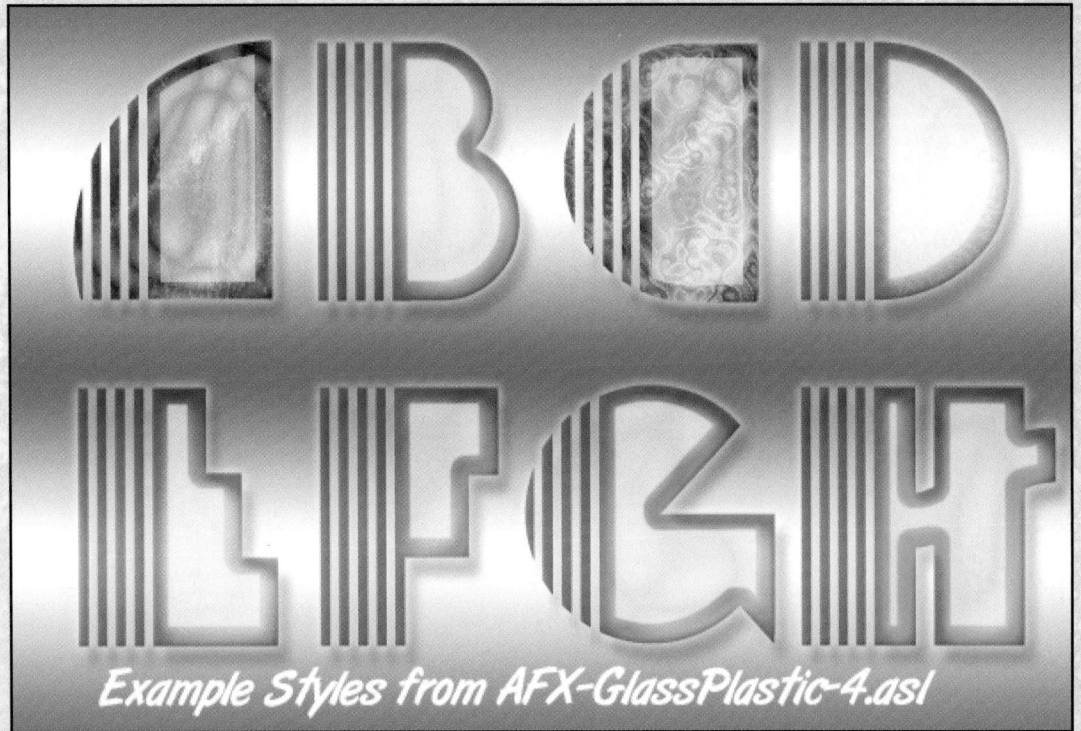

Example Styles from AFX-GlassPlastic-4.asl

CP29

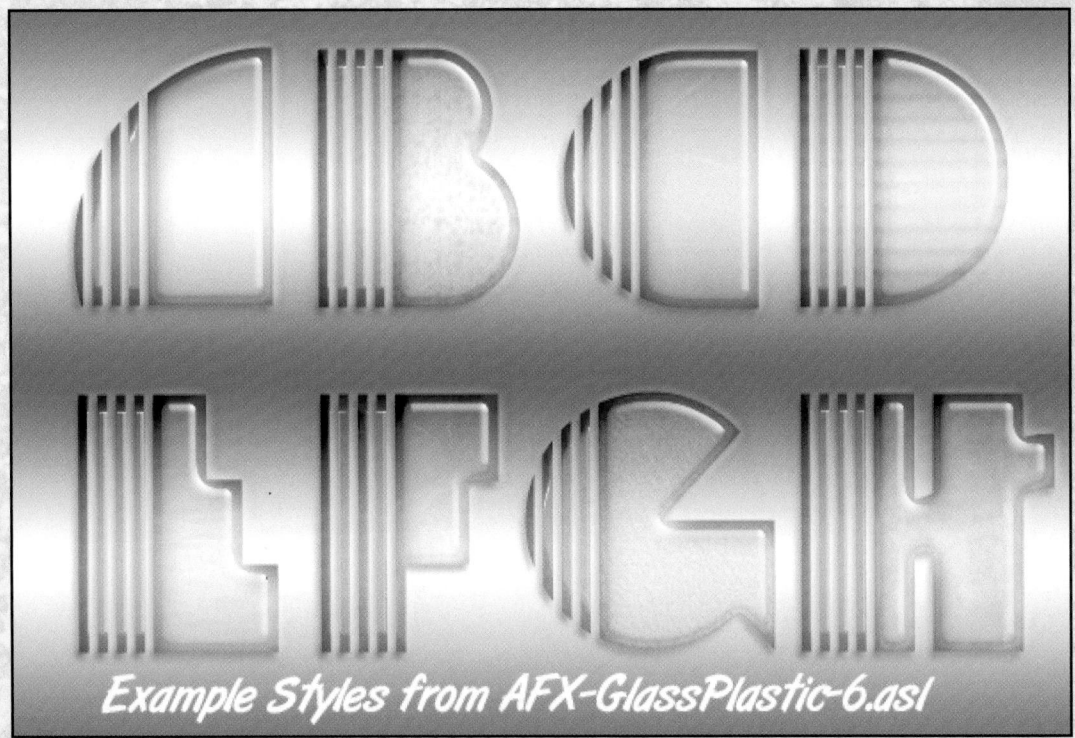

Example Styles from AFX-GlassPlastic-6.asl

CP30

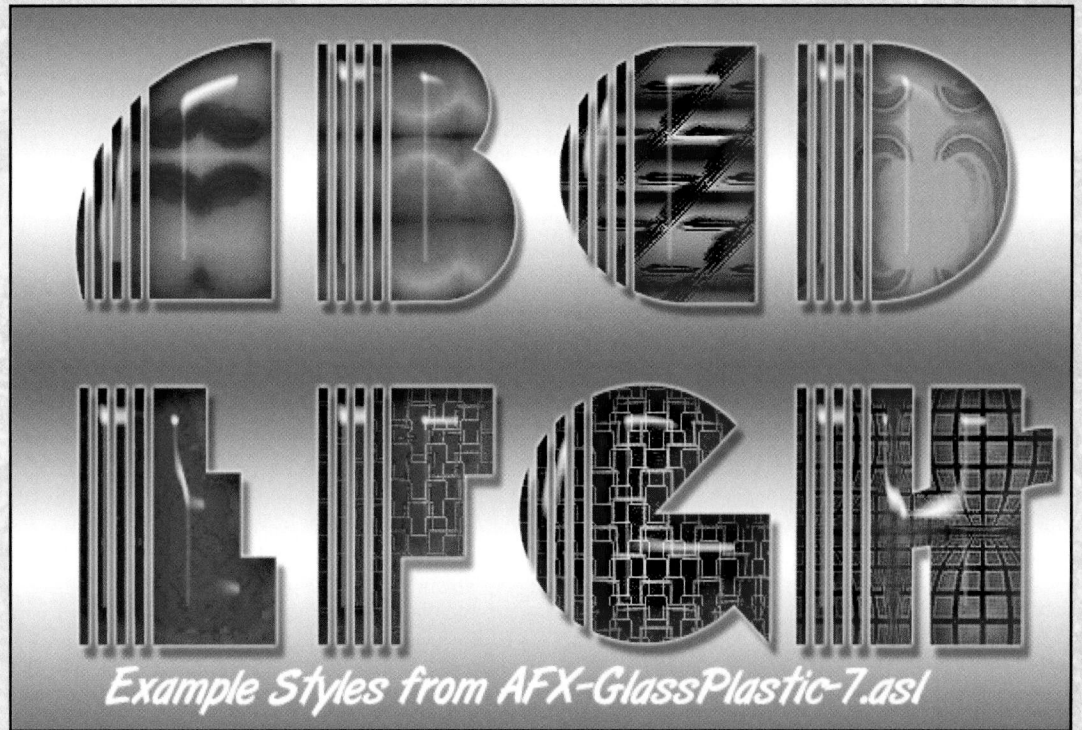

CP31

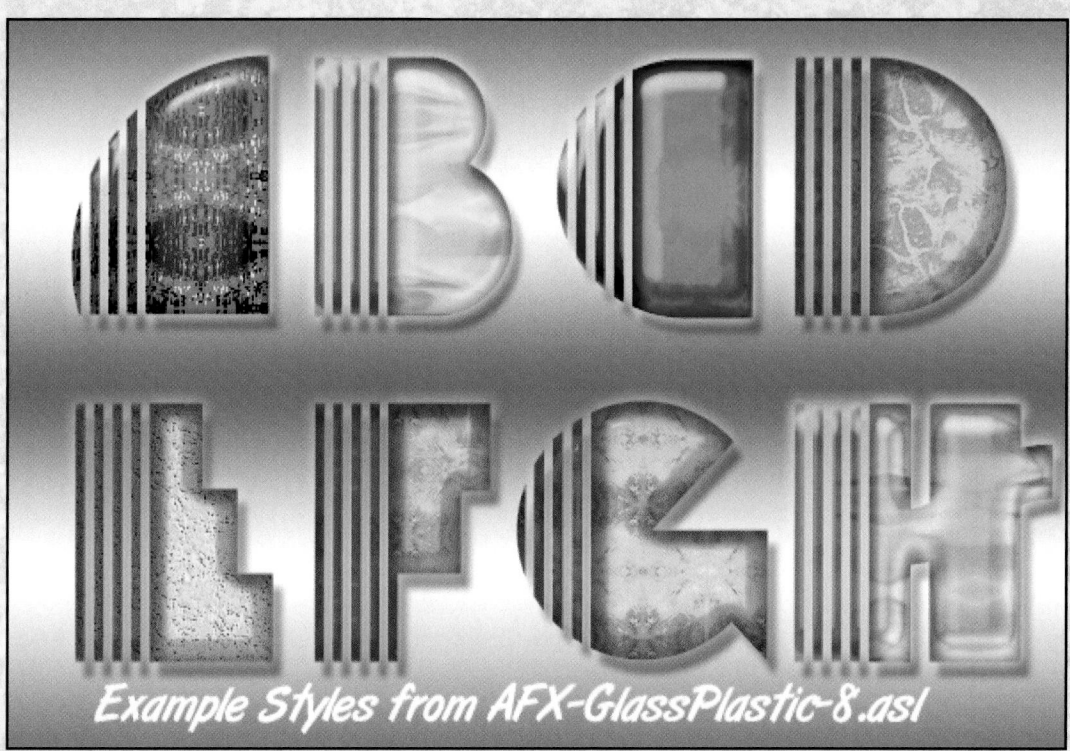

CP32

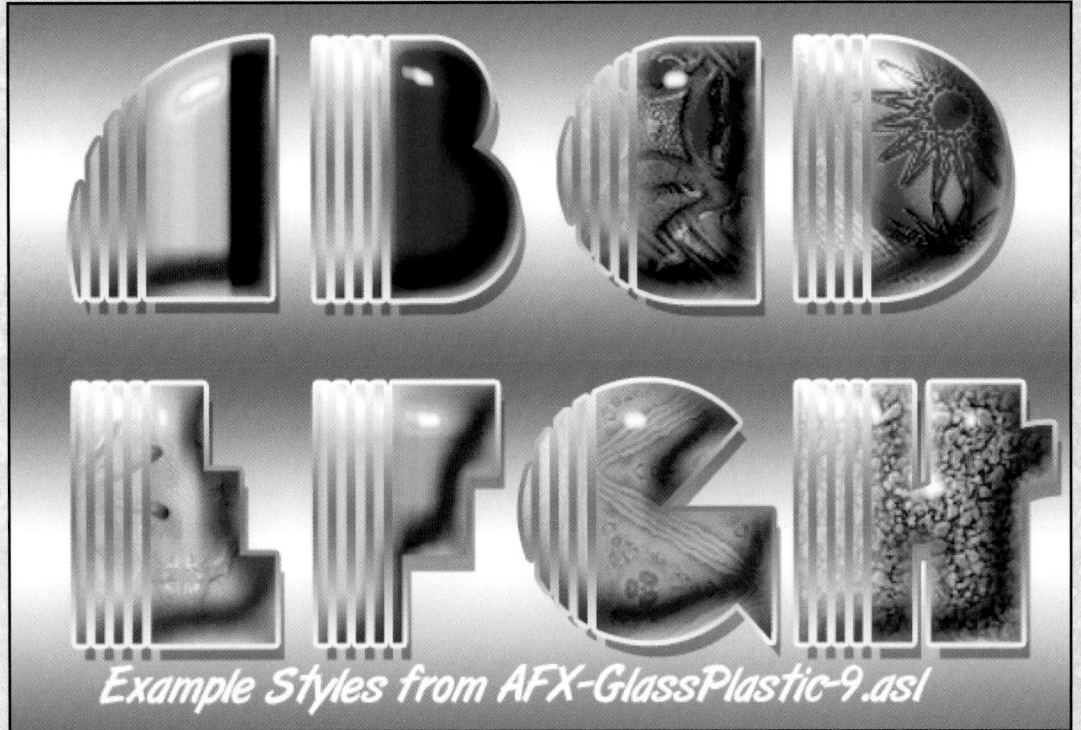

Example Styles from AFX-GlassPlastic-9.asl

CP33

Example Styles from AFX-MetalType-1.asl

CP34

Example Styles from AFX-PatternType-1.asl

CP35

Example Styles from AFX-PatternType-4.asl

CP36

Example Styles from AFX-PatternType-10.asl

CP37

Example Styles from AFX-PatternType-13.asl

CP38

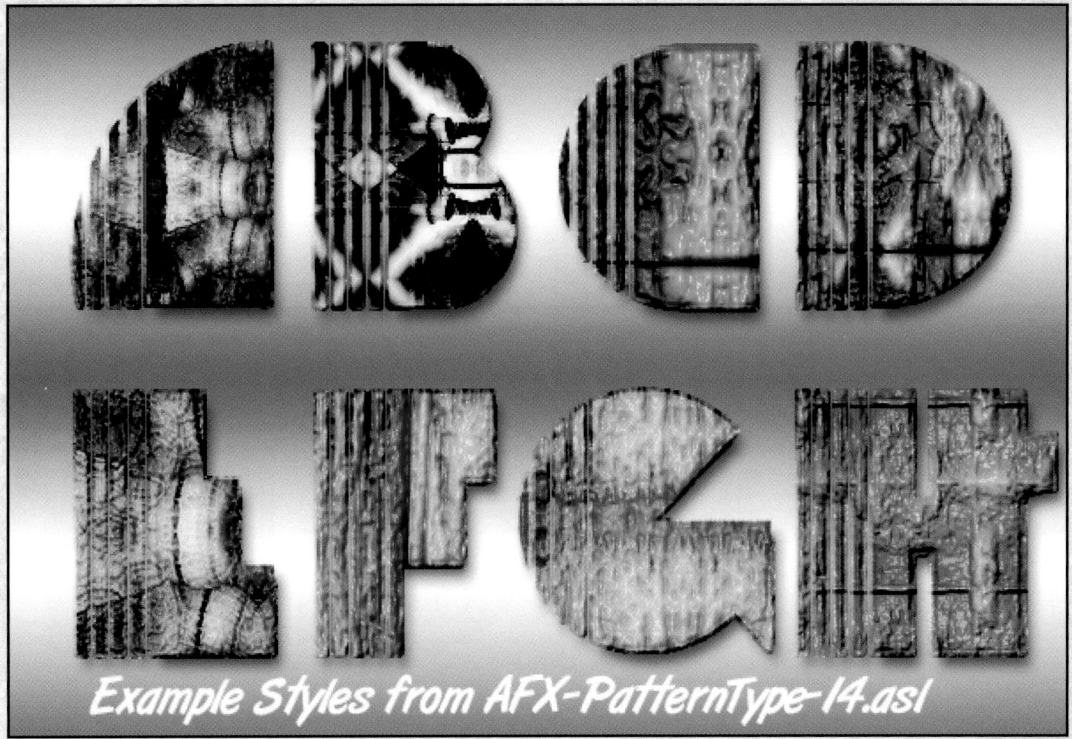

Example Styles from AFX-PatternType-14.asl

CP39

Example Styles from AFX-WoodStone-2.asl

CP40

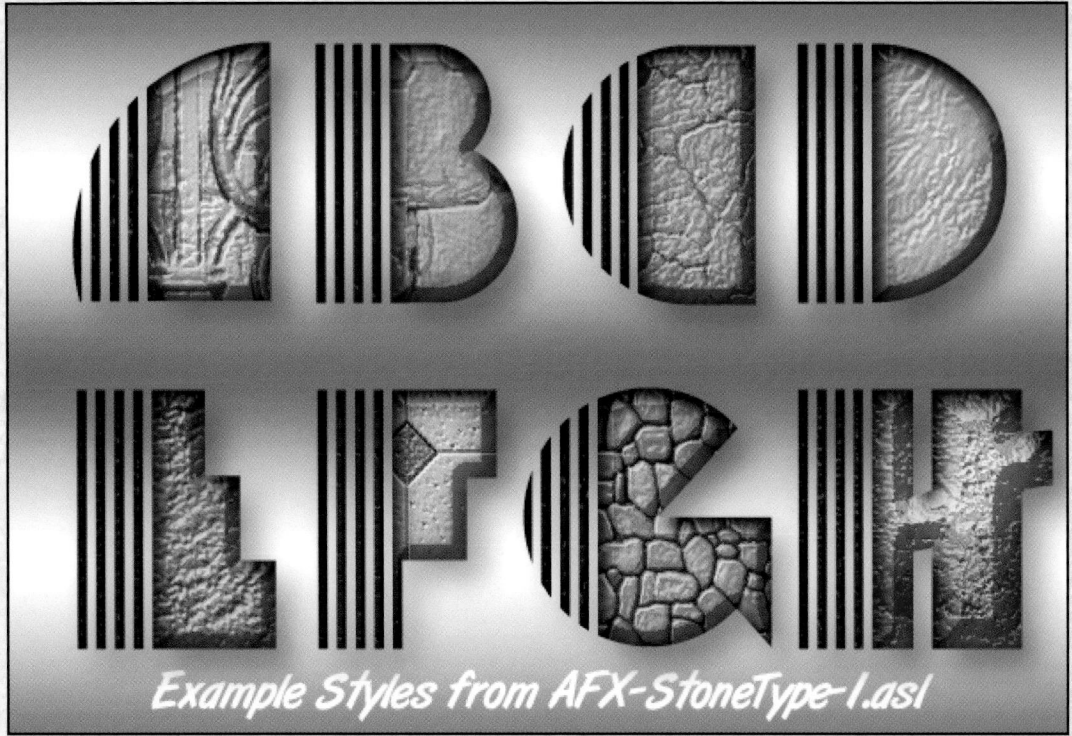

Example Styles from AFX-StoneType-1.asl

CP41

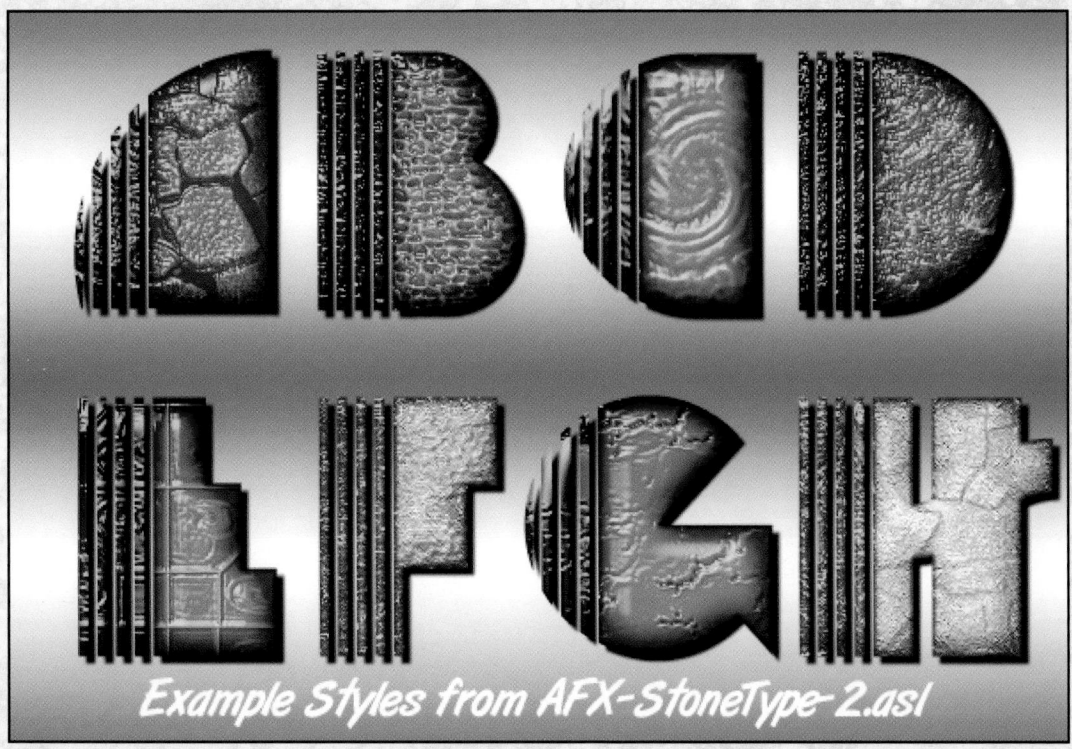

Example Styles from AFX-StoneType-2.asl

CP42

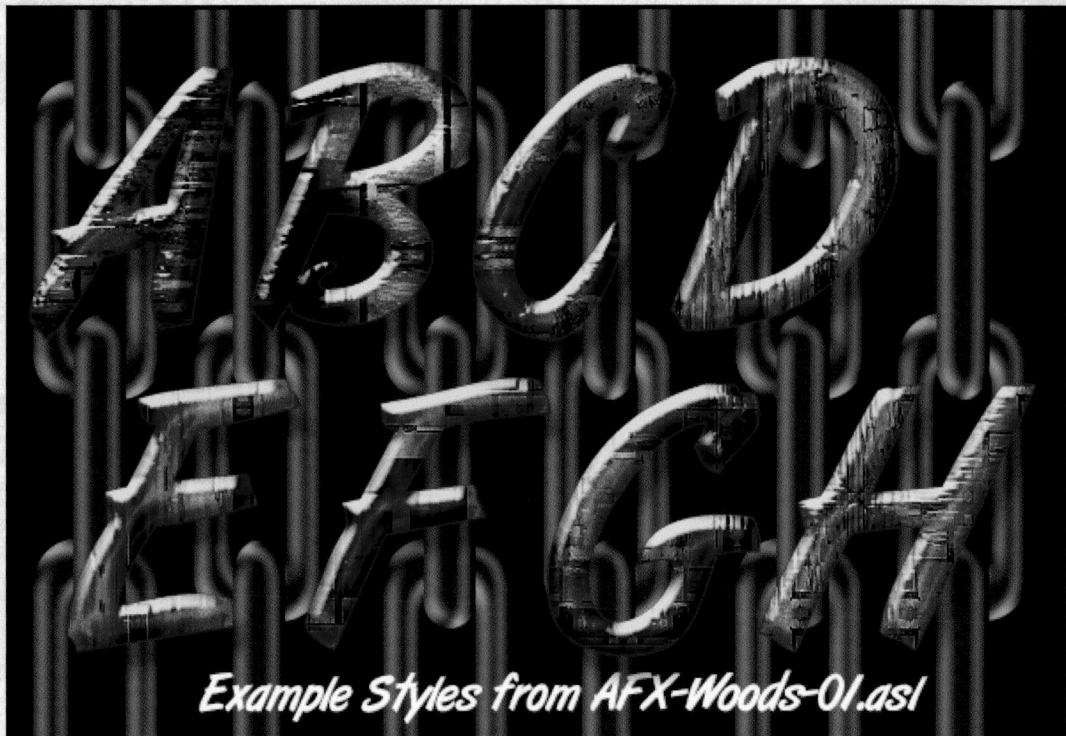

Example Styles from AFX-Woods-01.asl

CP43

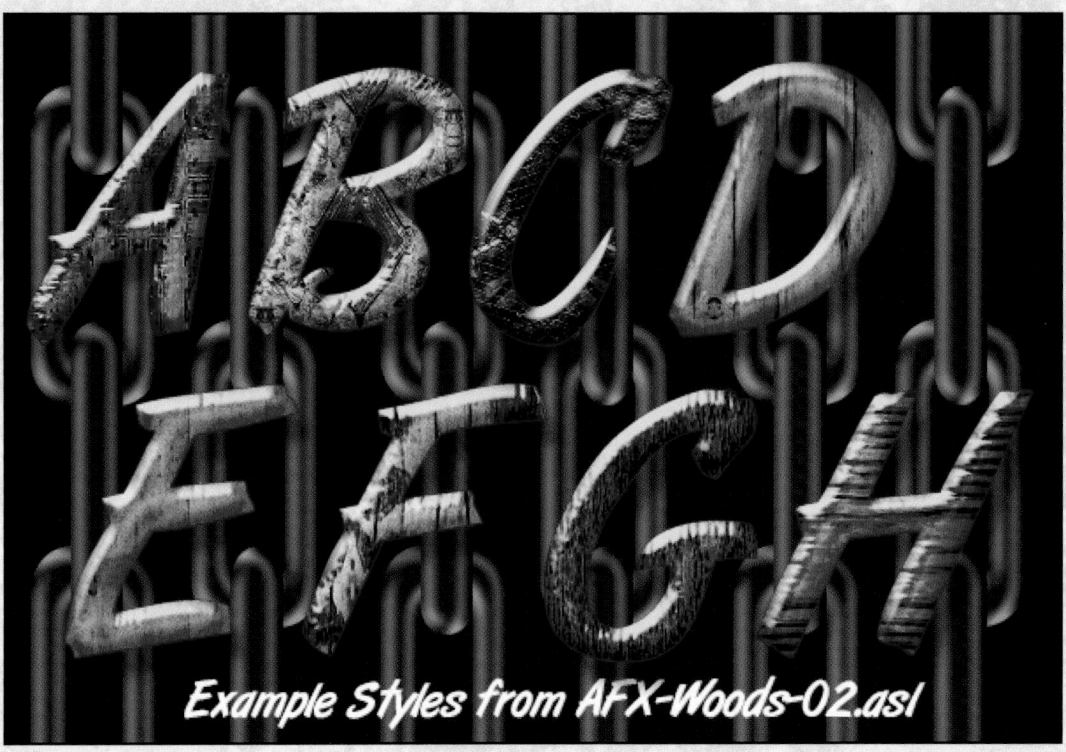

Example Styles from AFX-Woods-02.asl

CP44

Examples of layer styles included on the CD-ROM (continued)

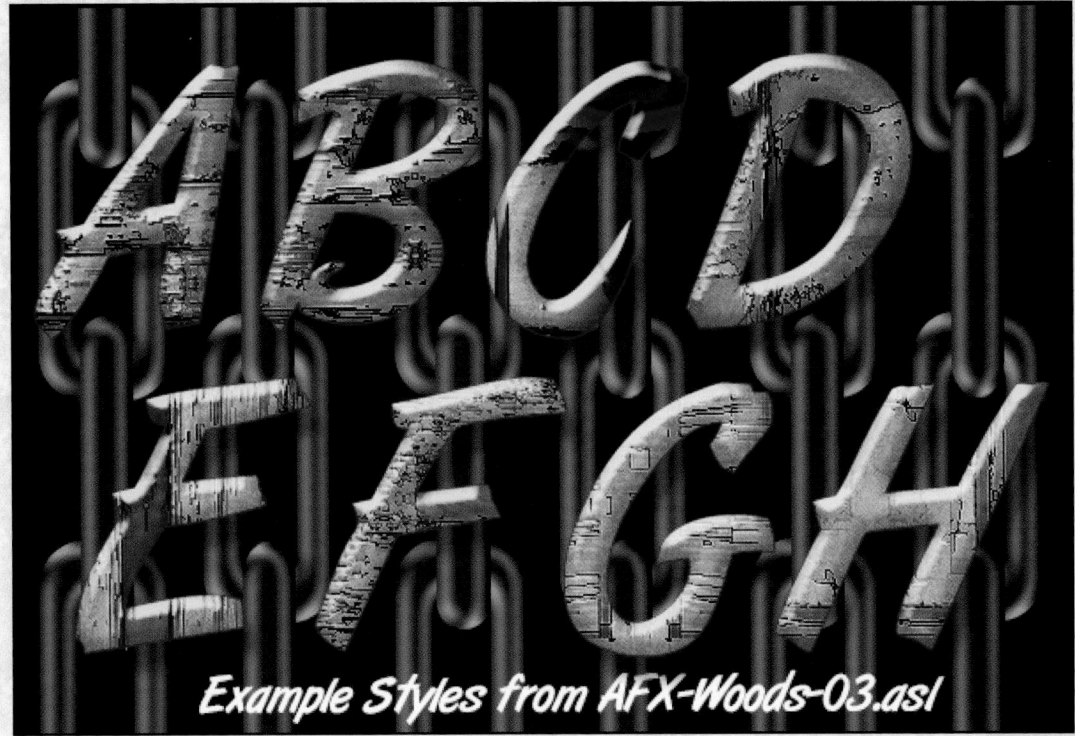

Example Styles from AFX-Woods-03.asl

CP45

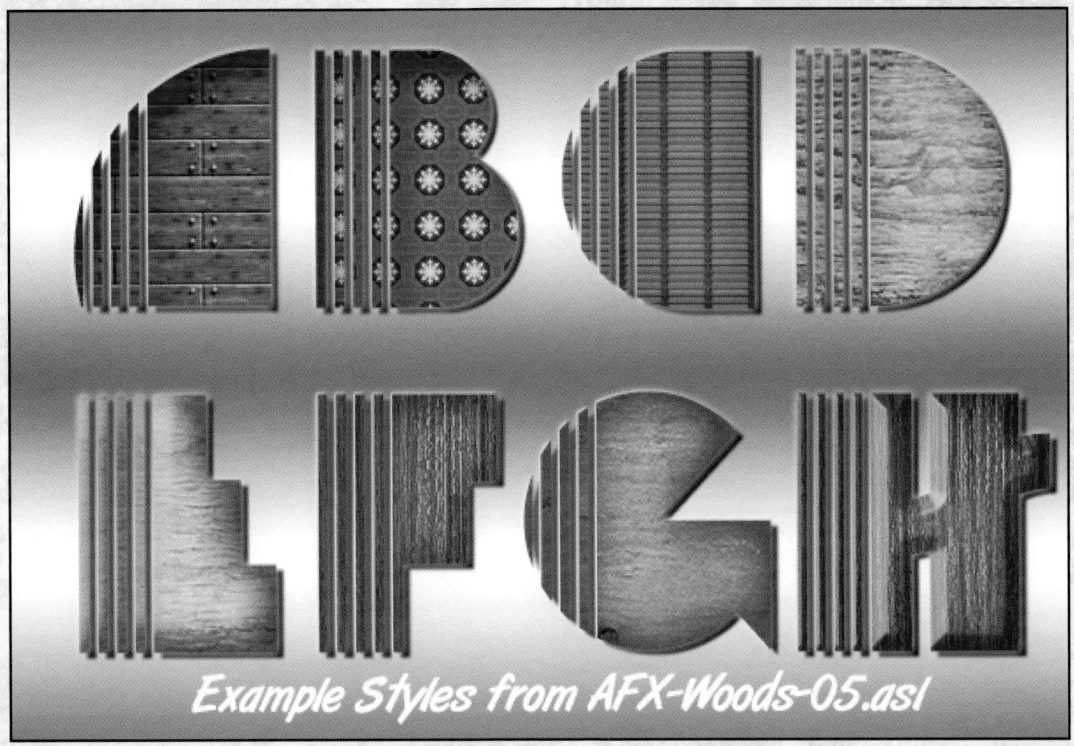

Example Styles from AFX-Woods-05.asl

CP46

CP47

Examples of natural patterns included on the CD.

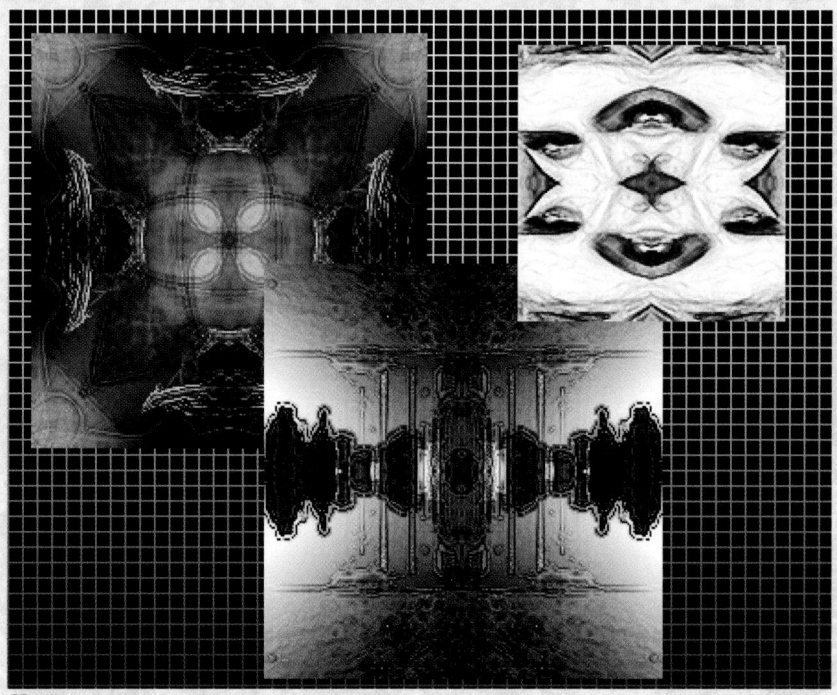

CP48

Examples of patterns using people and industrial images. All can be found on the CD.

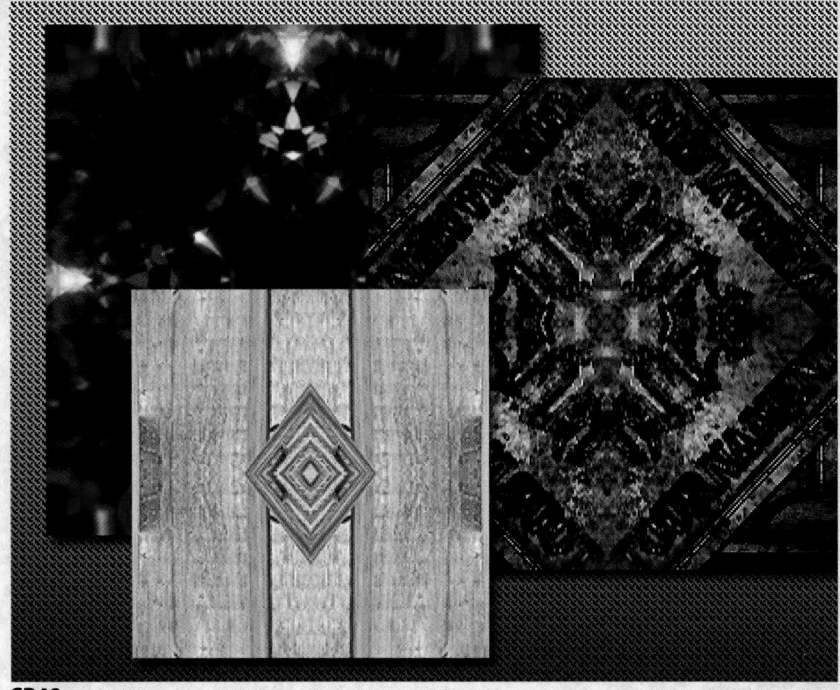

CP49

Patterns created from crystal, stone, and wood. Examples taken from the CD.

CP50

Cloud and stone photos, converted to seamless patterns. These can be found on the CD.

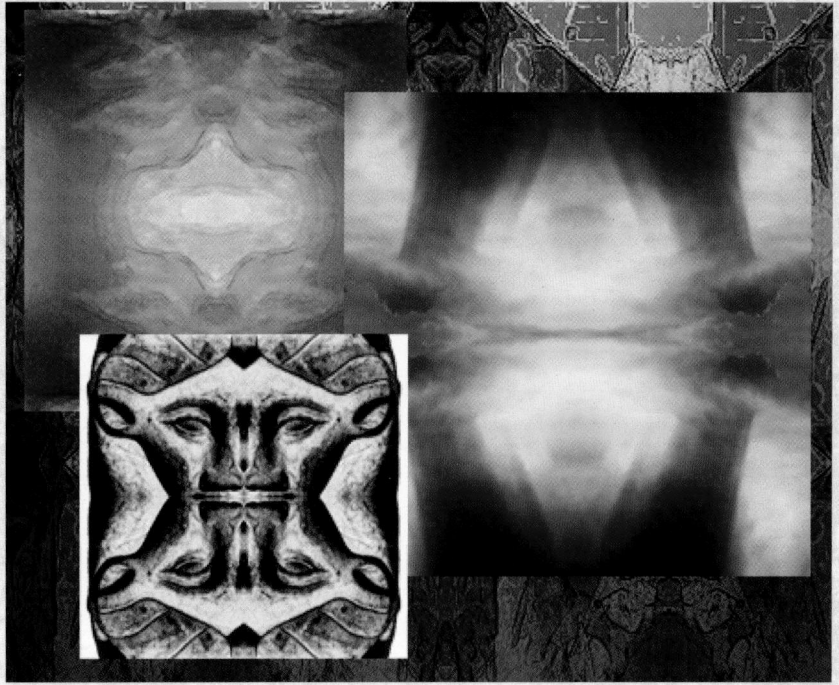

CP51

Examples of patterns on the CD using elements of fire, statuary, and sky.

CP52

More examples of patterns found on the CD using elements of human features and industrial photos.

BASIC WIRE

Moving into the digital age, this tutorial teaches you to create components found in the world of electronics. You will create wiring to apply to an electronic interface.

STEP 1: PREPARE THE IMAGE

- Open an image for use as a background (see **Figure 5.1**) or create a new image.
- Create a new layer named **Wire**.

5.1

STEP 2: MAKE THE WIRE

■ Select the **Rectangular Marquee** tool from the Toolbox. Set the following attributes in the Options bar:
   ■ Selection Type = **New Selection**
   ■ Feather = **0**
   ■ Style = **Normal**

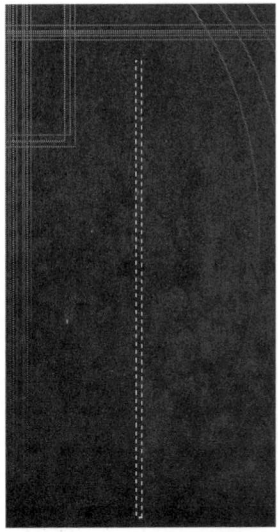

5.2

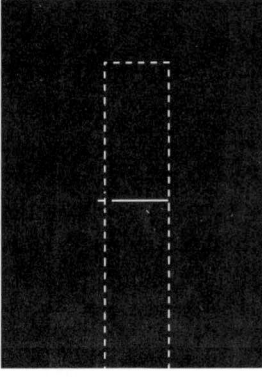

5.3

5.4

■ On the Wire layer, make a long, thin vertical selection, as shown in **Figure 5.2**. Extend the selection all the way to the bottom edge of the image.

■ Select the **Gradient** tool from the Toolbox.

■ Reset the default gradients. In the Gradient Picker, select the **Copper Gradient**.

■ Set the following attributes for the Gradient tool in the Options bar:
   ■ Gradient Type = **Linear Gradient**
   ■ Mode = **Normal**
   ■ Opacity = **100%**
   ■ Reverse = **Unchecked**

■ Using the ⌘/**Ctrl**+(+) key combination, zoom the image to a 600% view. Maneuver the image so that you can clearly see a portion of the selection. The extremely narrow selection makes seeing and applying the gradient easier.

■ Starting on either the left or right (L to R in this example), draw the gradient across the selection horizontally. Make the line straight by holding the **Shift** key down, or the reflections will be incorrect for the wire. See **Figure 5.3**.

■ Even working with a narrow selection, the wire may still be a bit wide. Choose **Image ➢ Transform ➢ Distort**.

■ In the Options bar, change the Width Value to **50%**.

■ Also in the Options bar, click the **Accept Change** icon. It appears as a checkmark on the right side of the bar. The new width is now applied to the layer. **Figure 5.4** shows the new wire.

PLASTIC-COATED WIRE

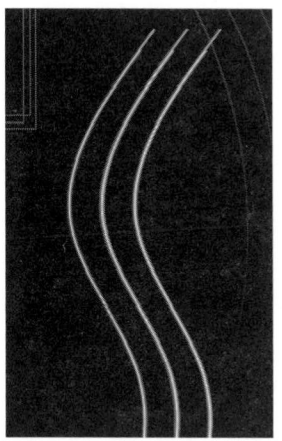

This tutorial requires the following from the CD-ROM:

- Wire Coat.grd (gradient set)

This tutorial shows a simple way to coat the bare wire with a layer of insulating plastic that is used in electronic devices.

STEP 1: GENERATE THE SELECTION

- ⌘/**Ctrl**+click the Wire layer to generate a selection.
- Create a new layer by clicking the **Add a Layer** icon on the bottom of the Layers palette.
- Name the new layer **Wire Coating**.
- Choose **Select ➢ Modify ➢ Expand**.
- In the Expand dialog box, enter a setting of **1**.
- Click **OK**.
- Click the **Rectangular Marquee** tool. In the Options bar, set the following attributes:
  - Selection Type = **Subtract from Selection**
  - Feather = **0**
  - Mode = **Normal**
- Use the **Rectangular Marquee** tool to draw around a short section of the top portion of the wire. After the wire is coated, the intent is to have a copper section exposed. See **Figure 5.5**. **Figure 5.6** shows the selection after the upper portion is no longer active.

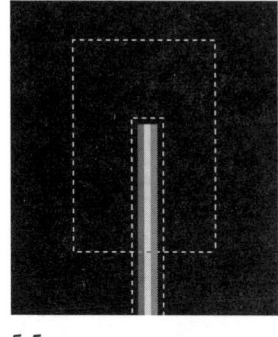

5.5

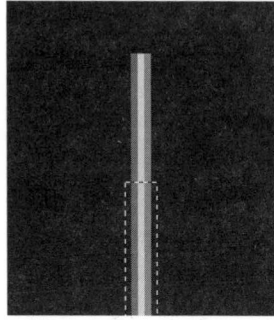

5.6

STEP 2: COAT THE WIRE

- Click the **Gradient** tool. In the Options bar, open the Gradient Picker and then the Gradient menu. Load the Gradient set **Wire Coat.grd**, which is found on the CD-ROM.
- Select the gradient Wire Coat 1 as soon as the gradient set is loaded into the Gradient Picker.
- Increase the zoom on the image to **600%** and move the image so that the selection, or a portion of it, is clearly seen.
- In the Gradient options, set the Gradient to **Linear Gradient**.

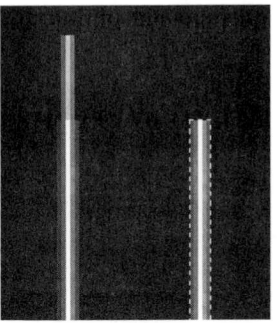

5.7

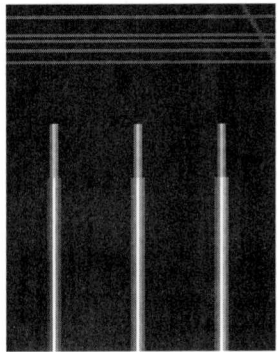

5.8

- Draw the Gradient across the selection from left to right, starting at the left edge of the active selection to the right edge of the selection. Stay as horizontal as possible to spread the gradient evenly.

STEP 3: DUPLICATE THE WIRE

Wires used for electronics never travel alone. This step shows a simple way to duplicate the wires and be able to distinguish among them.

- Duplicate the Wire Coating layer. Rename this layer **Wire Coating 2**.
- Select the **Move** tool. With the arrow keys, move the contents of Wire Coat 2 to the right a few clicks.
- ⌘/**Ctrl**+click Wire Coat 2 to generate a selection.
- Select the **Gradient** tool. In the Gradient Picker, select the Wire Coat 2 gradient.
- Again, zoom in to about **500%** and fill this selection with the new gradient, just as before. See **Figure 5.7**.
- Duplicate the Wire layer; rename the duplicate **Wire 2**. With the arrow keys move Wire 2 beneath the new wire coating. Also, in the Layers palette, move the Wire 2 layer up so that it is directly below Wire Coat 2.
- Repeat the processes above to create a third wire and coating. When you fill with the gradient, this time choose Wire Coat 3 from the Gradient palette. Move these further off to the right and place the Wire Coating 3 layer at the top of the stack in the Layers palette. Place Wire 3 directly below it. See **Figure 5.8**.

The Layers palette should look like **Figure 5.9**.

- Select Wire Coating 3 at the top of the Layers palette. Press ⌘/**Ctrl+E** to merge it with Wire 3 below it.

■ Select Wire Coating 2 in the Layers palette. Press ⌘/**Ctrl**+**E** to merge it with Wire 2.

■ Lastly, select Wire Coating 1 in the Layers palette. Again, press ⌘/**Ctrl**+**E** to merge it with the Wire 1 layer.

All three wires are completed.

STEP 4: APPLY THE BEND

In the real world, I doubt you have ever seen a perfectly straight wire, let alone a group of straight wires together. This next step shows how to add some character to the wires just created.

■ Select Wire 1 in the Layers palette.

■ Choose **Filter** ➢ **Distort** ➢ **Shear**. The use of this filter is the primary reason the wires were created vertically as opposed to horizontally. The Shear filter uses a vertical perspective.

■ Add **2** to **3** points to the shear line in the Shear dialog box. Move the points slightly to the right or left of center, as shown in **Figure 5.10**.

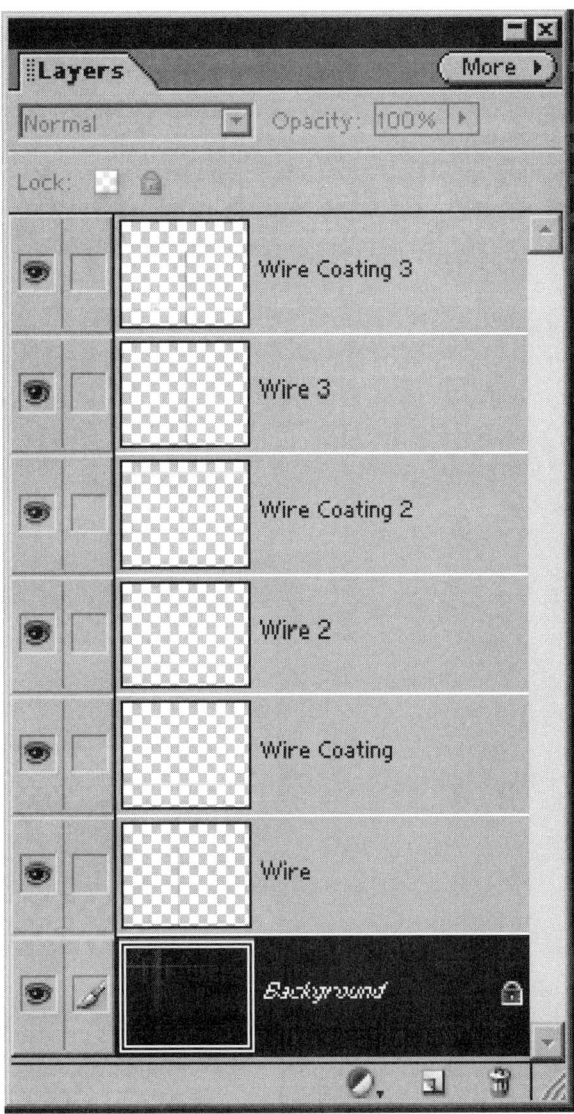

5.9

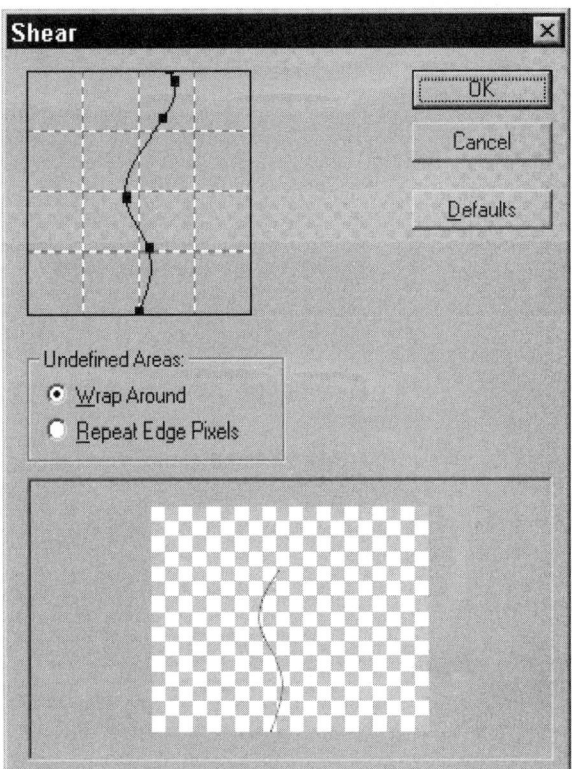

5.10

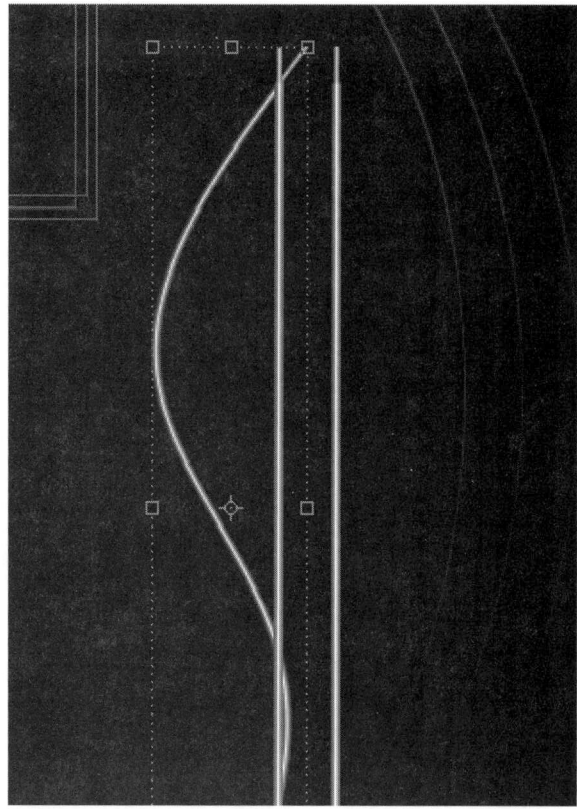

5.11

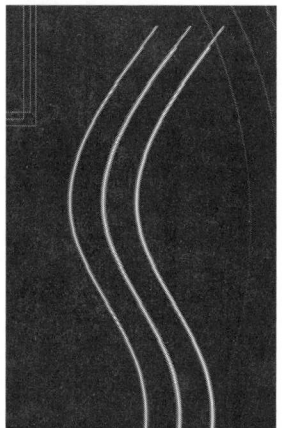

5.12

- Click **OK. Figure 5.11** shows the newly twisted wire.
- Select Wire 2 in the Layers palette. Press **⌘/Ctrl+F** to repeat the shear effect on this layer.
- Select Wire 3 in the Layers palette. Again, press **⌘/Ctrl+F**. All three wires have an identical bend, as shown in **Figure 5.12**.

WIRE BUNDLES

F or the next tutorial you will combine the wires into bundles.

STEP 1: DUPLICATE WIRES

■ Duplicate each of the wires twice. Move the layers so that they are interspersed but close together, as shown in **Figure 5.13**.

That was pretty easy. The result certainly looks like a bundle of wires. As stated before, rarely do all wires in a group have exactly the same bend. This next step fixes that.

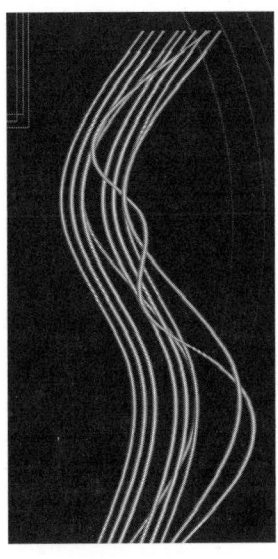

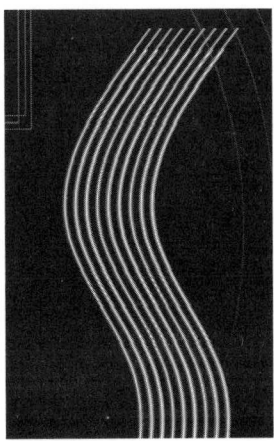

5.13

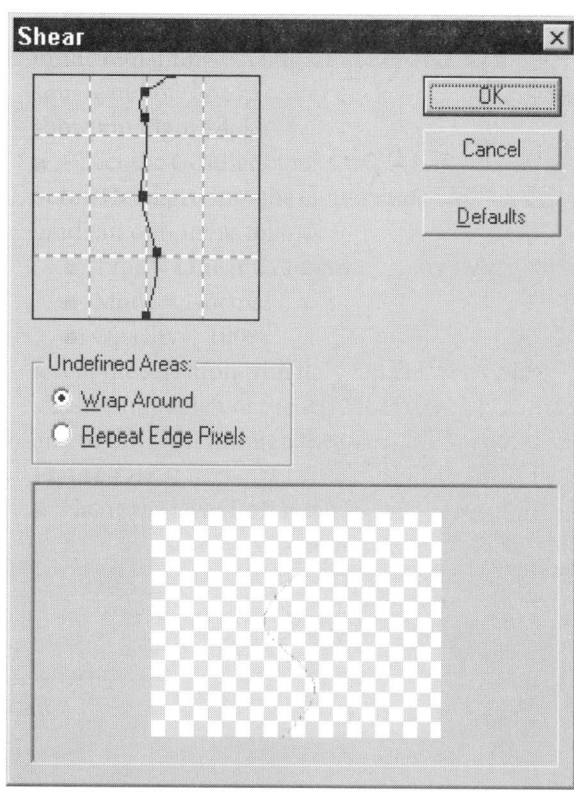

5.14

STEP 2: TWIST AND MIX

- Select a wire from the center of the group by clicking the wire's layer.
- Choose **Filter ➢ Distort ➢ Shear**.

In the Shear dialog box, change the point positions a bit; you may even add a couple of extra points for more character in the wire. See **Figure 5.14**.

- Run the Shear filter on more wires, changing the settings slightly each time. **Figure 5.15** shows alterations to three wires in the group.
- Select a wire from the group that has twisted over the top of another. See **Figure 5.16**.
- Select the **Polygonal Lasso** tool from the Toolbox. In the Options bar, enter the following settings:
  - Selection Type = **New Selection**
  - Feather = **0**
  - Anti-aliased = **Checked**

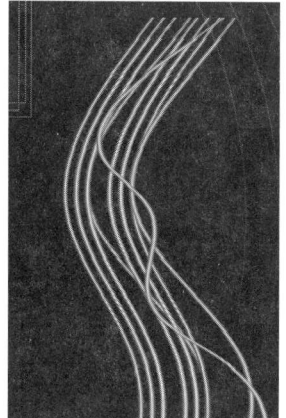

5.15

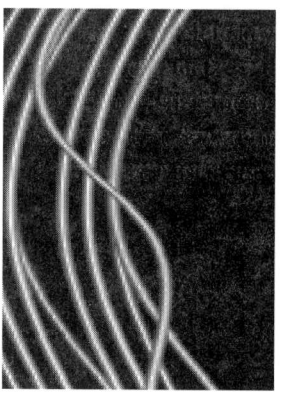

5.16

- Select a portion of the wire where it overlaps another wire, as in **Figure 5.17**.
- Choose **Layer** ➢ **New** ➢ **Layer via Cut**.
- Name the new layer **Wire Clip 1**.
- Move the layer down in the Layers palette so that it resides below the wire it overlapped. Doing this makes the wire appear to be wound around the other wire, as shown in **Figure 5.18**.

Repeat this process as many times as you want with other wires. **Figure 5.19** shows the finished wire group.

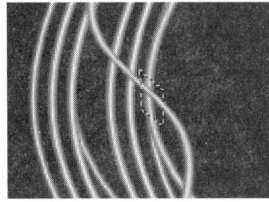

5.17

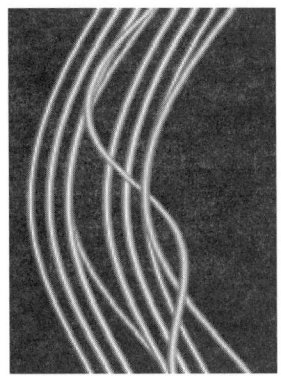

5.18

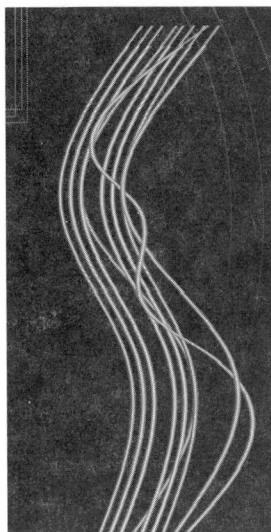

5.19

CIRCUITS – METHOD 1

The filters and blending modes of certain tools in Elements allow for quick creation of other electronic patterns. This tutorial covers one way to create an easy electronic circuit board.

STEP 1: PREPARE THE IMAGE

- Create a new image. Set the following attributes in the New Image dialog box:
    - Name = **Circuits-1**
    - Width = **300**
    - Height = **300**
    - Resolution = **100 dpi**
    - Mode = **RGB**
    - Contents = **White**
- Choose **Edit ➤ Fill** and fill the background with black, **100%** opacity.
- Create a new layer.

- Starting on the left side of the image and drawing horizontally to the right side of the image, fill the new layer with the gradient. See **Figure 5.20**.
- Fill the layer with the gradient again, this time vertically. The image should now look similar to **Figure 5.21**.

STEP 2: FROM GRADIENT TO CIRCUITS

- Click the **Gradient** tool in the Toolbox.
- Open the Gradient Picker in the Options bar and then open the Gradient menu. Select **Reset Gradients** from the menu.
- Select the **Copper** gradient in the Color Picker to make it active. In the Options bar, enter the following settings for the Gradient tool:
    - Gradient Type = **Linear Gradient**
    - Mode = **Difference**
    - Opacity = **100%**
    - Reverse = **Unchecked**

5.20

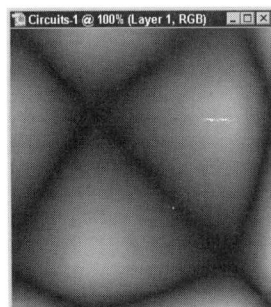

5.21

- Choose **Filter** ➢ **Noise** ➢ **Add Noise**. Enter the following settings in the Add Noise dialog box:
  - Amount = **25%**
  - Distribution = **Gaussian**
  - Monochromatic = **Checked**
- Click **OK**.
- Choose **Filter** ➢ **Texture** ➢ **Grain**. Enter the following settings in the Grain dialog box:
  - Intensity = **50**
  - Contrast = **50**
  - Grain Type = **Clumped**
- Click **OK**.
- Choose **Filter** ➢ **Pixilate** ➢ **Mosaic**. Enter a cell size of **8**.
- Click **OK**.

- Choose **Filter** ➢ **Stylize** ➢ **Find Edges**.
- Click **OK**. See **Figure 5.22**.
- Choose **Filter** ➢ **Stylize** ➢ **Glowing Edges**. Enter the following settings:
  - Edge Width = **1**
  - Edge Brightness = **20**
  - Smoothness = **2**
- Click **OK**. See **Figure 5.23**.
- Choose **Layer** ➢ **New Fill Layer** ➢ **Solid Color**. Select **Color** as the adjustment type.
- When the Color Picker appears, enter a Color number value of **#02A434**, or R = **2**, G = **164**, and B = **52**.
- Click **OK**.
- In the Layers palette, set the blending mode of the color fill layer to **Linear Light** and change the opacity to **50%**.
- Select Layer 1 (the circuits layer) in the Layers palette.
- Choose **Enhance** ➢ **Adjust Brightness/Contrast** ➢ **Brightness/Contrast**.
- In the Brightness/Contrast dialog box, set the Brightness to **–100** and Contrast to **+40**.
- Click **OK**.

Figure 5.24 (CP13) shows the completed circuit image.

5.22

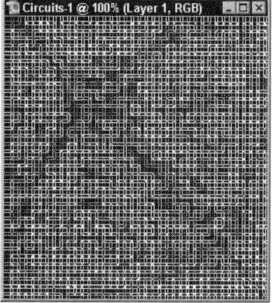

5.23

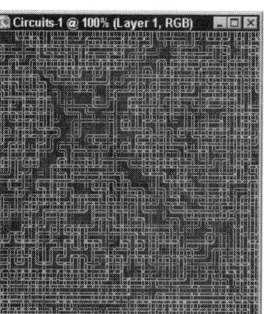

5.24 (CP13)

CIRCUITS – METHOD 2

This tutorial demonstrates another way to achieve the circuits effects. There are no absolutes; a healthy knowledge of filters working together will soon have you experimenting with your own circuit patterns.

STEP 1: PREPARE THE IMAGE

- Select **File** ➢ **New**.
- In the New Image dialog box, enter the following:
    - Name = **Circuits-2**
    - Width = **300 pixels**
    - Height = **300 pixels**
    - Mode = **RGB Color**
    - Contents = **White**
- Click **OK**.
- Choose **Edit** ➢ **Fill** and fill the contents with black, **100%** Opacity.
- Click **OK**.
- Create a new layer.

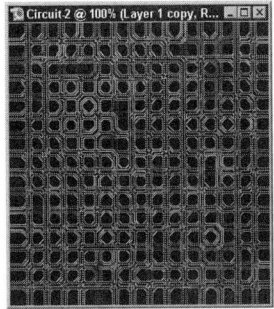

STEP 2: FROM GRADIENT TO PATTERNS

- Select the **Gradient** tool.
- In the Options bar, set the following options for the Gradient tool:
    - Gradient = **Copper**
    - Gradient Type = **Linear Gradient**
    - Mode = **Difference**
    - Reverse = **Unchecked**
- Starting at the top of the image and dragging the mouse to the bottom, fill the new layer with the Copper gradient.

- Click and drag the gradient in the upper-left corner to the lower-right corner in the same layer.
- Again, fill the layer with the gradient, only this time go from the left edge to the right edge, drawing the mouse across the image horizontally. See **Figure 5.25**.

Figure 5.26 shows the effect caused by applying the Copper gradient in Difference mode as in the steps above.

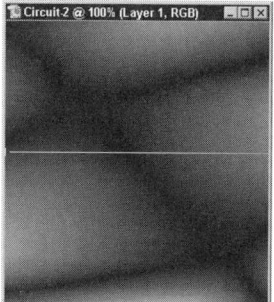

5.25

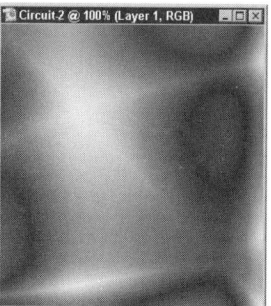

5.26

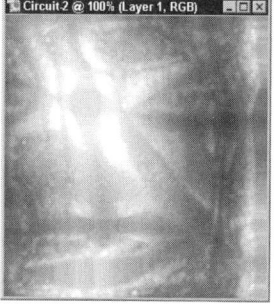

5.27

- Choose **Filter ➤ Artistic ➤ Paint Daubs**. Enter the following settings in the Paint Daubs dialog box:
  - Brush Size = **50**
  - Sharpness = **20**
  - Brush Type = **Light Rough**
- Click **OK**. See **Figure 5.27**.
- Choose **Filter ➤ Pixilate ➤ Mosaic**. Enter a cell size of **20**.
- Click **OK**.
- Choose **Filter ➤ Stylize ➤ Glowing Edges**. Enter the following settings in the Glowing Edges dialog box (see **Figure 5.28**):
  - Edge Width = **5**
  - Edge Brightness = **14**
  - Smoothness = **10**

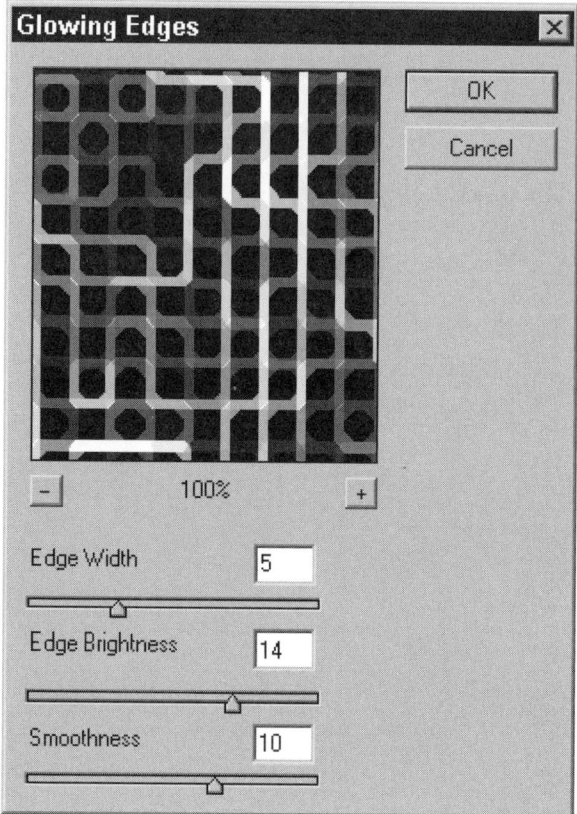

5.28

■ Click **OK**.

■ Choose **Filter** ➢ **Stylize** ➢ **Find Edges**. See **Figure 5.29**.

■ Choose **Image** ➢ **Adjustments** ➢ **Invert** (⌘/Ctrl+I).

■ Choose **Filter** ➢ **Stylize** ➢ **Glowing Edges**.

Enter the following settings in the Glowing Edges dialog box:

    ■ Edge Width = **1**

    ■ Edge Brightness = **2**

    ■ Smoothness = **3**

■ Click **OK**.

■ Make a duplicate of the circuits layer.

■ Choose **Image** ➢ **Adjustments** ➢ **Threshold**.

Set the Threshold Level to **215**.

■ Click **OK**.

■ Set the blending mode of the duplicate circuits layer to **Darken**. Change the opacity to **55%**. See **Figure 5.30**.

Changing the blending modes for the duplicate circuits layer offers some interesting variations on the circuitry pattern. For example, **Figure 5.31** shows the image with the duplicate layer set to Difference mode at 45% opacity.

Keep these settings, because from this point, you launch straight into the next effect — Circuit Lights.

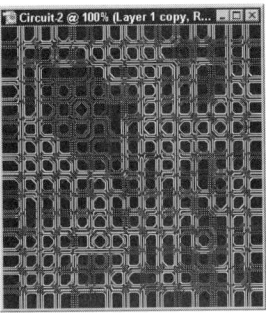

5.30

5.29

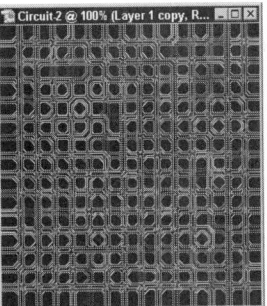

5.31

CIRCUIT BOARD LAMPS

T his tutorial requires the completion of Tutorial 26. The image created in Tutorial 26 is used for the continuation of this tutorial.

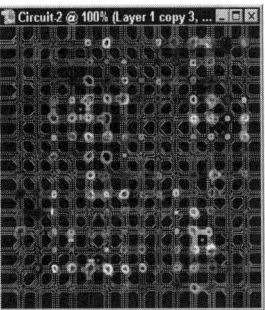

STEP 1: ADD LAMPS TO A CIRCUIT BOARD

■ Using the image created in Tutorial 26, choose **Layer ➢ New Fill Layer ➢ Solid Color**.
■ In the Color Picker, enter a color value of **#FB5EE3**, or R = **251**, G = **94**, and B = **227**.
■ Click **OK**.
■ Set the blending mode of the fill layer to **Darken**. See **Figure 5.32**.
■ Duplicate the original circuits layer and drag it to the top of the Layers palette.
■ Choose **Filter ➢ Stylize ➢ Glowing Edges**. Enter the following settings in the dialog box:
  ■ Edge Width = **2**
  ■ Edge Brightness = **13**
  ■ Smoothness = **15**
■ Click **OK**. See **Figure 5.33**.
■ Select the **Magic Wand** from the Toolbox.
■ Click the black area between the neon-type light circles.

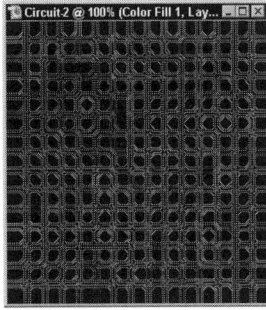

5.32

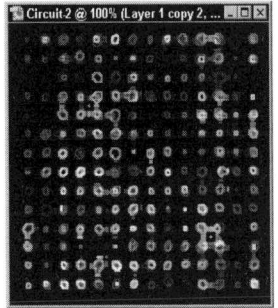

5.33

153

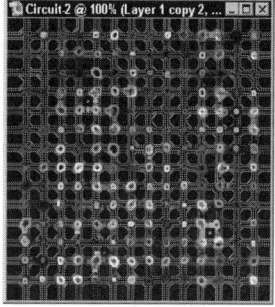

5.34

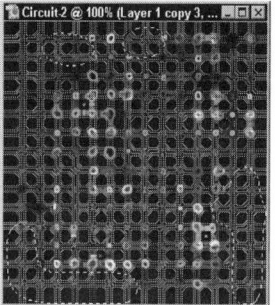

5.35

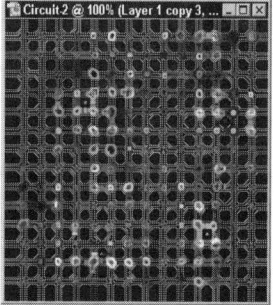

5.36

- With the black selected, press the **Delete** key. See **Figure 5.34**.
- Click the **Selection Brush** in the Toolbox. In the Options bar, set the following attributes:
    - Brush Type = **Rounded, Feathered**
    - Size = **45 pixels**
    - Mode = **Selection**
    - Hardness = **0**
- Paint a few vertical and horizontal selections through the lamps layer.
- Press the **Delete** key. See **Figure 5.35**.

Figure 5.36 shows the completed circuit board, lamps and all.

APPLYING WIRES AND CIRCUITS TO AN INTERFACE

W e have learned to create wires and circuit patterns, so you may be asking yourself, what are these techniques good for? Actually these techniques are quite popular for users of Photoshop. They are used to dress up artwork, to a degree, but are most often used for designing Web site interfaces. This tutorial shows how to take what you've learned and apply it to an interface design.

This tutorial uses the following, found on the CD-ROM:

■ Interface Template 2.psd

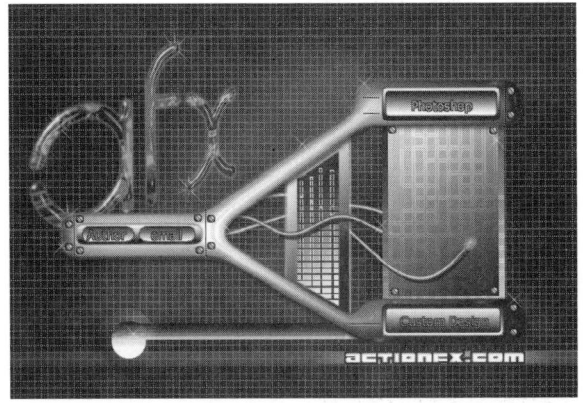

STEP 1: PREPARE THE IMAGE

■ Open **Interface Template 2.psd**, found on the CD-ROM. See **Figure 5.37**.
■ Create a new layer at the top of the Layers palette: Name this layer **Wire 1**.

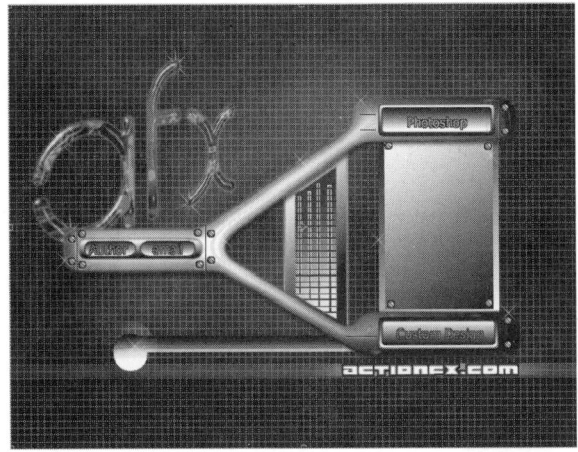

5.37

- Using new layers atop the layer stack, perform Tutorials 22 and 23 to create three differently toned wires. See **Figures 5.38** and **5.39**.

5.38

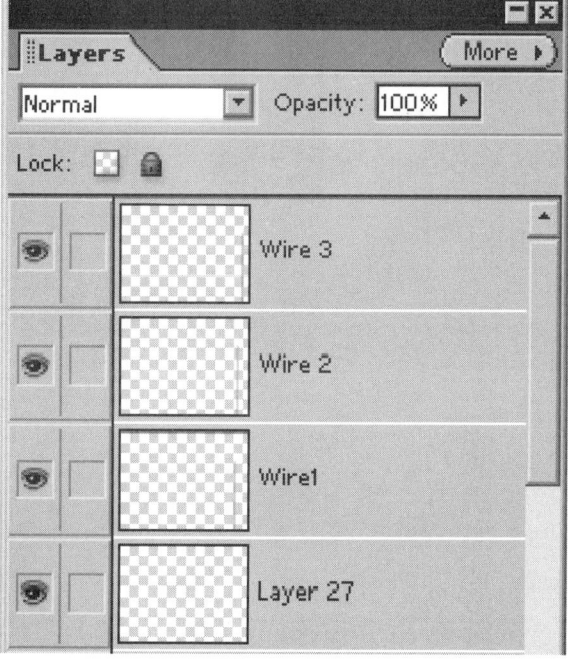

5.39

STEP 2: WARP THE WIRE

- Select the Wire 1 layer.
- Choose **Filter ➢ Distort ➢ Wave**. Enter the following settings in the Wave dialog box:
  - Number of Generators = **5**
  - Type = **Sine**
  - Wavelength: Min. = **62**; Max = **62**
  - Amplitude: Min = **5**; Max = **5**
  - Scale: Vertical = **100%**; Horizontal = **100%**
  - Undefined Areas = **Repeat Edge Pixels** (this setting is unimportant)
- Click **OK**. See **Figure 5.40**.

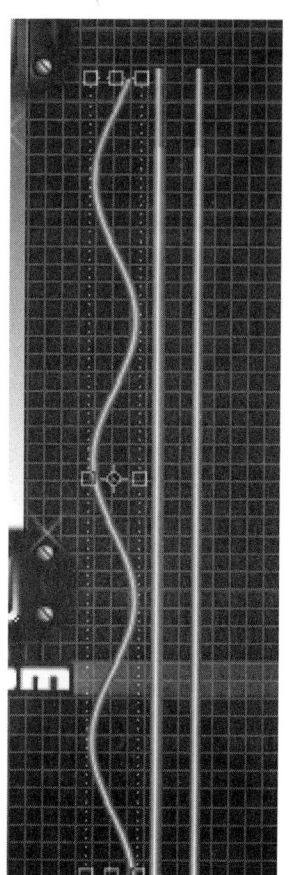

5.40

■ Choose **Image ➤ Rotate ➤ Layer 90 Degrees Right**.

■ Move the Wire 1 layer to the bottom of the layer stack in the Layers palette; place it just above the background layer.

■ Click the **Move** tool (V) in the Toolbox. Position Wire 1 behind the main body of the interface, as shown in **Figure 5.41**.

STEP 3: CROSS THE WIRE OVER THE INTERFACE

■ Click the **Rectangular Marquee** tool.

■ Select the portion of the wire that passes behind the metal plate portion of the interface. See **Figure 5.42**.

■ Choose **Layer ➤ New ➤ Layer via Cut**.

■ In the Layers palette, move the newly cut layer to the top of the layer stack. See **Figures 5.43** and **5.44**.

STEP 4: MAKE WIRES 2 AND 3

■ Select the Wire 2 layer in the Layers palette.

■ Move Wire 2 so that it is centered on the image. You need only move it horizontally and not vertically.

■ Choose **Filter ➤ Distort ➤ Shear**.

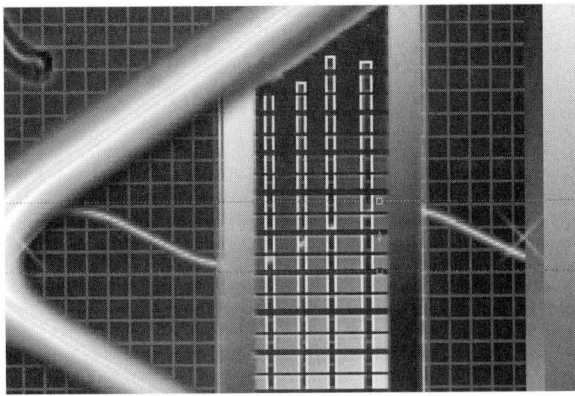

5.41

5.43

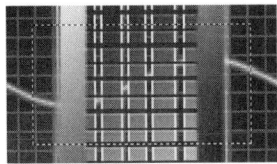

5.42

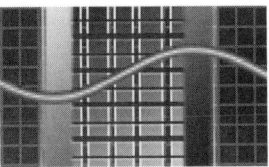

5.44

- In the Shear dialog box, add a few points to the shear line and move them slightly off-center to the left and right, as shown in **Figure 5.45**.
- Choose **Layer ➢ Rotate ➢ Layer 90 degrees Right**.

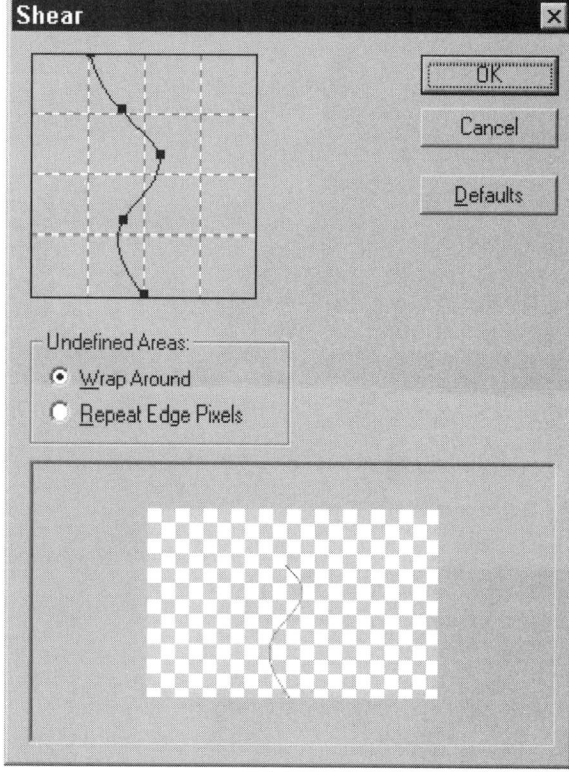

5.45

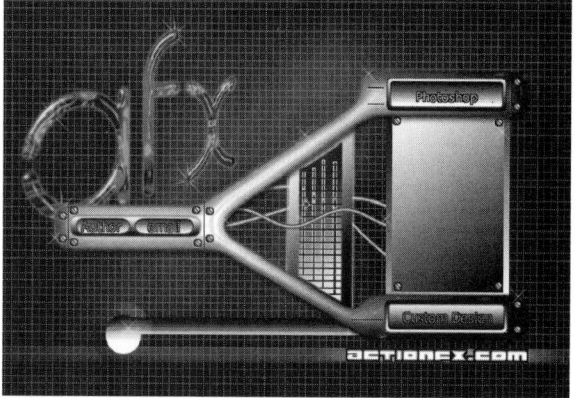

5.46

- Again, move the layer to the bottom of the layer stack, just above the background. Use the **Move** tool to slide the wire into place close to Wire 1.
- Repeat the above process with Wire 3. Change the point settings in the Shear dialog box slightly, rotate the layer, and place it behind the interface. See **Figure 5.46**.
- Pick one of the wires that you want to pass in front of the interface. In this case, Wire 2, or the green wire, is perfect. Click the layer holding the wire.
- Select the **Rectangular Marquee** tool. Select an area that holds the section to pass over the interface, as shown in **Figure 5.47**.
- Choose **Layer ➢ New ➢ Layer via Cut**.
- Name the new layer **Green Wire Section** or name it appropriate to the color of the wire you clipped.
- Place the layer at the top of the layer stack in the Layers palette. The copper end now appears to cross in front of the metal plate, as shown in **Figure 5.48**.
- As the wire passes between the interface and the light source, a shadow helps dress up the effect. Click the **Layer Styles** tab. Load the **Drop Shadows** layer style set, and click the **Hard Edge** style. See **Figure 5.49**.

Time to make sparks!

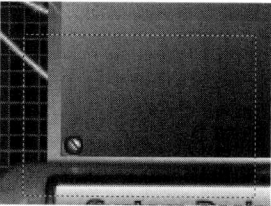

5.47

5.48

STEP 5: SPARKS

- Zoom the image in to **400%** or so and position it so that the copper end of the wire is visible.
- Select the **Polygonal Lasso** in the Toolbox.
- With the **Lasso** tool, select the tip of the wire, as shown in **Figure 5.50**.
- Choose **Enhance ➢ Adjust Brightness/Contrast ➢ Brightness/Contrast**. Set the Brightness slider to **15** and the Contrast slider to **75**.
- Click **OK**.
- Choose **Layer ➢ New ➢ Layer via Copy**.
- Click the **Layer Styles** tab. Load the **Outer Glows** style set.
- Click the layer style named **Fire**.
- Create a new, blank layer beneath the one to which the Fire style is applied.
- Select the layer with the Fire style applied, and press ⌘/**Ctrl+E** to merge it with the blank layer beneath it.
- Choose **Enhance ➢ Adjust Color ➢ Hue/Saturation** (⌘/**Ctrl+U**). Enter the following settings in the Hue/Saturation dialog box:
  - Hue = **+173**
  - Saturation = **+100**
  - Lightness = **0**
- Click **OK**. See **Figure 5.51**.

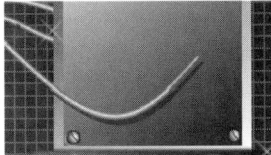

5.49

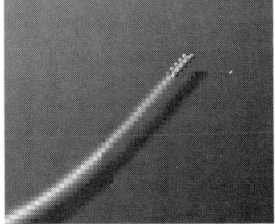

5.50

STEP 6: ADD THE CIRCUIT PATTERN

For a final touch, this step will walk through a possible application for the circuitry patterns worked on earlier. This effect is a bit subtle compared to those tutorials, but the process is nearly identical.

- Select the metal plate layer. If you are unsure which layer the plate resides on, select the **Move** tool (V) from the Toolbox. Move it over the metal plate and right-click the mouse. A list pops up, revealing all the layers that reside beneath that point. This helps find layers in multilayered.psd files quickly, which is useful if you have a file that has many unnamed layers, as is the case here. See **Figure 5.52**.
- In this case, the metal plate is found in Layer 2. Select Layer 2.
- Create a new layer just above Layer 2. Rename the layer **Circuits**.
- Press **D** to reset the default colors.
  - Click the **Gradient** tool.
  - In the Options bar, select the **Foreground to Background** gradient.
  - Set the blending mode for the gradient to **Difference**.
  - Reverse = **Checked**

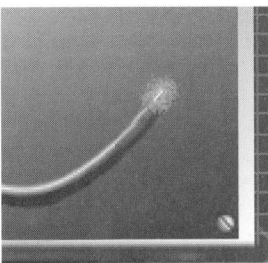

5.51

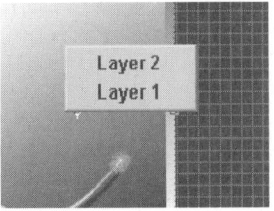

5.52

- ⌘/**Ctrl**+click Layer 2 to bring up the selection. Make sure that the Circuits layer remains active in the Layers palette.

- Fill the Circuits layer several times with the gradient, from different points and at different angles. The results are similar to **Figure 5.53**.

- Choose **Filter** ➤ **Noise** ➤ **Add Noise**. Enter the following in the Add Noise dialog box:
  - Amount = **10%**
  - Distribution = **Gaussian**
  - Monochromatic = **Checked**

- Click **OK**.

- Choose **Filter** ➤ **Pixilate** ➤ **Mosaic**. Enter a cell size of **14**.

- Click **OK**.

- Choose **Filter** ➤ **Stylize** ➤ **Find Edges**.

- Choose **Filter** ➤ **Stylize** ➤ **Glowing Edges**. Enter the following in the Glowing Edges dialog box:
  - Edge Width = **2**
  - Edge Brightness = **4**
  - Smoothness = **4**

- Click **OK**.

- In the Layers palette, set the blending mode for the Circuits layer to **Darken** and the opacity to **20%**. See **Figure 5.54** (**CP14**).

There you have it! This chapter gives you a good foundation for creating electronic images and components for use in your own designs. As always, the key word is experiment.

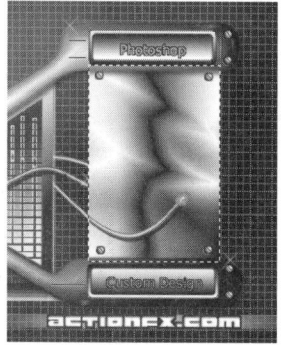

5.53

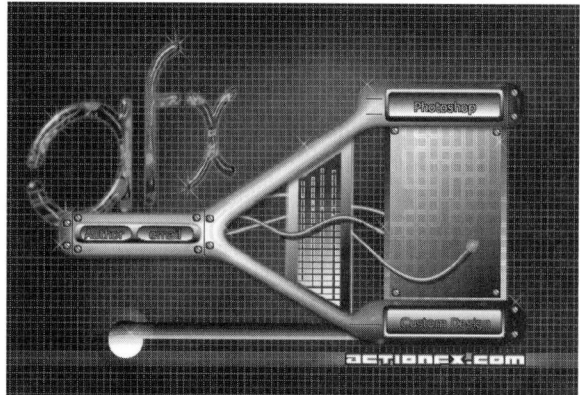

5.54 (CP14)

6

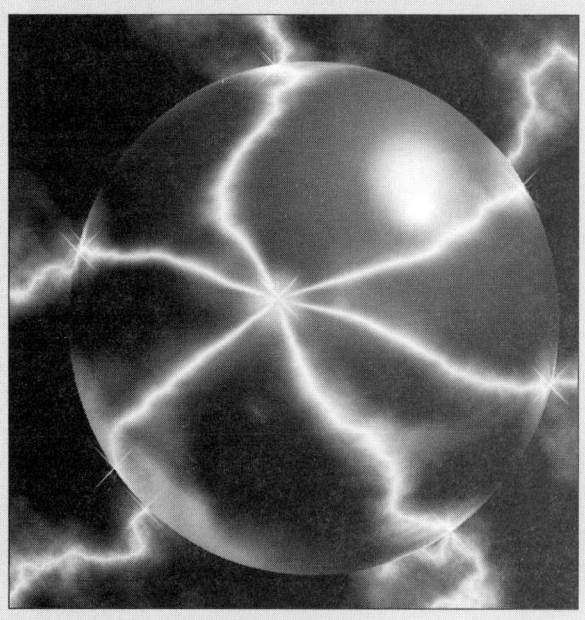

GETTING A GRASP ON INTANGIBLES: VAPORS, RAYS, AND ELECTRICITY

You have spent the previous five chapters creating objects with physical attributes. Adobe Elements isn't locked into objects with shape, texture, and density, however. This chapter looks at intangible elements, adding yet another tier to what a little imagination and Adobe Elements can accomplish. You look at electricity, create smoke, get a visit from a couple specters, and finish up with a medical exam!

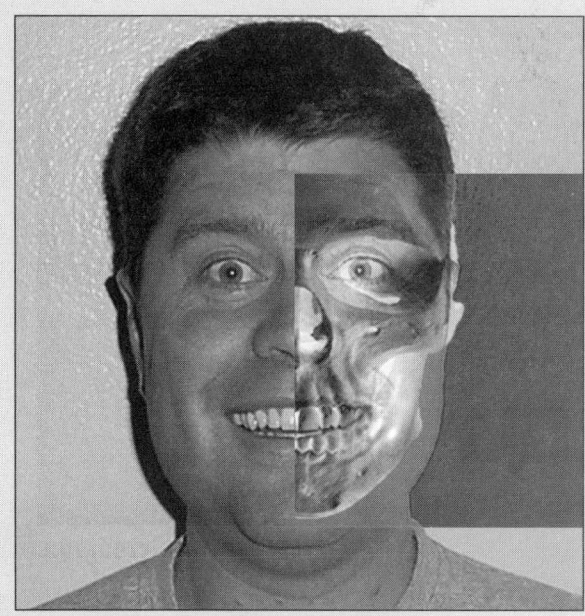

LIGHTNING

I have found a few tutorials on the Internet that teach Photoshop users methods of creating lightning. I have a few techniques that I used in the past, but for this tutorial, I have to give credit to my good friend Colin Smith of the Photoshop Café (`www.photoshopcafe.com`). Although this is not a duplication of his tutorial on the subject, the concept is the same. It is easy to perform and produces great results.

The previous chapter took you through the development of electronic components. In order for those items to work in the physical world, they need juice. This tutorial shows how to generate electricity, or at least a visual replication of such.

STEP 1: PREPARE THE IMAGE

- Create a new image. In the New Image dialog box, enter the following attributes:
    - Name = **Lightning**
    - Width = **300 pixels**
    - Height = **300 pixels**
    - Resolution = **100 dpi**
    - Mode = **RGB color**
    - Contents = **White**

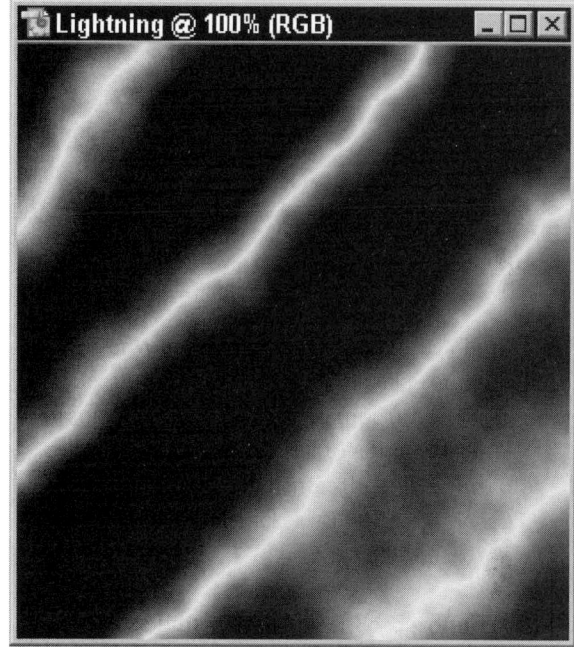

- Click **OK**.
- Press the **D** key to reset the foreground/background colors.
- Select the **Gradient** tool. In the Options bar, click the Gradient window to open the Gradient Editor.

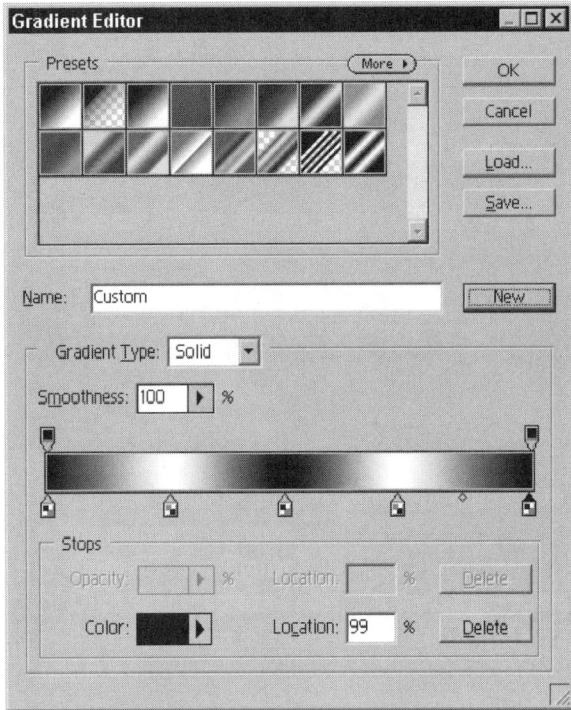

6.1

6.2

6.3

■ The Gradient Editor is in the lower portion of the Gradient dialog box. **Figure 6.1** shows which gradient to use. You create this gradient by adding black and white color stops, evenly dispersed along the Gradient Editor. This is done by clicking points directly beneath the Gradient Editor, choosing a color for the stop and setting the opacity. As soon as you have the gradient created, click **New** to save it and then click **OK**.

■ Starting in the upper-left corner of the image and drawing the gradient to the lower-right corner, fill the image with the gradient by clicking and dragging the mouse between the two opposing corners. When done, the image looks like **Figure 6.2**.

STEP 2: TURN A GRADIENT INTO LIGHTNING

■ Choose **Filter ➢ Render ➢ Difference Clouds**.
■ Choose **Image ➢ Adjustments ➢ Invert** (⌘/**Ctrl+I**). The lightning bolts start to take shape, as shown in **Figure 6.3**.
■ Choose **Enhance ➢ Brightness/Contrast ➢ Levels** (⌘/**Ctrl+L**).

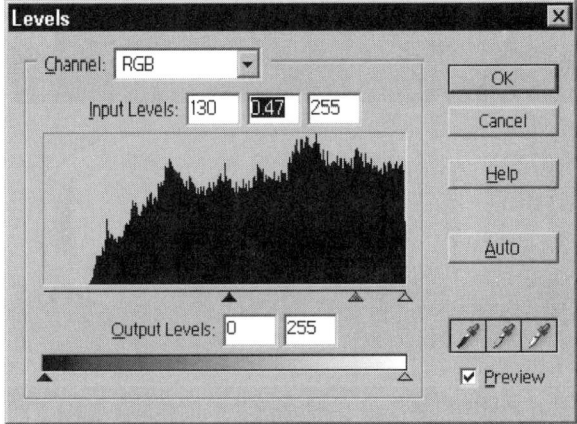

6.4

■ In the Levels dialog box, move the black and gray sliders to the right. Keep an eye on the image; the lightning forms as you move the sliders. See **Figure 6.4**. When you have crisp bolts, click **OK**.

■ Choose **Enhance** ➤ **Adjust Color** ➤ **Color Variations**.

■ You can change the highlights, midtones, and shadows of the bolts by manipulating the Add/Remove color icons at the bottom of the Color Variations dialog box. The first view window on the top-left shows the original image, and the view window on the right shows the corrected image (see **Figure 6.5**.) When satisfied with the color of your lightning bolts, click **OK**.

When done, you are left with several lightning bolts streaking across the image, as shown in **Figure 6.6**.

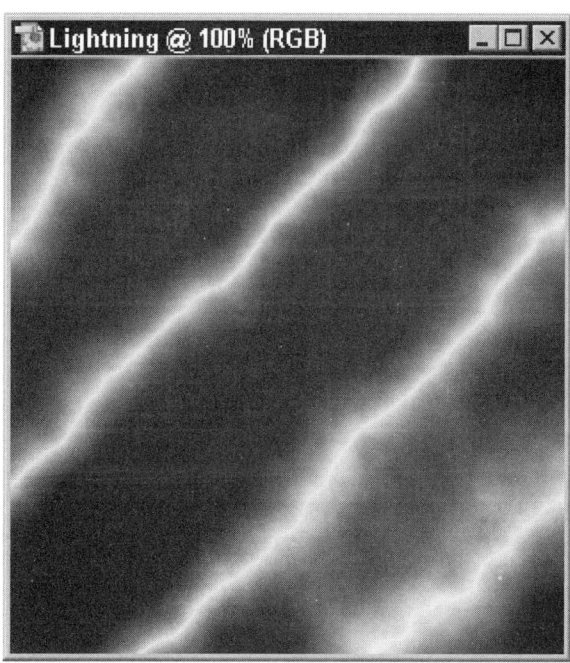

6.6

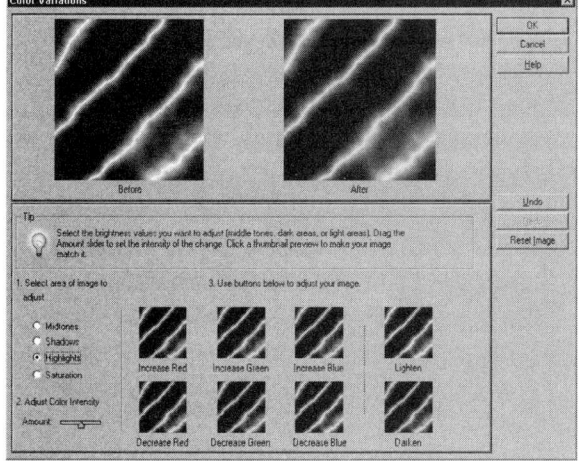

6.5

STATIC

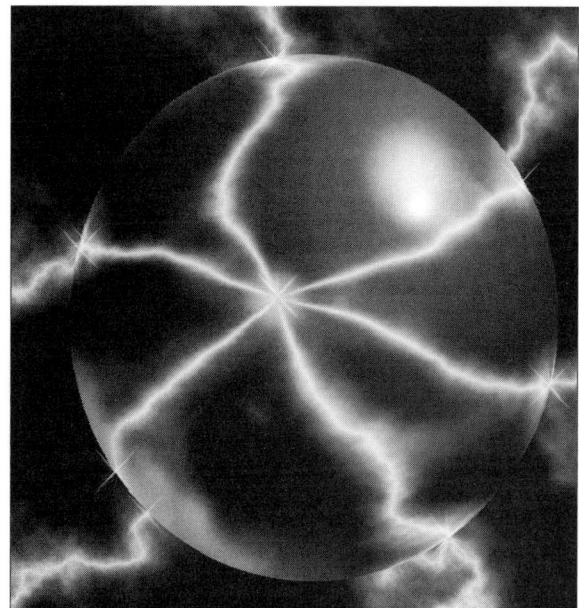

T his tutorial is a variation on the one previous, but rather than semistraight bolts traveling in parallel, this tutorial demonstrates how to create several bolts branching from a central point, as you see in those static balls sold at the local novelty shop.

STEP 1: PREPARE THE IMAGE

■ Choose **File ➢ New**. In the New Image dialog box, set the following attributes:
  - ■ Name = **Lightning 2**
  - ■ Width = **300 pixels**
  - ■ Height = **300 pixels**
  - ■ Resolution = **100 dpi**
  - ■ Mode = **RGB color**
  - ■ Contents = **White**
■ Click **OK**.
■ Select the **Gradient** tool. In the Options bar, click the Gradient window to open the Gradient Editor.

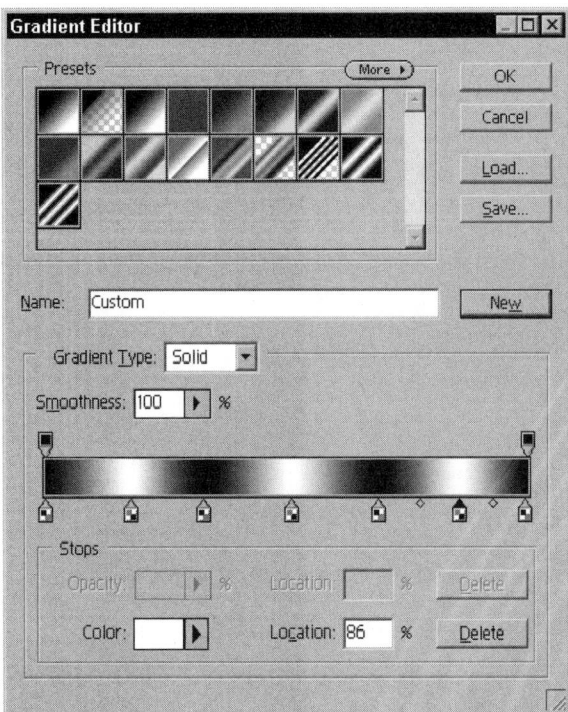

6.7

- The Gradient Editor is in the lower portion of the Gradient dialog box. **Figure 6.7** shows the gradient to use. You create this gradient by adding black and white color stops evenly dispersed along the Gradient Editor. As soon as you have it created, click **New** to save the gradient and then click **OK**.
- In the Options bar, set the following attributes for the gradient:
  - Gradient Type = **Angle Gradient**
  - Mode = **Normal**
  - Opacity = **100%**
  - Reverse = **Unchecked**
- Click in the center on the image and then draw the gradient to the border of the image. The gradient fill is shown in **Figure 6.8**.

STEP 2: CREATE THE ZAPPERS

- Choose **Filter ➢ Render ➢ Difference Clouds**. See **Figure 6.9**.
- Choose **Image ➢ Adjustments ➢ Invert** (⌘/**Ctrl+I**). As in the previous tutorial, the strings of electricity begin to take shape.
- Choose **Enhance ➢ Brightness/Contrast ➢ Levels** (⌘/**Ctrl+L**).

6.8

6.9

- In the Levels dialog box, move the black and gray sliders to the right. Keep an eye on the image; the lightning forms as you move the sliders. See **Figure 6.10**.
- Click **OK**. See **Figure 6.11**.
- In the last tutorial, color was added in the Color Variations dialog box. This time, you use the Hue/Saturation dialog box. Choose **Enhance ➢ Adjust Color ➢ Hue/Saturation**. Check the **Colorize** box and move the sliders until you are happy with the hue. Click **OK**.

Figure 6.12 (CP15) shows the result of applying the static tutorial to a sphere.

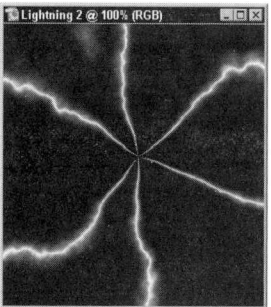

6.11

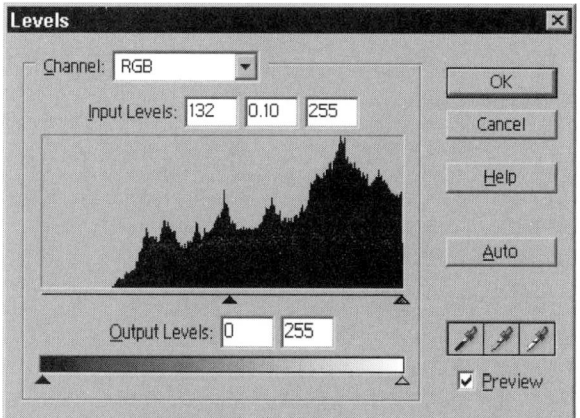

6.10

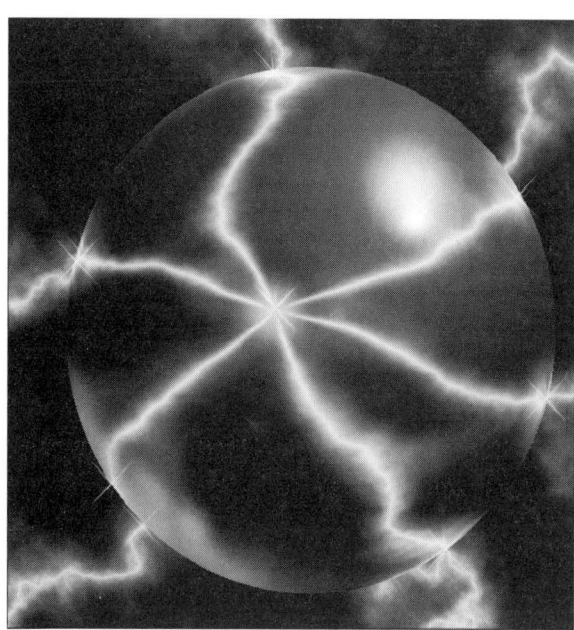

6.12 (CP15)

SMOKE

C ontinuing with the intangibles, vapors are another you can tackle using Elements. This tutorial shows how to create smoke from scratch.

STEP 1: PREPARE THE IMAGE

- Choose **File** ➢ **New**. In the New Image dialog box, set the following attributes:
    - Name = **Smoke**
    - Width = **800 pixels**
    - Height = **600 pixels**
    - Resolution = **100 dpi**
    - Mode = **RGB color**
    - Contents = **White**
- Click **OK**.
- Choose **Edit** ➢ **Fill**. Fill the background layer with black, **100%** opacity.
- Click **OK**.
- Create a new layer by clicking the **Add a Layer** icon on the bottom of the Layers palette or choose **Layer** ➢ **New** ➢ **Layer** (**Shift+⌘/Ctrl+N**).

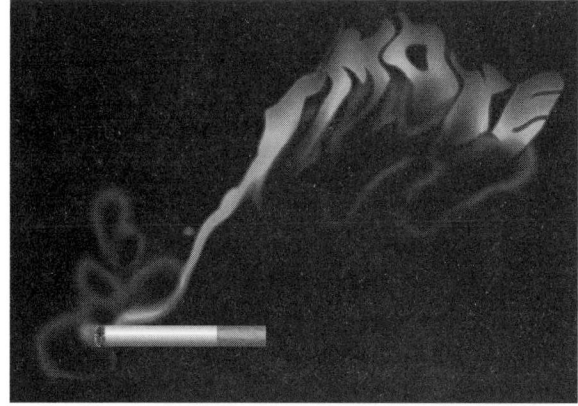

STEP 2: GENERATE VAPOROUS TYPE

- Select the **Type Mask** tool in the Toolbox. In the Options bar, set the following attributes for the type selection:
    - Font Style = **Normal**
    - Font = Any font will do, although one with a combination of thick and thin areas works best
    - Font Size = **160 pixels**
    - Anti-aliased = **Selected**
    - Justify = **center**

- Enter your text in the center of the image. See **Figure 6.13**.
- Choose **Edit ➢ Fill**. Fill the selection with white, **100%** opacity.
- Press the **D** key to reset the foreground and background colors. Black is now in the foreground.
- Choose **Edit ➢ Stroke**. Set the following attributes in the Stroke dialog box:
  - Width = **4 pixels**
  - Color = **Black**
  - Location = **Inside**
  - Mode = **Normal**
  - Opacity = **100%**
- Click **OK**.
- Choose **Filter ➢ Blur ➢ Gaussian Blur**. Enter a blur radius of **6** pixels.
- Click **OK**.

6.13

6.14

- Using the shortcut keys, press **⌘/Ctrl+I** to invert the colors of the fill.
- Choose **Enhance ➢ Brightness/Contrast ➢ Brightness/Contrast**. Increase the Brightness to **20** and the Contrast to **60**.
- Click **OK**. **Figure 6.14** shows the resulting text.
- Create a new layer just above the background layer but beneath the text.
- Select the **Gradient** tool. In the Options bar, set the following attributes:
  - Gradient Type = **Foreground to Background (Black to White)**
  - Gradient Style = **Linear Gradient**
  - Mode = **Normal**
  - Opacity = **100%**
  - Reverse = **Unchecked**
- Starting just above the text and proceeding straight down to just below the text, fill the selection with the gradient.
- Choose **Select ➢ Deselect**.
- In the Layers palette, click the small eye next to the original text layer to render it invisible.
- Make sure that the gradient filled layer is selected before proceeding.

STEP 3: WARP INTO SMOKE

- Choose **Filter ➢ Distort ➢ Wave**.
- In the Wave dialog box, set the following attributes:
  - Number of Generators = **30**
  - Type = **Sine**
  - Wavelength: Min. = **15**, Max. = **584**
  - Amplitude: Min. = **29**, Max. = **62**
  - Scale: Horiz. = **32**, Vert. = **31**
  - Undefined Areas = **Repeat Edge Pixels**
- Click **OK**.

See **Figure 6.15** for an example of the Wave dialog box settings. You may also use the Randomize button to adjust the settings until you have smoke in the viewer with which you are happy.

- Click **OK**. **Figure 6.16** shows the smoke effect thus far.
- Click the eye icon for the text layer again to make it visible.
- Make a copy of the Smoke layer and select it.
- Choose **Filter ➢ Blur ➢ Gaussian Blur**. Enter a blur radius of **2** pixels.
- Click **OK**.

- Merge the two smoke layers by choosing **Layer ➢ Merge Down** (**⌘/Ctrl+E**). See **Figure 6.17**.
- Select the **Smudge** tool in the Toolbox (**F** key).
- Set the following attributes for the Smudge tool in the Options bar:
  - Brush Type = **Round, Feathered**
  - Brush Size = **50 pixels**
  - Mode = **Normal**
  - Strength = **50%**
  - Finger Painting = **Checked**
- Smear the edges of the smoky vapor by randomly clicking and dragging spots, especially on the lower edges, as shown in **Figure 6.18**.
- Duplicate the Smoke layer.
- Set the blending mode for the duplicate smoke layer to **Difference**, and the Opacity to **50%** to **60%**.

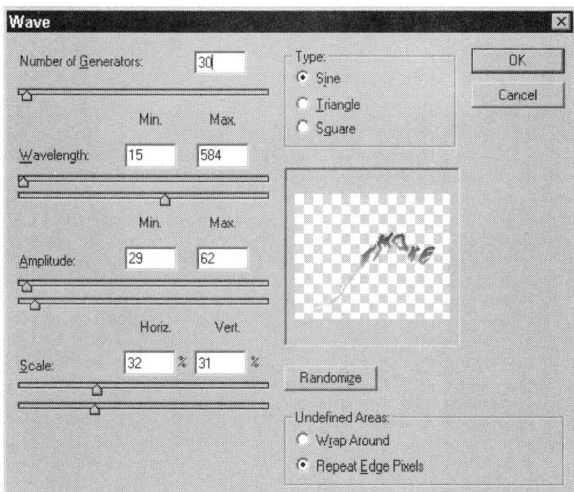

6.15

6.17

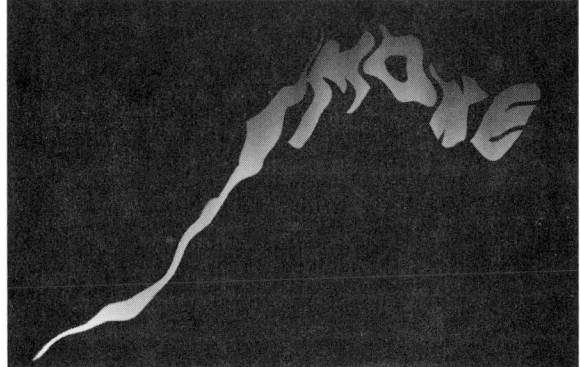

6.16

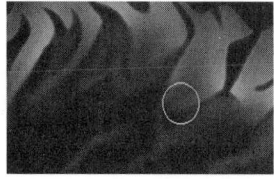

6.18

Figure 6.19 is the final smoke image. **Figure 6.20** replaces the text with a realistic source of the smoke.

6.19

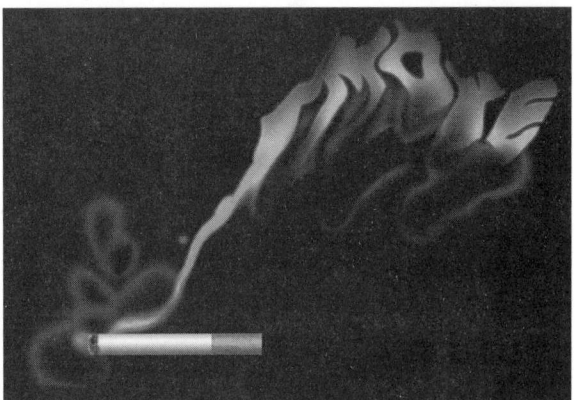

6.20

GHOSTS

This tutorial shows how to turn your friends into creepy specters in just a few steps. This is also an excellent warm-up for the next chapter, because here the Liquify tool is introduced for photo warping.

This tutorial requites the following from the CD-ROM:

- Stairwell.jpg
- ClawModel.psd

STEP 1: PREPARE THE IMAGE

- Find and open the image **Stairwell.jpg**.
- Select the **Magnetic Lasso** tool. In the Options bar, enter the following settings:
  - Selection Type = **New Selection**
  - Feather = **0**
  - Anti-aliased = **Selected**
  - Width = **10 pixels**
  - Edge Contrast = **20%**
  - Frequency = **20**
  - Pen Pressure = **Unchecked**
- In the lower-left of the image is a banister. Select it with the **Magnetic Lasso** by drawing around the edge of the banister and the book lying atop it. See **Figure 6.21**.
- Choose **Layer ➢ New ➢ Layer via Copy**.

STEP 2: INSERT A PERSON

- Open the image **ClawModel.psd**, found on the CD-ROM.

6.21

- Note that ClawModel.psd (see **Figure 6.22**) has two layers: a white background and a layer with the model. Select the model layer and drag it into the Stairwell image (see **Figure 6.23**).
- Drag the claw model layer beneath the banister layer in the Layers palette.

STEP 3: WARP THE SUBJECT

■ Choose **Filter** ➤ **Distort** ➤ **Liquify**. The model appears in the center of the huge Liquify dialog box, with no background or banister appearing.

■ Along the left-hand side of the Liquify dialog box is a series of tools. Select the **Warp** tool, found at the top of the tool buttons.

■ On the right side of the dialog box are settings for brush size and other tool options. Set the following options for the Warp tool:

- ■ Brush Size = **64**
- ■ Pressure = **50**

■ Click and drag points along the edge of the subject, dragging away from the body in curvy, swirling motions, as shown in **Figure 6.24**.

Most ghosts (or so I'm told) have a misty, distorted quality to them; I assume it has to do with having no physical body. By bloating certain areas of the face and visible body parts, the creepiness can be increased dramatically.

■ Select the **Bloat** tool from the left side of the dialog box. Set the following attributes for the Bloat tool:

- ■ Brush Size = **400**
- ■ Pressure = **50**

6.23

6.24

6.22

6.25

- Starting with the extended hand, increase the size of the appendage by clicking and holding the cursor over it, as shown in **Figure 6.25**.
- Continue warping other portions of the image, adjusting the tool selection and brush sizes as needed. For example, a smaller brush for the Bloat tool was used to increase the size of the eye in **Figure 6.26**, so as not to distort the rest of the face. In addition, the Warp tool was again used, this time to warp the lower portion of the body and to add to the liquid quality of the form.
- When satisfied with the distortions, click **OK**.
- Select the **Move** tool. Position the model so that the lower portion extends from behind the banister, as shown in **Figure 6.27**.

STEP 4: TRANSFORM FLESH TO MIST

- In the Layers palette, set the opacity of the model layer to **75%**, or until you can see the wall behind the model through her body.

- Choose **Image ➢ Adjustments ➢ Invert** (⌘/**Ctrl+I**).
- Choose **Enhance ➢ Adjust Color ➢ Remove Color** (⌘/**Ctrl+Shift+U**) to remove the color from the model.
- ⌘/**Ctrl**+click the model layer to generate a selection.
- Choose **Select ➢ Feather**. Enter a Feather radius of 4.
- Click **OK**.
- Choose **Select ➢ Inverse** (⌘/**Ctrl+Shift+I**).
- Choose **Filter ➢ Blur ➢ Gaussian Blur**. Enter a blur radius of **10** pixels.
- Click **OK**.
- Choose **Enhance ➢ Adjust Color ➢ Hue/Saturation**. In the Hue/Saturation dialog box enter the following settings:
  - Hue = **200**
  - Saturation = **14**
  - Lightness = **0**
  - Colorize = **Checked**

6.26

6.27

■ Click **OK**. See **Figure 6.28**.

■ Select the **Rectangular Marquee** tool. In the Options bar, set the following attributes:

  ■ Selection Type = **New Selection**
  ■ Feather = **15 pixels**
  ■ Style = **Normal**

■ Select the bottom portion of the model, as shown in **Figure 6.29**.

6.28

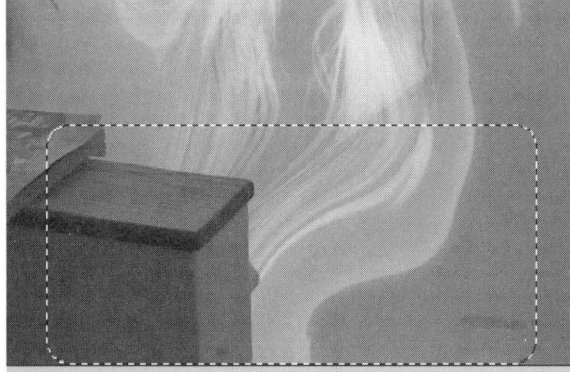

6.29

■ Choose **Filter ➢ Blur ➢ Gaussian Blur**. Enter a blur radius of **7** pixels.

■ Click **OK**.

■ ⌘/**Ctrl**+click the model layer to generate a selection in the form of the ghost.

■ Create a new layer beneath the model layer.

■ Press the **D** key, followed by the **X** key to place white in the foreground color box.

■ Choose **Edit ➢ Stroke**. Enter the following settings in the Stroke dialog box:

  ■ Stroke Width = **6**
  ■ Color = **White**
  ■ Location = **Center**
  ■ Mode = **Normal**
  ■ Opacity = **100%**

■ Click **OK**.

■ Choose **Filter ➢ Blur ➢ Gaussian Blur**. Enter a blur radius of **5** pixels.

■ Click **OK**. See **Figure 6.30** (**CP16**) for the final ghost!

6.30 (CP16)

X-RAY

This tutorial requires the following from the CD-ROM:

- Face-1.jpg
- Skull.psd

The last tutorial in this chapter rethinks the idea of seeing past or through the skin. In the ghost tutorial the entire entity was somewhat transparent. What if, instead of peering through the misty form of a wraith without a body, you could peer right through the skin of a living, breathing person? It would save a lot on medical testing, to be sure. Without further ado, put your subject on the slab and see what makes him tick!

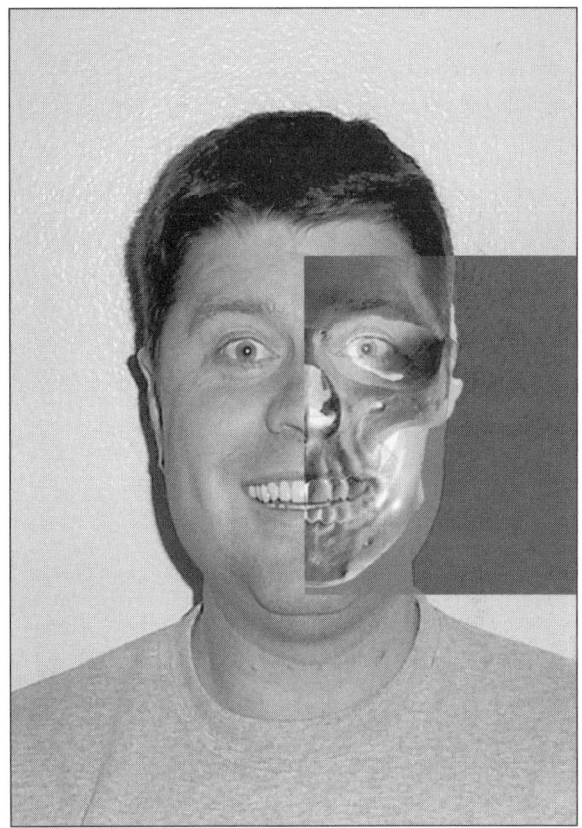

STEP 1: PREPARE THE IMAGE

- Find and open **Face-1.jpg**. See **Figure 6.31**.
- Find and open **Skull.psd**. As with the ClawModel image in the last tutorial, this image has two layers. See **Figure 6.32**.
- Click the Skull layer and drag it onto the Face-1.jpg image. A new layer is created, containing the skull.

STEP 2: FIT BONE TO FLESH

- Select the Skull layer in the Layers palette.
- Choose **Edit ➢ Transform ➢ Distort**.
- In the Options bar, change the width of the layer to **70%** and the height to **65%**. See **Figure 6.33**.
- Click the **Accept Change** icon in the Options bar.

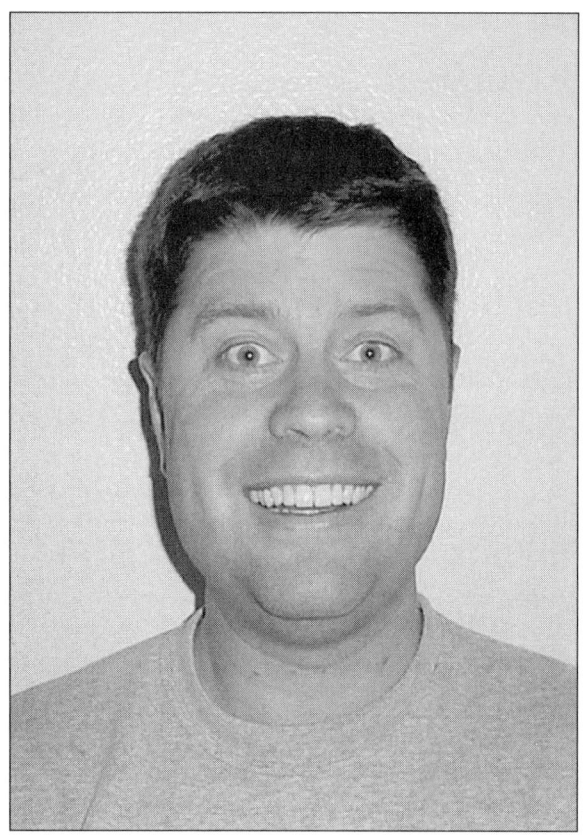

6.31

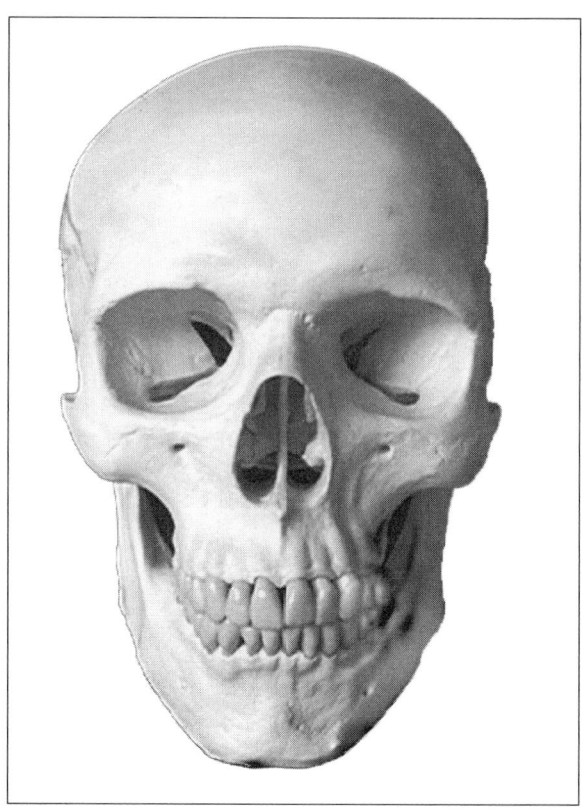

6.32

■ In the Layers palette, set the opacity for the Skull layer to **50%**.

■ Position the skull over the face so that the eye sockets and teeth line up with the face beneath. You may want to decrease the opacity of the layer temporarily to help positioning.

■ For this example, the skull is still a bit large for the face. Again, choose **Edit ➢ Transform ➢ Distort**. In the Options bar, set the width to **95%** and the height to **96%**.

■ Click the **Accept Change** icon.

■ Select the **Move** tool and reposition the skull over the face for the best fit, matching the teeth and eye sockets as before. See **Figure 6.34**.

STEP 3: TAKE AN X-RAY PHOTO

This step creates an area on a duplicate face layer that appears transparent, allowing the skull behind the face to be seen.

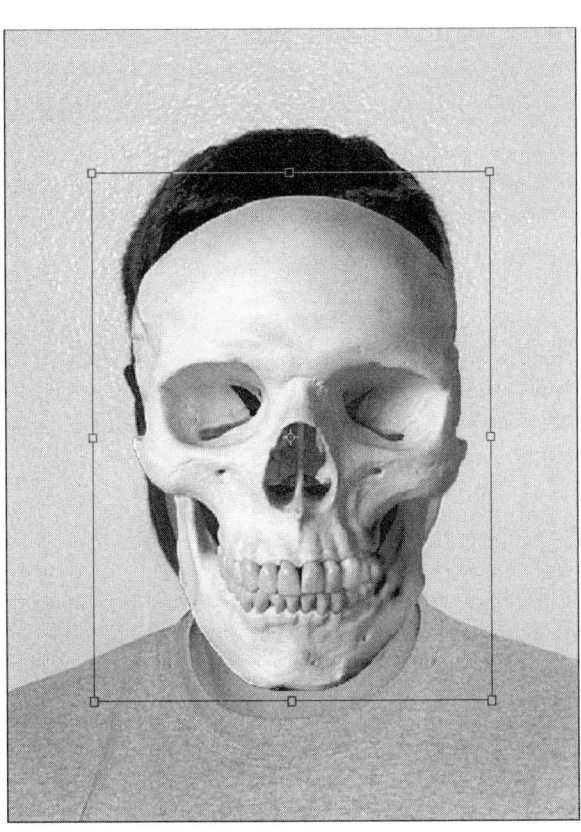

6.33

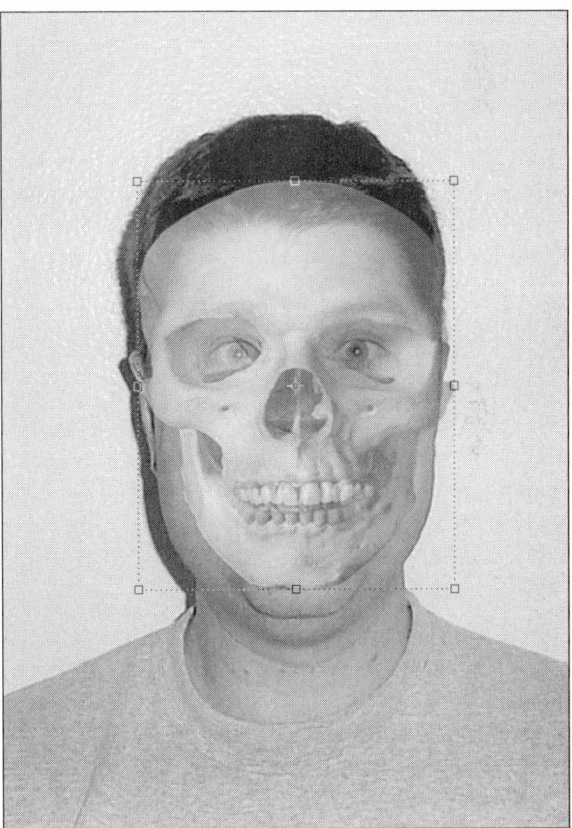

6.34

- In the Layers palette, duplicate the face layer and place the copy above the Skull layer. Select the duplicate face layer.
- Select the **Rectangular Marquee** tool. In the Options bar, set the following attributes:
  - Selection Type =**New Selection**
  - Feather = **0**
  - Style = **Normal**
- Select a portion of the face, as shown in **Figure 6.35**.
- Choose **Layer ➢ New ➢ Layer via Cut**. Doing this places the selected portion of the face on its own layer, where you can manipulate it separately from the rest of the face.
- In the Layers palette, select the cutout layer. Set the blending mode to **Difference**.

- Choose **Enhance ➢ Adjust Color ➢ Remove Color**.
- Choose **Enhance ➢ Brightness/Contrast/Brightness/Contrast**. Increase the brightness to +**100**.
- Click **OK**. See **Figure 6.36 (CP17)** for the X-ray!

Manipulating faces of friends, family and co-workers is extremely fun, made even more enjoyable by the reaction of the subject involved. At first people may seem reluctant to pose for your experimentation, but trust me: as soon as they see the result, and the snickering stops, they will ask what other things you can turn them into!

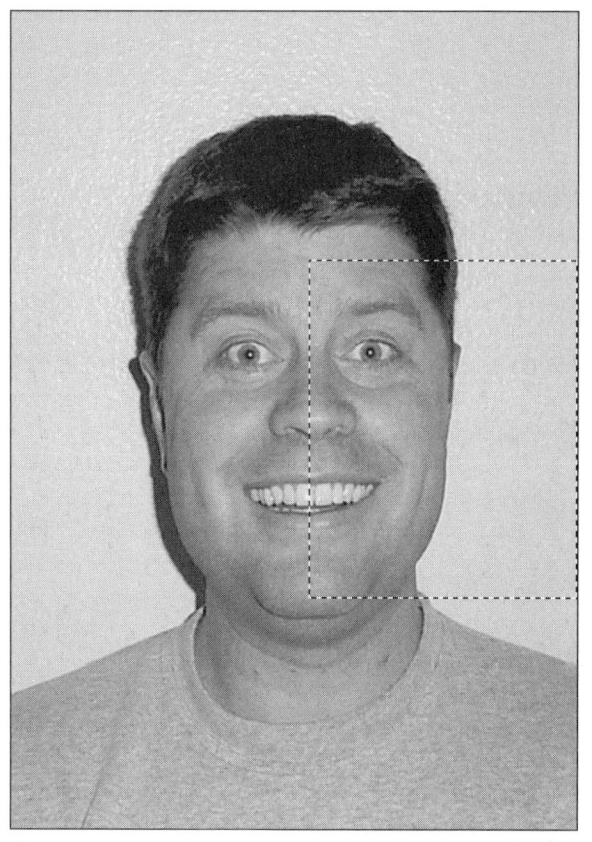

6.35

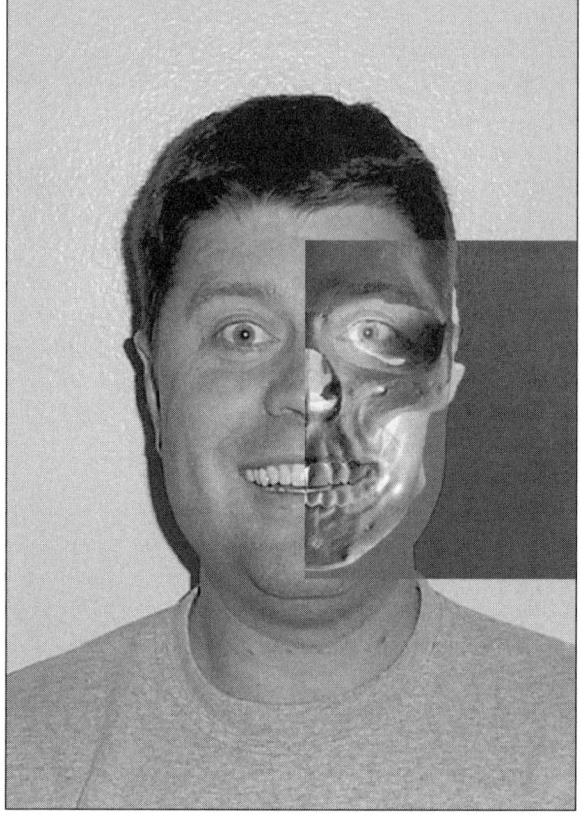

6.36 (CP17)

7

I SHOULD HAVE BEEN A DOCTOR: ALTERING HUMANS AND CRITTERS

This topic is a personal favorite of mine, and I must admit my friends and family are nervous whenever I take out the camera. They can't fool me; though they complain, very rarely do they run away and hide. Most just grumble or smirk and eventually submit to a pose, knowing full well that they may end up in the laboratory of my imagination.

The popularity of manipulating people and animals (or critters) is increasingly apparent. Take a walk through your local superstore greeting card section or shopping mall stationery store. One line of cards has animals warped into comical distortions and poses. Several tabloid newspapers take particular pride in displaying all manner of creatures on their covers. Bat Boy, Dog Boy, Gator Boy, Alien Babies . . . how do they do it? Photoshop, of course.

Many of those same tools used in Photoshop 7.0 to distort the animal photos are present in Photoshop Elements 2, lying in wait for the mad scientist in you to take control of the science and create creatures of your own.

GIVING FRIENDS A FACE LIFT

This tutorial requires the following from the CD-ROM:

- Face-2.jpg

This tutorial extends what you learned about the Liquify tools in the previous chapter. This tutorial takes a friendly face (in this case, my good friend Brent, who always wanted to be famous) and gives him a Hollywood make-over!

STEP 1: PREPARE THE IMAGE

- Open **Face-2.jpg**, found on the CD-ROM. See **Figure 7.1**.
- In the Layers palette, create a copy of the background layer.

STEP 2: REMOVE GLASSES

- Click the **Selection Brush** tool in the Toolbox. Set the following attributes in the Options bar:
    - Brush Type = **Rounded, Feathered**
    - Brush Size = **16 pixels**
    - Mode = **Selection**
    - Hardness = **0%**

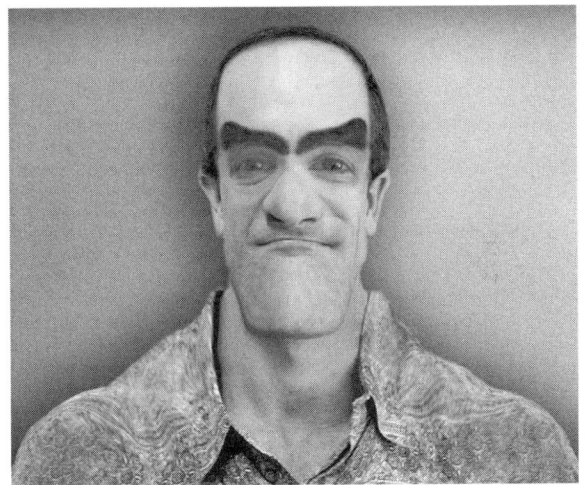

7.1

185

- Paint a selection around the frame and metal areas, as shown in **Figure 7.2**.
- Select the **Clone Stamp** tool. Set the following attributes in the Options bar:
    - Brush Type = **Rounded, Feathered**
    - Size = **10 pixels**
    - Mode = **Normal**
    - Opacity = **65%**
    - Aligned = **Unchecked**
- To begin deleting the glasses, take a sample of the skin on the nose by pressing **Alt**+click, as shown in **Figure 7.3**.
- Apply the **Clone Stamp** tool to areas within the selection that have the same general tone and texture as the nose. See **Figure 7.4**.
- Note that the glasses also cover the eyebrows. To cover this section, paint a selection over the eyebrows and take a sample of hair from the model's head. Stamp it into the eyebrow region with the **Clone Stamp** tool, as shown in **Figure 7.5**. The larger the selection, the bushier the eyebrows!

Figure 7.6 is the reworked shot of the model, sans glasses and with new, improved eyebrows in place.

STEP 3: RECEDE THE HAIRLINE

- Choose **Filter ➢ Distort ➢ Liquify**.
- Use the **Zoom** tool and the **Move** tool to increase the size of the face. Move the face into a centered position in the Liquify viewer.
- Select the **Bloat** tool. Set the Brush Size to **64** and the Brush Pressure to **50**.
- Lightly bloat the forehead just below the hairline, evenly across the width of the forehead. See **Figure 7.7**.

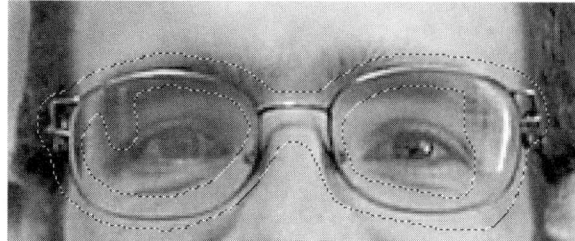

7.2

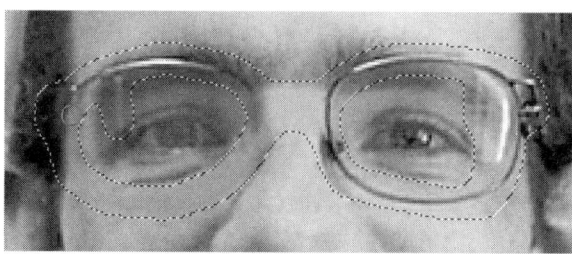

7.4

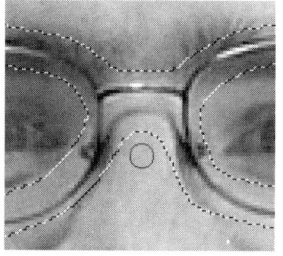

7.3

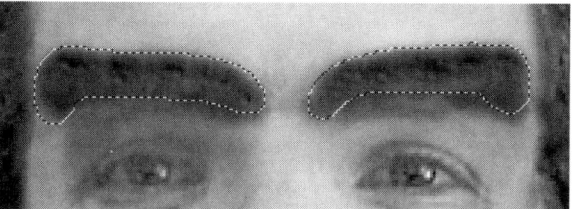

7.5

- Select the **Warp** tool.
- Starting in the center of the forehead, start slowly clicking the mouse on the skin and, holding the mouse button down, pushing the forehead and hairline up. Use short strokes so as not to distort the forehead and to keep an even hairline. You may also choose to add a bit of character to the eyebrows, as shown in **Figure 7.8**.
- The Liquify process has a habit of eating memory, and this can cause Elements to shut down or perform an illegal operation. For that reason, click **OK**.

STEP 4: ALTER FACIAL CHARACTERISTICS

- Again, choose **Filter ➤ Distort ➤ Liquify**.
- Select the **Bloat** tool.

- Set the Brush Size to **40**. Expand the sides of the nose just above the nostrils, as well as the ball of the nose.
- Increase the Brush Size to **80**.

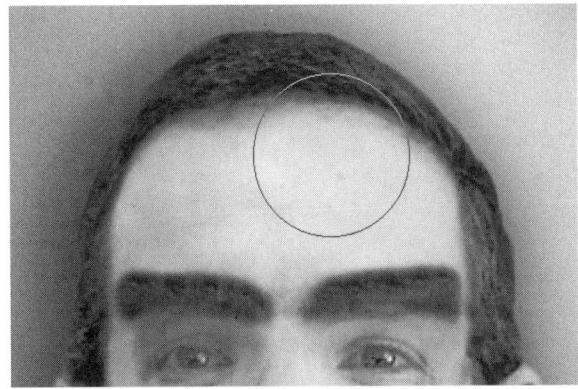

7.7

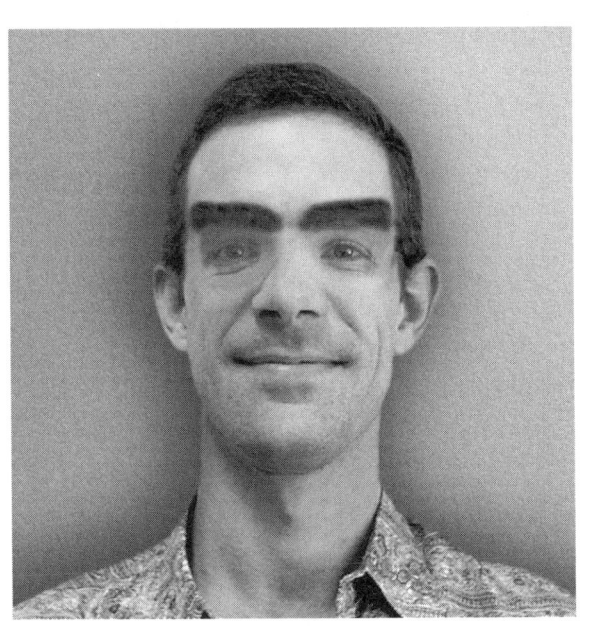

7.6

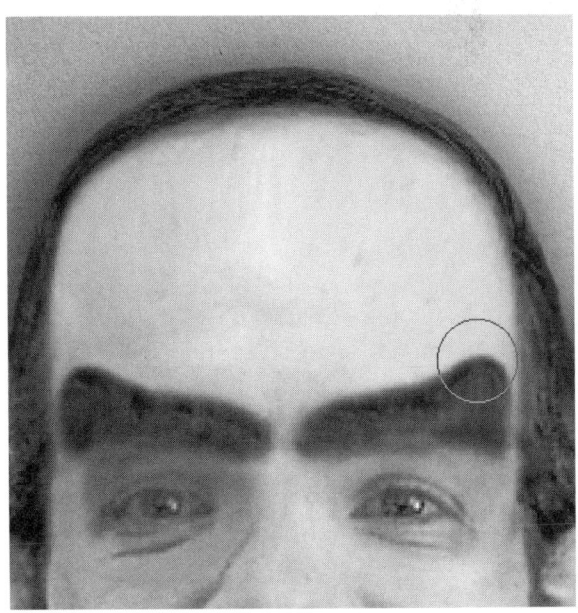

7.8

■ Apply the **Bloat** tool to each eye but not so much that the eyes distort beyond normal eye shape.

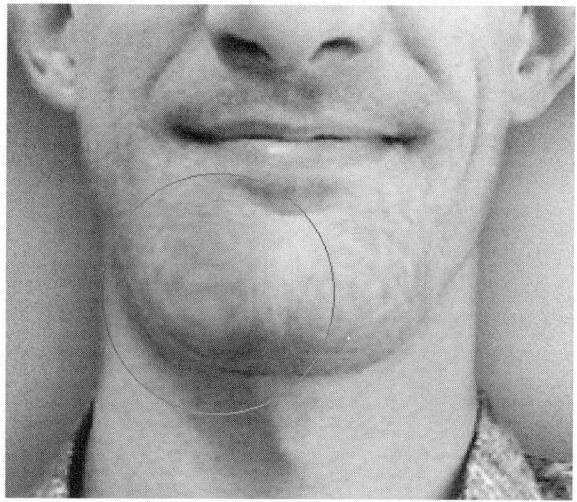

7.9

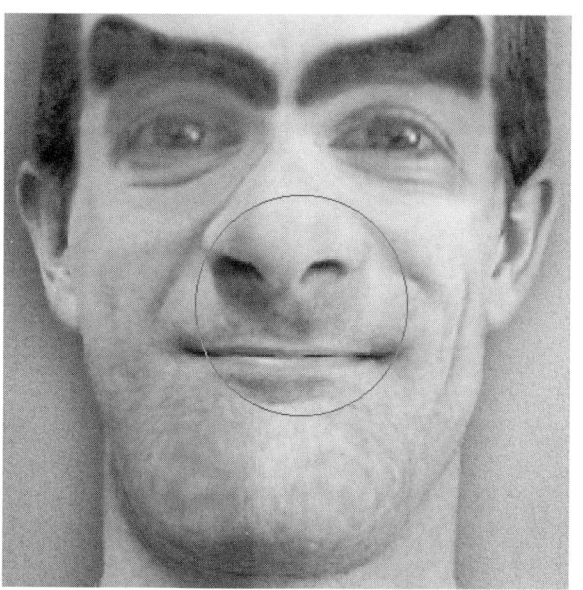

7.10

■ Expand the chin, first applying the **Bloat** tool to one side and then the other. See **Figure 7.9**.

■ Select the **Pucker** tool. Set the Brush Size to **42**, leaving the Brush Pressure at **50**.

■ Center the tool over an ear and apply the **Pucker** tool. Repeat the process on the other ear, reducing their size.

■ Apply the **Pucker** tool to the mouth, starting in the center and moving the **Pucker** tool back and forth to the edges. Apply evenly so that the lips are still recognizable as lips!

■ Apply the **Pucker** tool to the bridge of the nose between the eyes to draw them closer together without changing their size. **Figure 7.10** shows the Pucker tool in action.

■ Select the **Warp** tool. Set the Brush Size to **75** to **85**.

■ Center the tool on the edge of the face in the cheekbone/ear area and draw the face inward as if to narrow the head. Do so on both sides of the

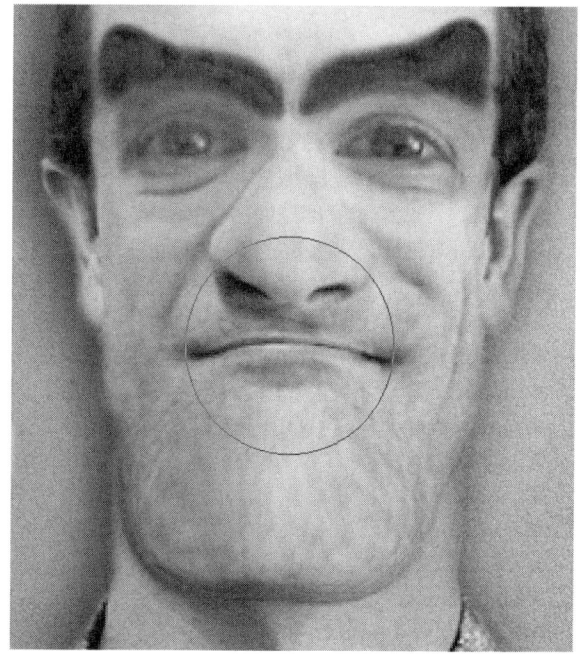

7.11

skull. Continue to move portions of the face slightly (see **Figure 7.11**) until you are satisfied with the new features and symmetry. **Figure 7.12** shows Brent's new head.

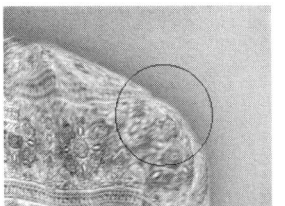

7.13

STEP 5: BULK UP

The desired effect is to create a fuller figure beneath the clothing.

- Increase the size of the Warp tool to **120** or so. Start with the shoulders and drag them outward, as though creating muscles. See **Figure 7.13**.
- Drag the sides of the neck out to thicken it, and also the areas on the tops of the shoulders above the collar bone. See **Figure 7.14**.
- Click **OK**.
- To eliminate some of the blurring in the shirt pattern, select the **Clone Stamp** and sample an area that hasn't suffered much distortion. Stamp the sharper pattern over the areas of heavy blurring. **Figure 7.15** shows the new, improved Brent!

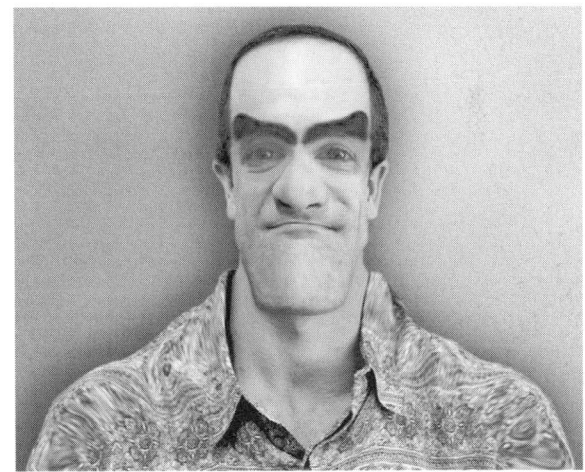

7.14

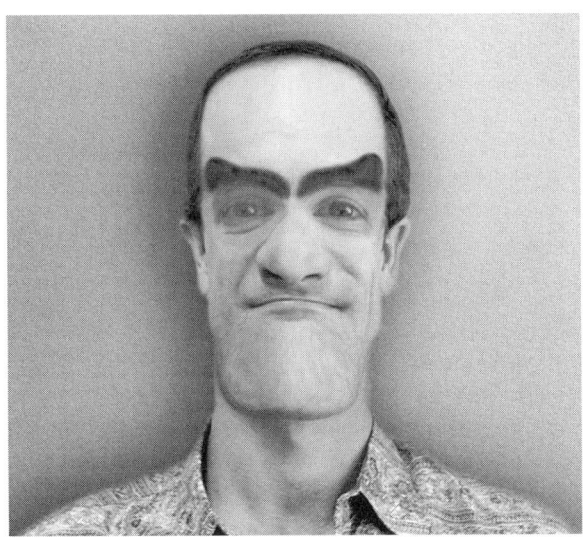

7.12

7.15

FUN WITH CRITTERS: WORKING WITH ANIMALS

T his tutorial requires the following from the CD-ROM:

- Kitty-1.jpg

STEP 1: PREPARE THE IMAGE

- Find and open the image **Kitty-1.jpg**. See **Figure 7.16**.
- In the Layers palette, duplicate the background layer.

STEP 2: WARP KITTY!

- Choose **Filter ➢ Distort ➢ Liquify**.
- Select the **Pucker** tool. Set the Brush Size to **100**, and the Brush Pressure to **50**.

7.16

7.17

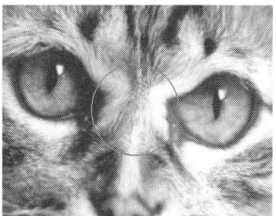

7.18

7.19

- Run the **Pucker** tool over the mouth, nose, and whiskers to decrease their size, as shown in **Figure 7.17**. This emphasizes the eyes, the main trait you are enhancing.
- Apply the **Pucker** tool to the area between the eyes (see **Figure 7.18**) to draw them closer together.
- Select the **Bloat** tool. Set the Brush Size to **150**.
- Center the tool over one of the eyes. Bloat the eye to increase the size, but be careful not to distort the pupil too much. Increase the size of the second eye in proportion to the first. See **Figure 7.19**.
- Click **OK**.

STEP 3: COLOR THE EYES

- Select the **Magnetic Lasso** tool in the Toolbox.
- Draw a selection around the perimeter of the eyes, as shown in **Figure 7.20**.
- Create a new layer in the Layers palette.
- Click the foreground color in the Toolbox. In the Color Picker, enter color **#8BFCF0**, or R = **139**, G = **252**, and B = **240**.
- Click **OK**.

7.20

- Select the **Paintbrush** tool in the Toolbox. Set the following attributes in the Options bar:
  - Brush Type = **Rounded, Feathered**
  - Brush Size = **70**
  - Mode = **Soft Light**
  - Opacity = **36**
  - Airbrush = **Selected**
- Lightly spray along the edges of the pupil, as shown in **Figure 7.21**.
- Set the blending mode for the paint layer to **Overlay**, opacity to **100%**.
- Choose **Select ➤ Deselect (⌘/Ctrl+D)**.

7.21

STEP 4: FROM PICTURE TO PAINTING

- Duplicate the background copy layer. Keep it beneath the paint layer.
- Choose **Enhance ➤ Adjust Color ➤ Remove Color**.
- Choose **Filter ➤ Brush Strokes ➤ Ink Outlines**.
- In the Ink Outlines dialog box (see **Figure 7.22**), apply the following settings:
  - Stroke Length = **48**
  - Dark Intensity = **15**
  - Light Intensity = **15**
- Click **OK**.
- In the Layers palette, change the blending mode of the desaturated layer to **Multiply**.
- Duplicate the desaturated layer. Again, make sure it remains beneath the paint layer.
- Choose **Image ➤ Adjustments ➤ Invert (⌘/Ctrl+I)**.

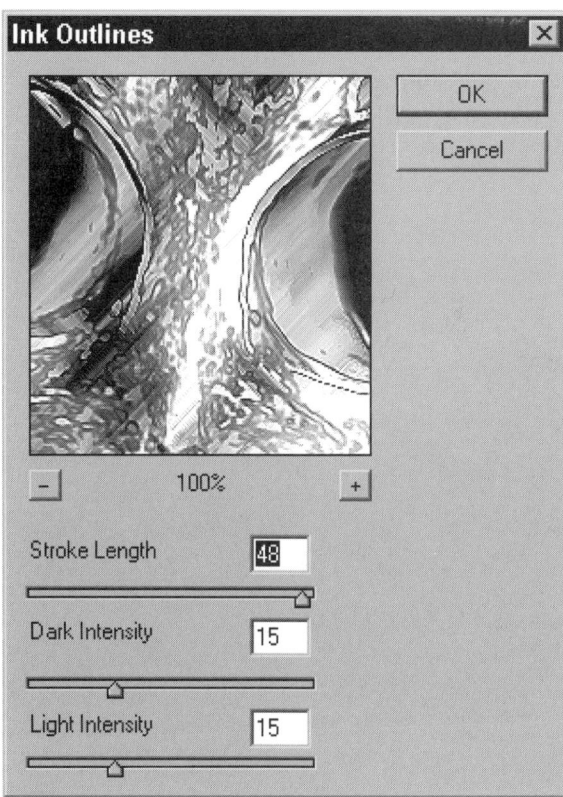

7.22

7.23

- Choose **Filter** ➢ **Stylize** ➢ **Glowing Edges**. Set the following in the Glowing Edges dialog box:
  - Edge Width = **1**
  - Edge Brightness = **20**
  - Smoothness = **15**
- Click **OK**.
- In the Layers palette, set the blending mode to **Soft Light**, and the opacity to **75%**. **Figure 7.23** shows the completed Kitty Art.

MERGING PHOTOS 1

Many ways exist to merge photos together, with differing applications. This tutorial is actually two tutorials. The first creates the ever-popular Dog Boy, morphing a human and man's best friend into something nature never intended. The second tutorial shows how to take two normal photos and create a rather comical situation.

This tutorial requires the following from the CD-ROM:

- Face-4.jpg
- DogModel-1.psd

STEP 1: PREPARE THE IMAGE

- Open the image **Face-4.jpg**, found on the CD-ROM (see **Figure 7.24**).
- Select the **Magnetic Lasso** tool from the Toolbox. Set the following attributes for the tool in the Options bar:
  - Selection Type = **New Selection**
  - Feather = **0**
  - Anti-aliased = **Checked**
  - Width = **10 pixels**
  - Edge Contrast = **10%**
  - Frequency = **11**
  - Pen Pressure = **Unchecked**

7.24

■ Make a selection around the model's body. In this case, my good friend Ted has stood in as the model. See **Figure 7.25**.

■ Choose **Layer ➢ New ➢ Layer via Copy**.

■ Create a new layer beneath the copy you made in the previous step.

7.25

7.26 (CP18)

■ Fill the empty layer with a radial gradient. In this example, a white to blue radial gradient was applied, starting behind the figure and drawn outward. See **Figure 7.26 (CP18)**.

STEP 2: MATCH HEADS

■ Select the top layer with the model separated from the background.

■ Choose **Image ➢ Transform ➢ Distort**.

■ In the Options bar, set the Width to **130%**.

■ Open **Dog-Model-1.psd**, found on the CD-ROM. See **Figure 7.27**.

■ Dog-Model-1.psd has two layers: a background and a layer with the dog's head separated from the background. Drag the dog's head layer over onto the model image.

■ Select the model layer.

■ Choose **Image ➢ Transform ➢ Distort**.

■ In the Options bar, set the Height to **85%**. Click the **Accept Change** icon.

7.27

■ Select the **Move** tool. Slide the model layer down so that it is again flush with the bottom of the image. See **Figure 7.28**.

■ Click the small eye next to the dog head layer in the Layers palette, rendering it invisible.

■ Select the model layer.

■ Select the **Magnetic Lasso** tool in the Toolbox.

■ Draw a selection around the head and neck, separating the flesh portion of the layer from the shirt as shown in **Figure 7.29**.

■ Choose **Layer** ➤ **New** ➤ **Layer via Cut**.

■ Select the dog head layer in the Layers palette, making it visible.

■ Choose **Image** ➤ **Transform** ➤ **Distort**.

■ Using the guides that appear around the head, widen the dog's head to cover the ears and hair of the model layer. See **Figure 7.30**.

■ Click the **Accept Change** icon in the Options bar.

■ ⌘/**Ctrl**+click the human head layer to generate a selection.

■ Create a new layer above the human head layer.

■ Select the **Clone Stamp** tool.

■ Select the dog head layer and sample a portion of the muzzle. Try to select more tan than black.

■ Go back to the empty layer and stamp the fur pattern over the chin of the human, as shown in **Figure 7.31**.

7.29

7.30

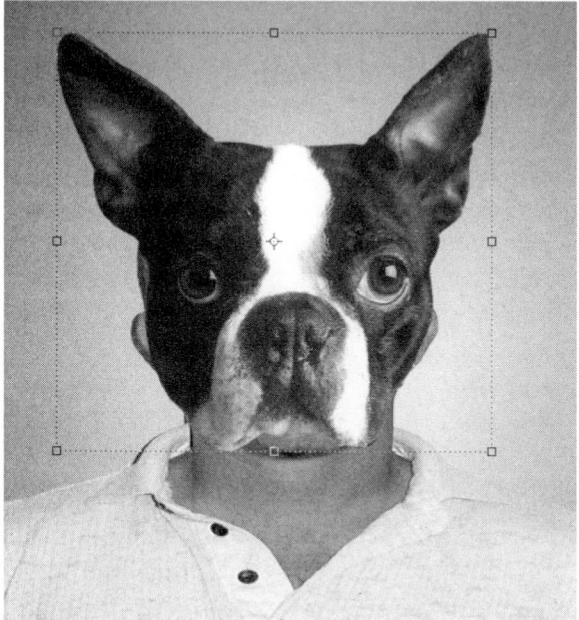

7.28

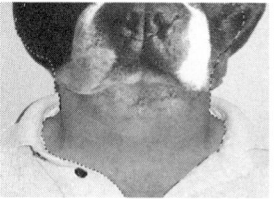

7.31

7.32

7.33

- Select the dog head layer again. Click the **Clone Stamp** tool and set the following attributes in the Options bar:
  - Brush Type = **Round, Feathered**
  - Brush Size = **100**
  - Mode = **Normal**
  - Opacity = **100%**
- Sample the portion of the dog's forehead where the black and white meet. See **Figure 7.32**.
- ⌘/**Ctrl**+click the human head layer to generate a selection.
- In the Layers palette create a new layer above the human head layer.
- Starting just beneath the chin and a bit to the left, stamp the fur pattern down the length of the neck to the shirt collar. Repeat the process, this time using the fur on the other side of the forehead and stamping to the right of the chin down the length of the neck. See **Figure 7.33**.
- On the dog head layer take another sample, this time of black fur only.
- On the layer with the fur-neck fill, completely cover the remaining portions of the neck with fur. See **Figure 7.34**.
- Select the **Burn** tool. In the Options bar, set the following attributes:
  - Brush Type = **Round, Feathered**
  - Brush Size = **39**
  - Range = **Highlights**
  - Exposure = **52%**

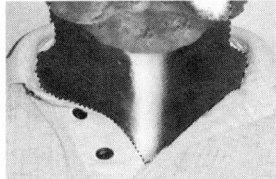

7.34

■ Darken the area just below the chin with the **Burn** tool to give the illusion of shadow. See **Figure 7.35.**

■ Select the top most layer (the dog head layer). Press ⌘/**Ctrl+E** and merge it with the layer beneath it. Continue merging until all that remain are the dog head layer, the gradient background, and the original background layer.

■ ⌘/**Ctrl**+click the dog head layer to generate a selection.

■ Move the selection to the left about an inch with the **Move** tool.

■ Create a new layer beneath the dog head layer in the Layers palette.

■ Choose **Edit ➤ Fill.** In the Fill dialog box, set the Fill Type to **Color,** the Color to **black,** and the Opacity to **60%.**

■ Click **OK.**

■ Choose **Filter ➤ Blur ➤ Gaussian Blur.** Enter a blur radius of **5** to **10** pixels, and click **OK. Figure 7.36 (CP19)** shows the new Dog Boy.

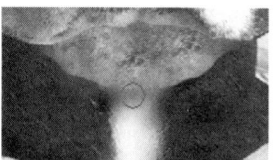

7.35

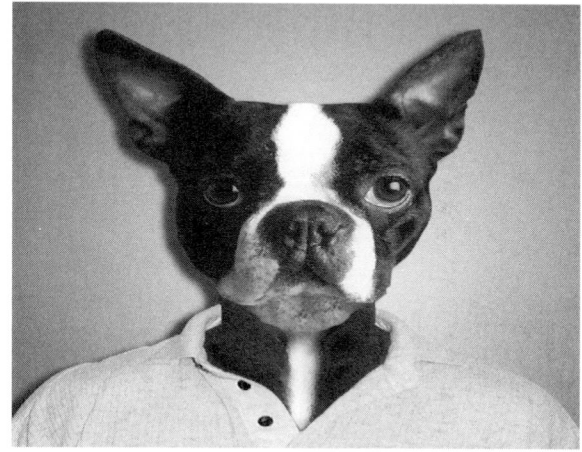

7.36 (CP19)

MERGING PHOTOS 2

T his tutorial requires the following from the CD-ROM:

- Cowboy-1.jpg
- Dog-1.jpg

This tutorial takes a slightly different turn by applying the name Dog Boy to a totally different situation. In short, this tutorial will show one technique for taking existing photos and merge elements of both, creating a unique situation for the subjects and perhaps a chuckle for the viewer.

STEP 1: PREPARE THE IMAGE

- Find and open **Cowboy-1.jpg**, located on the CD-ROM. See **Figure 7.37**.
- Duplicate the background layer.
- Select the **Magic Wand** tool. In the Options bar, set the following attributes:
  - Selection Type = **Add To Selection**
  - Anti-aliased = **Checked**
  - Contiguous = **Checked**

- Click the sky and blue areas in the background. By having the Magic Wand in Add To Selection mode, all the areas you click are added to the selection. See **Figure 7.38**.
- Choose **Select ➢ Inverse**.
- Choose **Layer ➢ New ➢ Layer via Copy**.
- In the Layers palette, select the background layer.
- Select the **Eyedropper** tool. Take a sample of the darker portion of the sky. Swap the foreground and background colors and take another sky sample, this time of the light area of the sky.

7·37

7·38

- Select the **Gradient** tool. In the Options bar, set the following attributes:
  - Gradient = **Foreground to Background**
  - Gradient Type = **Radial Gradient**
  - Mode = **Normal**
  - Opacity = **100%**
  - Reverse = **Unchecked**
- Choose **Select ➤ Deselect**.
- Starting in the center of the background layer and drawing outward to the edge of the photo, fill the background layer with the gradient. See **Figure 7.39**.

STEP 2: REMOVE THE HORSE

- Select the background copy layer. It should now contain only the cowboy and the horse.
- Select the **Polygonal Lasso** tool. Clip around the horse, leaving the cowboy, fence and reins as shown in **Figure 7.40**.

7.39

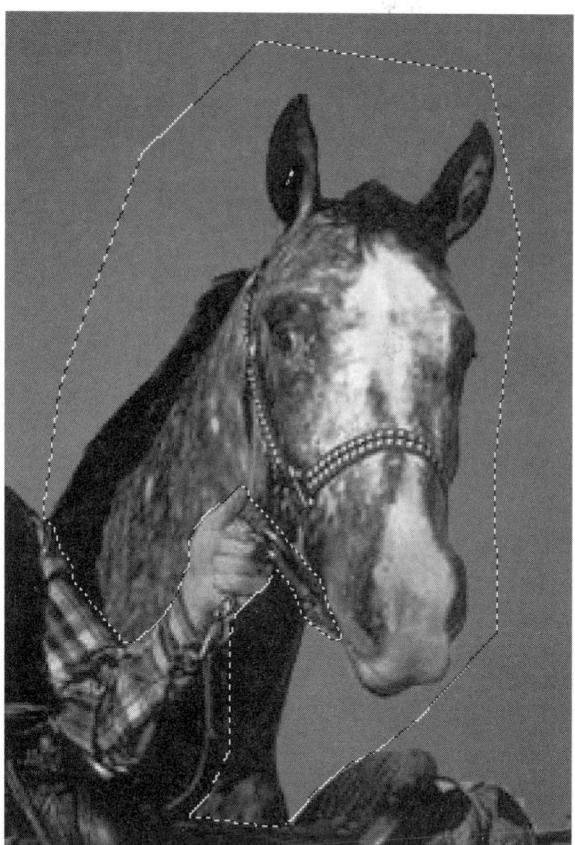

7.40

■ Press **Delete** to erase the horse from the layer. See **Figure 7.41**.

STEP 3: ADD THE DOG

■ Open the image **Dog-1.jpg**, found on the CD-ROM. See **Figure 7.42**.

■ Select the **Magnetic Lasso** tool. In the Options bar, set the following attributes:

  ■ Selection Type = **New Selection**
  ■ Feather = **0**
  ■ Anti-aliased = **Checked**

  ■ Width = **10**
  ■ Edge Contrast = **10%**
  ■ Frequency = **10**
  ■ Pen Pressure = **Unchecked**

■ Draw a selection around the dog with the **Magnetic Lasso**, as shown in **Figure 7.43**.

■ Choose **Layer ➤ New ➤ Layer via Copy**.

■ Drag and drop the dog layer onto the cowboy image.

■ In the Layers palette, drag the dog layer beneath the cowboy layer but above the gradient-filled background.

7.41

7.42

■ Select the **Move** tool. Position the dog behind the fence, roughly in the same place that held the horse. Line up the end of the reins with the shadow around the dog's neck. See **Figure 7.44**.

STEP 4: AGE THE PHOTO

■ Select the cowboy layer.
■ Choose **Enhance ➢ Adjust Color ➢ Hue/Saturation**. Enter the following settings in the Hue/Saturation dialog box:
  ■ Hue = **0**
  ■ Saturation = **–48**
  ■ Lightness = **+11**

■ Click **OK**.
■ Select the dog layer.
■ Choose **Filter ➢ Distort ➢ Liquify**.
■ Click the **Warp** tool. Drag the legs out a bit so that they can be seen through the fence.
■ Click **OK**.
■ Select the **Burn** tool.
■ Darken the area beneath the chin of the dog and where it appears the arm of the cowboy passes between the light source and the dog. See **Figure 7.45**.
■ Select the cowboy layer in the Layers palette.
■ Choose **Layer ➢ Merge Visible**.

7.44

7.43

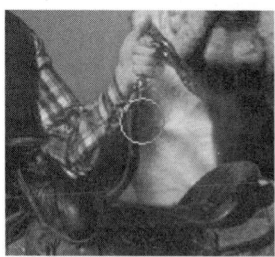

7.45

7.46 (CP20)

- Choose **Enhance ➤ Adjust Color ➤ Hue/Saturation**. Enter the following settings in the Hue/Saturation dialog box:
    - Hue = **0**
    - Saturation = **–30**
    - Lightness = **+14**
- Click **OK**.
- Duplicate the background layer.
- Choose **Enhance ➤ Adjust Color ➤ Remove Color**.
- Choose **Enhance ➤ Adjust Color ➤ Hue/Saturation**. Enter the following settings in the Hue/Saturation dialog box:
    - Hue = **40**
    - Saturation = **30**
    - Lightness = **0**
    - Colorize = **Checked**
- Click **OK**.
- Choose **Filter ➤ Noise ➤ Add Noise**. Enter the following settings in the Add Noise dialog box:
    - Amount = **8**
    - Distribution = **Gaussian**
    - Monochromatic = **Checked**
- Click **OK**.
- Set the layer blending mode to **Overlay**. See **Figure 7.46 (CP20)** for the new Dog Boy image.

MORPH AND LIQUIFY

The final tutorial in this chapter is a closer look at morphing and liquefying. This tutorial takes a single photo and, using only those elements in the photograph, transforms the subject from one entity into something totally different. This effect is a personal favorite of mine; I hope you enjoy it!

This tutorial requires the following from the CD-ROM:

- Boy.jpg

STEP 1: PREPARE THE IMAGE

- Open **Boy.jpg**, found on the CD-ROM. See **Figure 7.47 (CP21)**.
- Choose **Enhance ➤ Auto Contrast**.

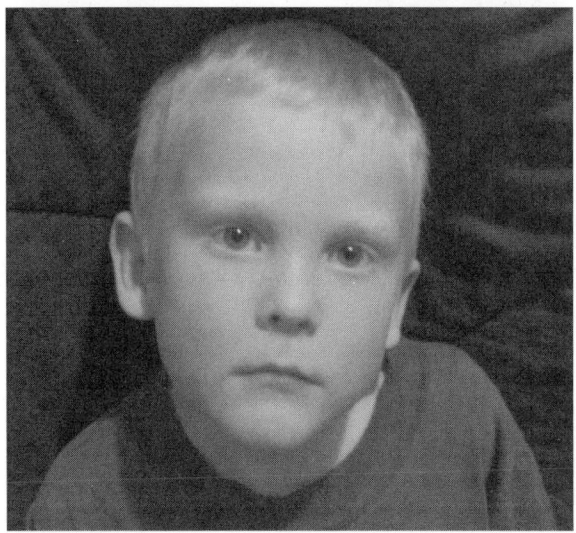

7.47 (CP21)

STEP 2: SEPARATE BOY FROM BACKGROUND

- Select the **Magnetic Lasso** tool.
- Draw a selection around the boy's face with the **Magnetic Lasso**. See **Figure 7.48**.
- Choose **Layer ➢ New ➢ Layer via Copy**.
- Select the face copy layer.

STEP 3: EYES, NOSE, AND MOUTH

- Choose **Filter ➢ Distort ➢ Liquify**.
- Select the **Bloat** tool. Set the Brush Size to **64**.

- Bloat both eyes evenly with the Bloat tool, as shown in **Figure 7.49**.
- Set the Brush Size for the Bloat tool to **100**.
- Again, center the **Bloat** tool cursor over each eye and bloat them evenly, as shown in **Figure 7.50**.
- Select the **Warp** tool. Set the Brush Size to **36**.
- Starting at the outer corners of the eyes, drag the **Warp** tool up and away from the center of the image.

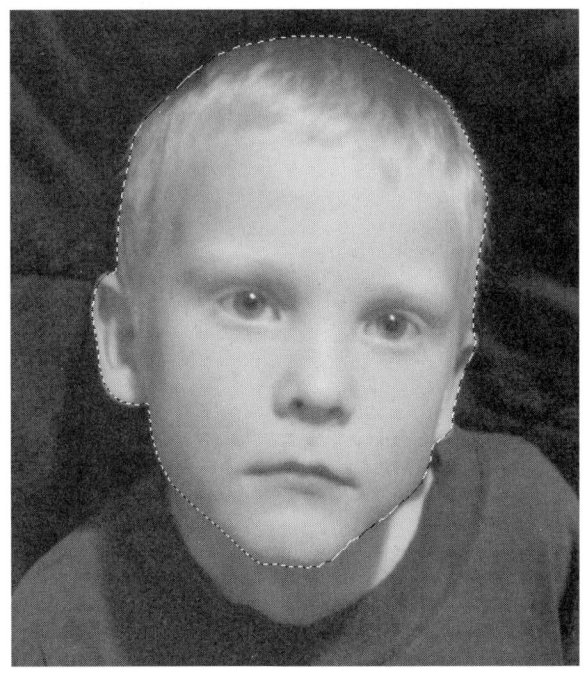

7.48

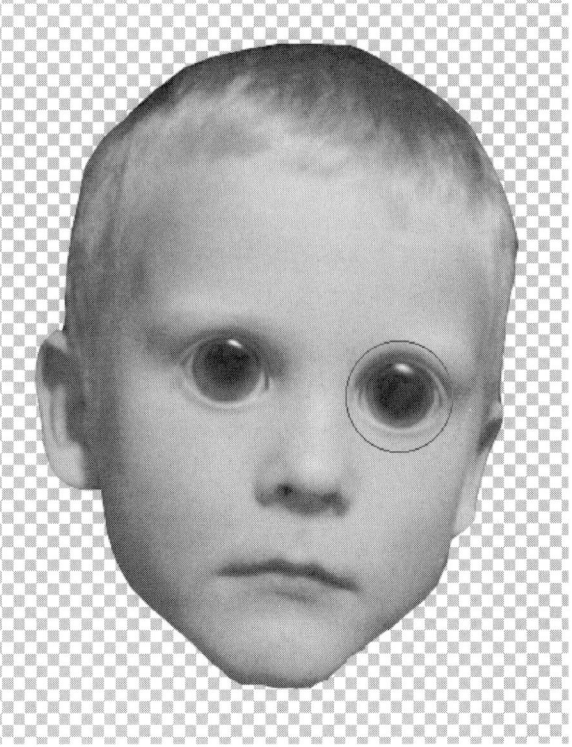

7.49

The key to a good alien is the eyes, which are an exaggerated olive shape. To achieve the pointy shapes shown in **Figure 7.51**, you may want to decrease the size of the brush when working toward the outer edges.

■ Select the **Pucker** tool. Set the Brush Size to **90**.

■ Apply the **Pucker** tool to the nose, reducing its size. When you have shrunk the nose quite a bit, move to the mouth and reduce it, as shown in **Figure 7.52**.

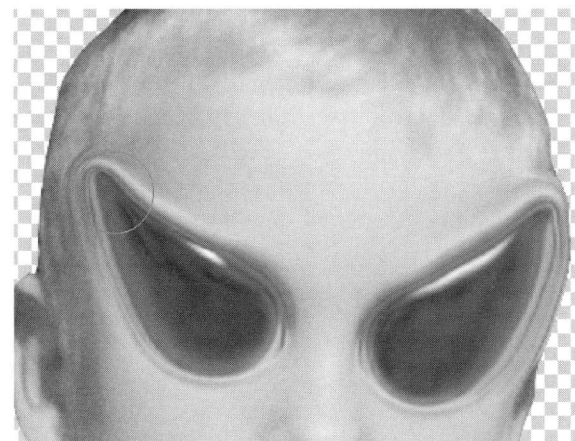

7.51

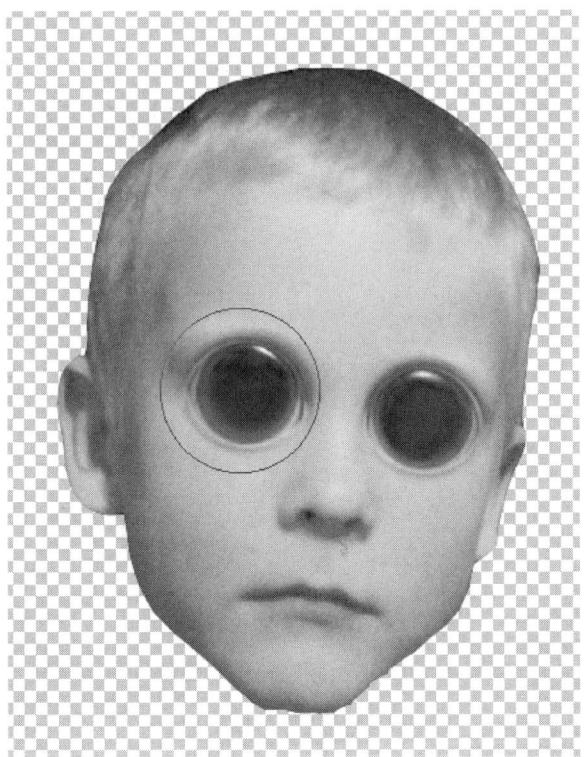

7.50

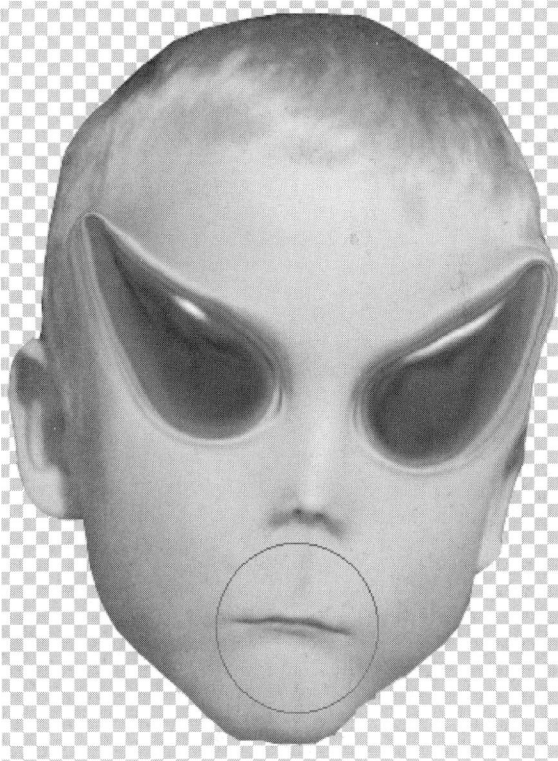

7.52

STEP 4: CHANGE FACIAL STRUCTURE

■ Select the **Warp** tool. Set the Brush Size to **42**.

■ Starting below the hairline, move the skin of the forehead up in short, even movements (see **Figure 7.53**). Continue to do this across the expanse of the forehead until the hairline is nearly invisible, and the tone/shape of the forehead is even (see **Figure 7.54**).

■ Run the **Warp** tool along the edges of the face. Push the ears in and methodically mold them so that they are even with the side of the face.

■ Continue narrowing the cheeks and chin (see **Figure 7.55**) by using the **Warp** tool until the head takes on a distinct alien shape. You also want to fix any distortions in the shape of the top of the head.

■ After the head has your approval, click **OK**.

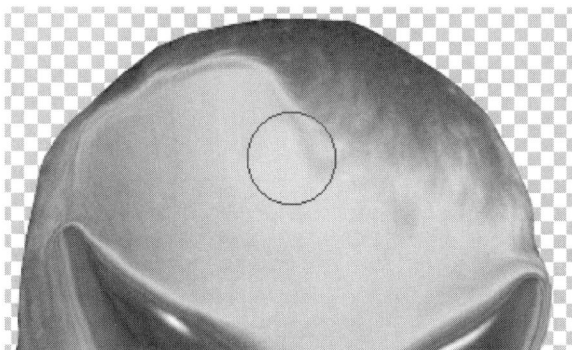

7.53

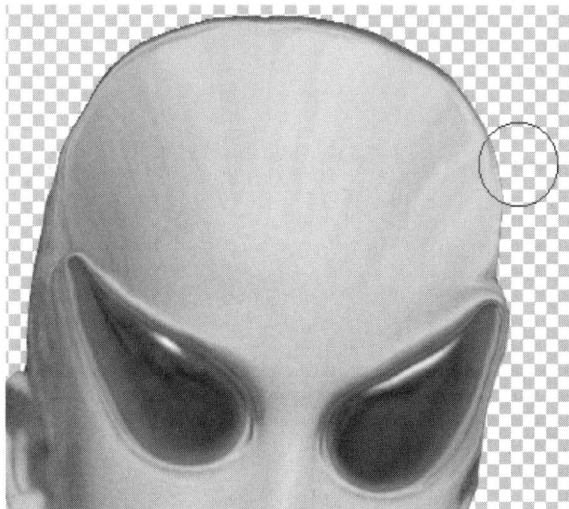

7.54

7.55

- Choose **Image** ➢ **Transform** ➢ **Distort**. In the Options bar, enter the following settings:
  - Width = **125%**
  - Height = **110%**
  - Angle = **−10**
- Select the **Clone Stamp** tool.
- ⌘/**Ctrl**+click the face layer to bring up a selection of the head.
- Create a new layer.
- On the face layer, take a sample with the **Clone Stamp** tool (**Alt**+click) on an undistorted portion of the face, such as the area just above and between the eyes.
- In the new layer, stamp the pattern over the streaked areas. See **Figure 7.56**.

- Choose **Filter** ➢ **Blur** ➢ **Gaussian Blur**. Enter a blur radius of **18** pixels.
- Click **OK**.
- Press ⌘/**Ctrl**+**E** to merge the blurred layer with the face. See **Figure 7.57**.

STEP 5: FINISHING TOUCHES

- Select the **Burn** tool. In the Options bar, set the following attributes:
  - Brush Type = **Round, Feathered**
  - Size = **85 pixels**
  - Range = **Shadows**
  - Exposure = **40**

7.56

7.57

- Run the **Burn** tool over the eyes to darken them, as shown in **Figure 7.58**.
- Run the **Burn** tool around the perimeter of the eyes also, including the area where the eyebrows should be.
- Select the **Dodge** tool. In the Options bar, set the following attributes:
  - Brush Type = **Round, Feathered**
  - Size = **36 pixels**
  - Range = **Shadows**
  - Exposure = **31**
- Create a few reflections on the dome of the head with the **Dodge** tool, as shown in **Figure 7.59**.
- Choose **Filter** ➤ **Render** ➤ **Lighting Effects**.

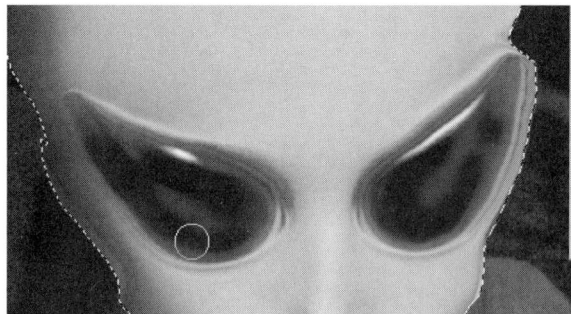

7.58

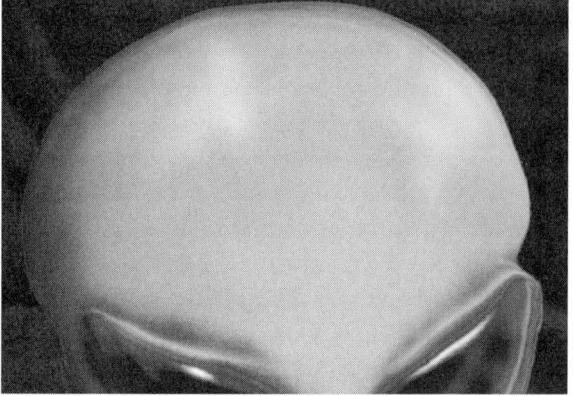

7.59

- In the Lighting Effects dialog box, set the following attributes:
  - Style = **Default**
  - Light Type = **Spotlight**
  - Intensity = **35**
  - Focus = **69**
  - Gloss = **10**
  - Material = **97 Metallic**
  - Exposure = **0**
  - Ambiance = **0**
- Set the light position so that it shines from the upper-right of the image, as shown in **Figure 7.60**.
- Click **OK**.
- Select the background layer.
- Press ⌘/**Ctrl+F** to reapply the **Lighting Effect** filter to the background layer. Repeat this step to increase the darkness of the background layer.
- Select the alien face layer.
- Choose **Enhance** ➤ **Adjust Color** ➤ **Hue/Saturation**. Enter the following settings in the Hue/Saturation dialog box:
  - Hue = **+5**
  - Saturation = **−50**
  - Lightness = **0**

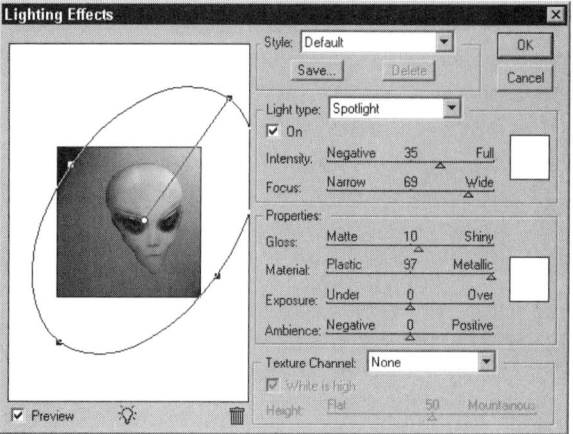

7.60

■ Click **OK**.

■ Select the **Smudge** tool and run it around the outer edges of the face where some distortions are still visible. **Figure 7.61 (CP22)** shows the finished Alien Boy image.

These tutorials show how easy it can be to generate totally new critters from the people and pets you know and love. Try the effects on your old photographs, and you'll have a wealth of material for your homemade greeting cards.

7.61 (CP22)

CHAPTER 8

INTERFACING WITH THE WEB

A designer wants the viewer to recognize the combination of graphics and information on the site as Frank's page or the small business site for Nuts 'n' Bolts Unlimited.

However, Photoshop Elements 2 does offer the image creation aspect of Web design; for those who develop sites around theme-driven graphics, Elements has you covered. Some creative methods for dicing images for placement online may be in order, but Elements covers the graphics end just fine.

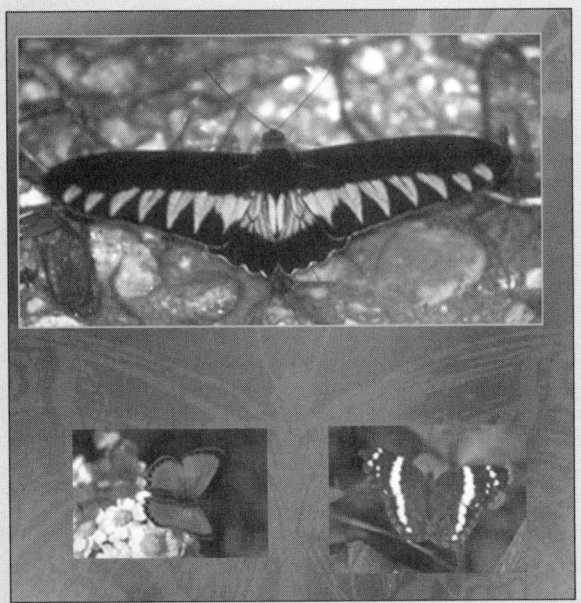

LINK 1

LINK 2

LINK 3

LINK 4

L

Green, Black and Evil

Known for its devious ferocity, the Green Backed Razor Wing
lures its prey by flitting gleefully across open meadows.
When an unsuspecting collector approaches, this meek
appearing villain of the insect world lashes out, striking
its startled prey with barbs and insults that would make a
sailor blush. Recommended treatments are extended therap
sessions and new hobbies, most frequently bowling.

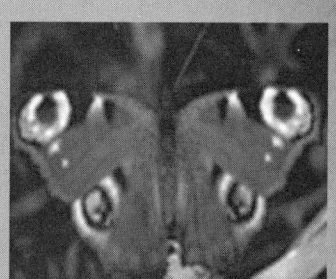

A NATURAL INTERFACE

BUTTERFLY CROSSING

LINK 1
LINK 2
LINK 3
LINK 4
LINK 5

Green, Black and Evil

Known for its devious ferocity, the Green Backed Razor Wing lures its prey by flitting gleefully across open meadows. When an unsuspecting collector approaches, this meek appearing villain of the insect world lashes out, striking its startled prey with barbs and insults that would make a sailor blush. Recommended treatments are extended therapy sessions and new hobbies, most frequently bowling.

This tutorial requires the following from the CD-ROM:

- Butterfly-1.jpg.jpg
- ButterF-2.abr

The key to themed Web sites is to maintain a certain feeling throughout the pages. The background, links, color of the text, headers, and so forth should all reflect the character of the site. In this tutorial the theme is nature, and specifically butterflies. Before you begin designing the page, all of the images you plan to use as thematic elements should be grouped together in one folder, ready to go at a moment's notice.

STEP 1: PREPARE THE BACKGROUND

■ Open the image **Butterfly-1.jpg**, found on the CD-ROM. See **Figure 8.1**.

■ Choose **Image** ➢ **Resize** ➢ **Image Size**. In the Image Size dialog box, set the following dimensions:
  ■ Constrained Proportions = **Unchecked**
  ■ Width = **1000 pixels**
  ■ Height = **600 pixels**
  ■ Resolution = **72 dpi**

■ Click **OK**.

■ Choose **Filter** ➢ **Blur** ➢ **Gaussian Blur**. Enter a blur radius of **30** pixels.

■ Click **OK**.

■ In the Layers palette, click the **Add a Layer** icon to create a new layer.

STEP 2: LINES AND GUIDES

■ If the rulers are not visible along the top and down the left-hand side of the screen, choose **View** ➢ **Rulers** (⌘/Ctrl+R).

■ In the Toolbox, click the **Rectangular Marquee** tool. In the Options bar, set the following attributes:
  ■ Selection Type = **Add To Selection**
  ■ Feather = **0**
  ■ Style = **Fixed Size**

  ■ Width = **1000 pixels** (the width of the image)
  ■ Height = **1 pixel**

■ In the upper-left corner of the image, place the mouse one half-inch down the left side ruler and click. Doing this creates a selection one-pixel high and 1000-pixels wide across the image.

■ Move the mouse down to the ⅝ inch mark. Click again, making another line selection. See **Figure 8.2**.

■ Change the settings for the Rectangular Marquee in the Options bar:
  ■ Selection Type = **Add To Selection**
  ■ Feather = **0**
  ■ Style = **Fixed Size**
  ■ Width = **1 pixel**
  ■ Height = **600 pixels**

■ Click a couple more times in the upper-left corner, this time creating vertical selections in addition to the horizontal ones already active. See **Figure 8.3**.

■ Click the foreground color to open the Color Picker. Enter a color value of **#FCA102**, or R = **252**, G = **161**, and B = **2**.

■ Click **OK**.

■ Choose **Edit** ➢ **Fill**. In the Fill dialog box, select **Foreground Color** at **100%** opacity as the fill color.

8.1

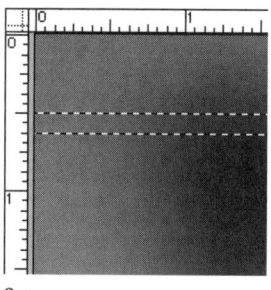

8.2

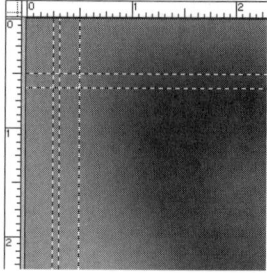

8.3

- Click **OK**.
- Choose **Select** ➤ **Deselect**. See **Figure 8.4**.

8.5

STEP 3: ADD IMAGES IN DESIGN

- Open the image **Butterfly-2.jpg**, found on the CD-ROM.
- Choose **Enhance** ➤ **Auto Contrast**.
- Select the **Magnetic Lasso** in the Toolbox. Set the following attributes in the Options bar:
  - Selection Type = **New Selection**
  - Feather = **0**
  - Anti-aliased = **Checked**
  - Width = **5 pixels**
  - Edge Contrast = **100%**
  - Frequency = **25**
  - Pen Pressure = **Unchecked**
- Draw a selection around the butterfly, as shown in **Figure 8.5**.
- You'll note that a few portions of the butterfly were not selected. Click the **Polygonal Lasso** tool and, in Add to Selection mode, select the remaining areas of the butterfly you would like added to the selection (antennae, and so on.). See **Figure 8.6**.

8.6

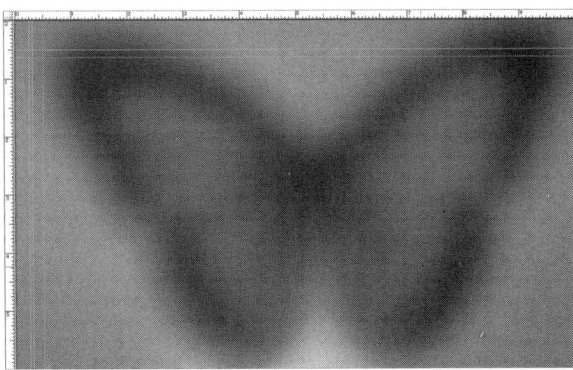

8.4

- Choose **Layer** ➢ **New** ➢ **Layer via Copy**.
- Drag the new butterfly layer into the original image. See **Figure 8.7**.
- The premise for adding the butterfly photo is to make it seem the insect has landed on the Web page. In order to get that illusion, some modifications must be made. Choose **Image** ➢ **Transform** ➢ **Distort**. In the Options bar, enter the following settings:
    - Width = **30%**
    - Height = **30%**
    - Angle = **–15**
- Click the **Accept Change** icon found on the Options bar.
- Select the **Move** tool (**V**). Move the butterfly so that it rests above the intersection of the lines in the upper-left corner. See **Figure 8.8**.
- Click the **Layer Styles** palette tab. Load the default Drop Shadows set and click the layer style called **Low**.
- Select **Layer** ➢ **Layer Styles** ➢ **Style Settings**. In the Style Settings dialog box, set the following:
    - Use Global Light = **Unchecked**
    - Angle = **80 degrees**
    - Shadow Distance = **15 pixels**
- Click **OK**.

STEP 4: BANNER PLACEMENT

This step shows a quick way to add a title to your Elements Web page image.

- Select the layer with the lines.
- Select the **Magic Wand** tool.
- Click the long rectangular empty space at the top on the image to create a selection, as shown in **Figure 8.9**.
- Click the **Add a Layer** icon and create a new layer. Move the new layer beneath the butterfly layer.
- Choose **Edit** ➢ **Fill**. Enter the following in the Fill dialog box:
    - Contents: Use = **Black**
    - Mode = **Normal**
    - Opacity = **50%**
- Click **OK**.
- Select the **Type** tool in the Toolbox. Enter the following settings for the Type tool in the Options bar:
    - Type Tool = **Horizontal Type**
    - Font = **Font of Choice**
    - Size = **30 points** (can resize after typing if needed)
    - Anti-aliased = **selected**
    - Justify = **Left Justify**
    - Color = **Foreground** (should be orange; refer to Step 2)

8.7

8.8

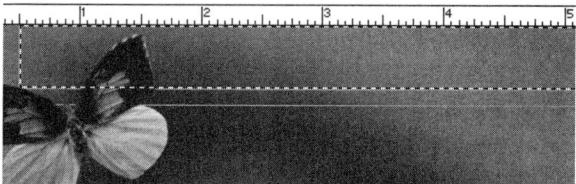

8.9

■ Type your header text or page title in the black area at the top of the page. Resize the font as needed. When done, select the **Move** tool and position the type. See **Figure 8.10**.

STEP 5: ADD LINK HOT SPOTS

■ Create a new layer. Name the layer **Links**.

■ Select the **Type** tool. In the Options bar set the following attributes:

    ■ Type Tool = **Horizontal**

    ■ Font Style = **Regular**

    ■ Font = This is up to you, although generally system fonts appear best on-screen. For this tutorial a font called Astro 867 is used.

    ■ Size = Again, this is up to you, but 8 to 10 points is a fair size setting. For this tutorial 8 points is used.

    ■ Anti-aliased = **selected**

    ■ Left Justify

■ Placement of the links for your personal page is entirely up to you. In this tutorial, I look at two options. The first option is the standard across-the-top link format. Take a look at **Figure 8.11**. When creating the initial graphics and layout, several lines were created both vertically and horizontally. These were not merely for aesthetics, but can serve a practical use as guides for the links. Start by clicking between the lines, next to the butterfly. Type your link names; I've used Link 1, Link 2, and so forth.

> **NOTE**
>
> Examples of system fonts would be Verdana, Arial, and so forth. These font families have an excellent shelf life, and for producing links and text they are hard to beat. Better still, they are already installed on your computer.

■ In Elements, you have an option that perhaps you hadn't considered. You can convert your links to a vertical typing format. Click the **Change the Text Orientation** icon to the right of the Options bar to change the text orientation from horizontal to vertical, or vice versa. See **Figure 8.12**.

8.10

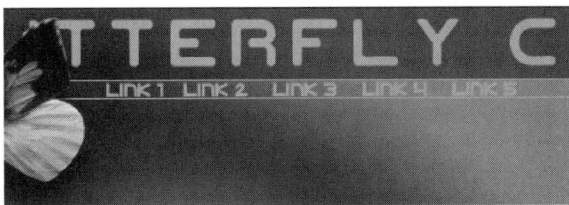

8.11

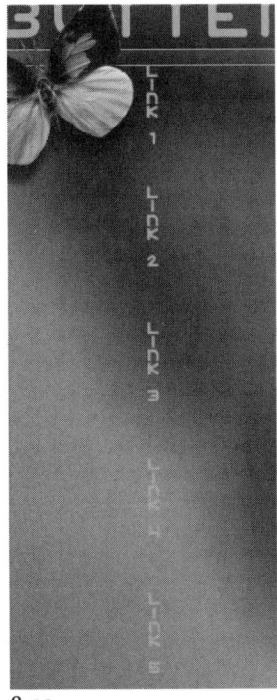

8.12

■ Select the **Move** tool.

■ Move the text next to the vertical lines created earlier on the left side of the image.

■ Sometimes the text color used initially doesn't quite fit the theme, is hard to read against the background, or simply doesn't appeal to you. Select the type layer and, with the mouse, highlight the type.

■ In the Options bar, click the color selector.

■ In the Color Picker, enter a color value of **#110285**, or R = **17**, G = **2**, and B = **133**.

■ Click **OK**.

■ The type is now a dark-blue color. This color may be difficult to see against the blue background. ⌘/**Ctrl**+click the type layer to create a selection around the text.

■ Create a new layer.

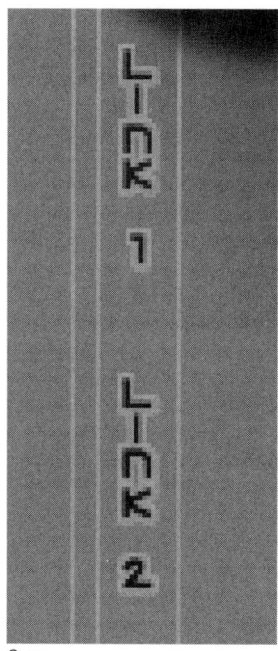

8.13

■ Choose **Edit** ➢ **Stroke**. Enter the following attributes in the Stroke dialog box:
  ■ Width = **1 pixel**
  ■ Color = **Foreground (orange)**
  ■ Location = **outside**
  ■ Mode = **normal**
  ■ Opacity = **100%**
■ Click **OK**.

■ The stroke may still be a bit dark. Choose **Enhance** ➢ **Adjust Brightness/Contrast** ➢ **Brightness/Contrast**. Enter the following in the Brightness/Contrast dialog box:
  ■ Brightness = **+25**
  ■ Contrast = **+100%**
■ Click **OK**.

■ Select the Links layer. Right-click the Links layer in the Layers palette and select **Simplify Layer** from the menu that appears.

■ Select the stroke layer, which is just above the Links layer.

■ Press ⌘/**Ctrl+E** to merge the stroke layer with the Links layer.

■ Right-click the Links layer in the Layers palette again. This time, rename the layer **Links-State 1**.

■ Duplicate the Links-State 1 layer. Rename the duplicate **Links-State 2**.

■ The purpose for having two identical links layers is for rollover transitions. In Web site design, two nearly identical images used in conjunction with a JavaScript create a rollover transition. Choose **Enhance** ➢ **Adjust Color** ➢ **Hue/Saturation** (⌘/**Ctrl+U**). Enter the following settings in the Hue/Saturation dialog box:
  ■ Hue = **–25**
  ■ Saturation = **0**
  ■ Lightness = **0**
■ Click **OK**. See **Figure 8.13**.

STEP 6: CREATE TEXT AND IMAGE VIEWING AREAS

- Press the **U** key to activate the **Shape** tools. In the Options bar, select the **Rounded Rectangle** tool and enter the following settings:
  - Radius = **10 pixels**
  - Click the **Create a New Shape Layer** icon.
  - Color = Foreground (orange)
- Draw the shape over the main body of the image, as shown in **Figure 8.14**.
- Right-click the shape layer and select **Simplify Layer** from the menu that appears.
- In the Layers palette, set the blending mode for the shape layer to **Soft Light**. See **Figure 8.15**.

STEP 7: ARTISTIC TOUCHES

- Select the **Paintbrush** tool in the Toolbox.
- In this last step, I've created brushes to follow the theme of this particular Web site. In the Options bar,

load the brush set **ButterF-2.abr** into the Brushes palette. This brush set is included on the CD-ROM.
- Open the **Brushes** menu and select brush **bf1**. Enter the following settings for the brush in the Options bar:
  - Brush Size = **200 pixels**
  - Mode = **Normal**
  - Opacity = **30%**
- Create a new layer above the simplified shape layer.
- In the Options bar, select **More Options**.
- In the Brush Options dialog box, change the Spacing to **25%**, and the Angle to **–66** degrees. See **Figure 8.16**.

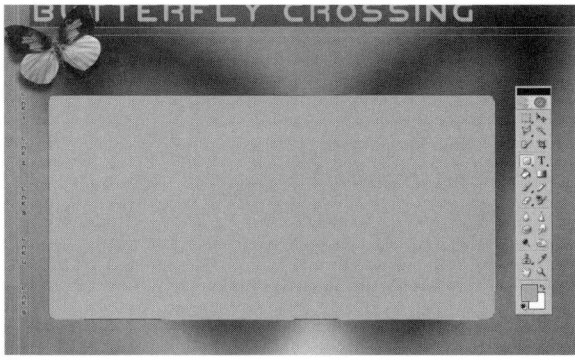

8.14

8.15

8.16

8.17

■ Using the brush in a stationary spray, add a butterfly to the layer. In this example, a corner of the shape was selected for position, as shown in **Figure 8.17**.

To demonstrate what this image may look like as a completed Web page, **Figure 8.18** (**CP23**) has been mocked up with additional images and text.

BUTTERFLY CROSSING

LINK 1
LINK 2
LINK 3
LINK 4
LINK 5

Green, Black and Evil

Known for its devious ferocity, the Green Backed Razor Wing lures its prey by flitting gleefully across open meadows. When an unsuspecting collector approaches, this meek appearing villain of the insect world lashes out, striking its startled prey with barbs and insults that would make a sailor blush. Recommended treatments are extended therapy sessions and new hobbies, most frequently bowling.

8.18 (CP23)

A TECHNICAL INTERFACE

The previous tutorial covered a standard Web layout using images and text links. Another form of interfacing is the use of images that look like machines of some sort, either realistic or out of the imagination of the designer. Some contain elements of both the fantastic and the realistic.

This tutorial could best be inserted into the latter category. You see a few previously covered items come into play and find out about some new techniques. The effects covered here are useful in interface design, but what I want you to focus on is the process involved in combining effects into a stylish, out-of-this-world navigation design. As a bonus, this tutorial also covers the creation of the popular blue gel buttons.

This tutorial requires the following from the CD-ROM:

- Tubes-Metals.grd
- Skull.psd
- AFX-grids.pat

STEP 1: PREPARE THE IMAGE

- Create a new image with the following dimensions/attributes:
    - Preset Size = **800 x 600 pixels**
    - Resolution = **72 dpi**
    - Background Color = **White**
- Click **OK**.

■ Select the **Shape** tool. In the Options bar, select the **Polygon** tool and enter the following attributes:
  ■ Sides = **3**
  ■ Create New Shape Layer = **Selected**
  ■ Color = **Black**
■ Draw a large triangle. A new layer is created to hold the shape. While drawing the shape, rotate it with the mouse to make the top edge horizontal, with one corner pointing straight down, as in **Figure 8.19**. Holding down the **Shift** key also helps keep it stationary.

8.19

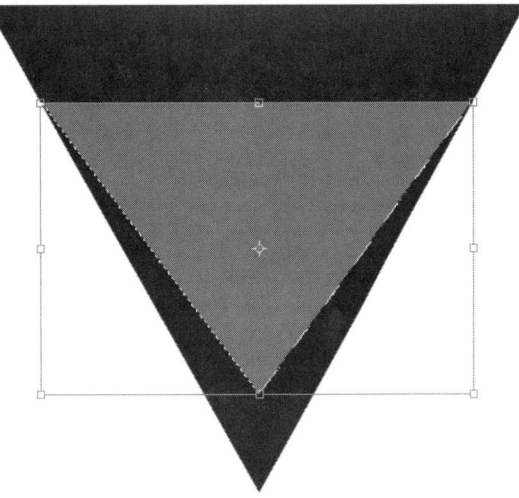

8.20

STEP 2: MAKE AN INTERFACE SHAPE

■ Right-click the shape layer in the Layers palette. Select **Simplify Layer** from the menu that appears.
■ Duplicate the triangle layer.
■ ⌘/**Ctrl**+click the duplicate triangle layer to generate a selection.
■ Choose **Edit** ➢ **Fill**. In the Fill dialog box, set the following attributes:
  ■ Contents: Use = **50% gray**
  ■ Mode = **Normal**
  ■ Opacity = **90%**
■ Click **OK**.
■ Choose **Image** ➢ **Transform** ➢ **Distort**. In the Options bar, enter the following settings:
  ■ Width = **80%**
  ■ Height = **60%**
  ■ Angle = **0**

See **Figure 8.20**. Note that the duplicate triangle has shrunk vertically as a result of the transform applied.

■ Warp the triangle more by moving the corner points around. Keep the points within the boundaries set by the larger triangle, as shown in **Figure 8.21**.

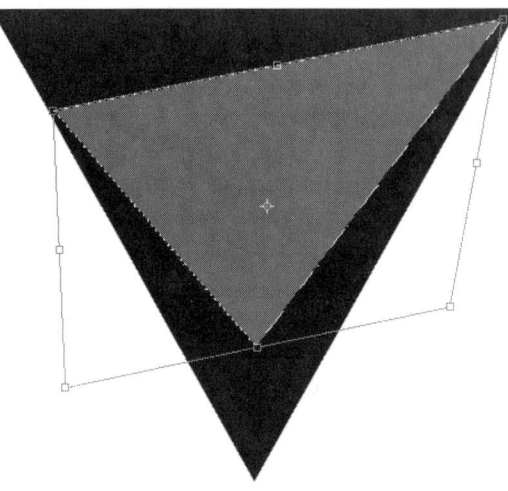

8.21

- When you are happy with the shape of the warped triangle, press **Return/Enter**.

STEP 3: BEVEL AND STYLE THE INTERFACE

- Select the larger triangle layer.
- Duplicate the layer. Make sure that the duplicate layer is active.
- ⌘/**Ctrl**+click the layer to select the triangle.
- Choose **Filter** ➢ **Blur** ➢ **Gaussian Blur**. Enter a blur radius of **15** pixels.
- Click **OK**.
- Open the **Layer Styles** palette. Load the **Glass Buttons** style set.
- Select the **Orange Glass** style to apply it to the blurred triangle.
- ⌘/**Ctrl**+click the distorted triangle layer, but keep the blurred triangle layer selected.
- Click the **Delete** key.
- ⌘/**Ctrl**+D to deselect.

See **Figure 8.22**. The layer style is now applied to the primary triangle shape you created first.

- Choose **Filter** ➢ **Blur** ➢ **Gaussian Blur**. Enter a blur radius of **4** pixels.
- Click **OK**.
- Select the **Rectangular Marquee** tool. Set the options in the Options bar as follows:
  - Selection Type = **New Selection**
  - Feather = **0**
  - Mode = **Normal**
- Make a narrow horizontal selection on one side of the styles layer, as shown in **Figure 8.23**, and press **Delete**.
- Move the selection around the sides of the styled triangle and add a few more deleted sections. See **Figure 8.24**.

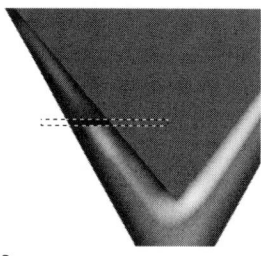

8.23

8.22

8.24

STEP 4: MANIPULATE THE VIEW SCREEN

- Select the warped triangle layer.
- Set the foreground color to light gray and the background to dark gray.
- ⌘/**Ctrl**+click the warped triangle layer.
- Create a new layer above the warped triangle layer.
- Select the **Gradient** tool.
- In the Options bar, load the **Tubes-Metals** gradient set, found on the CD-ROM. Click in the gradient viewer to open the Gradient Editor and change the colors of the gradient stops to the foreground and background colors. For example, the lighter stops change to the foreground color, and the darker stops change to the background color.

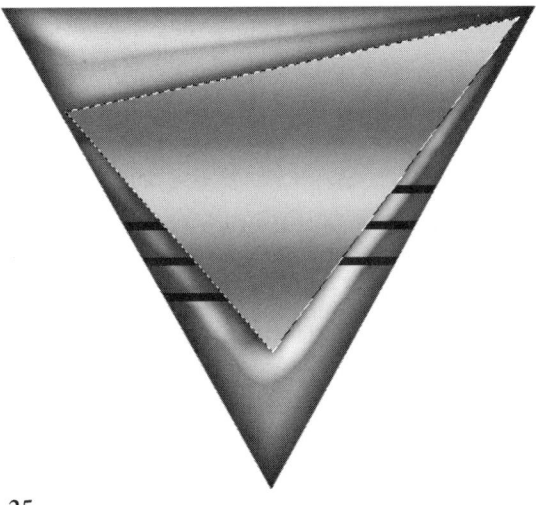

8.25

- Click **OK**.
- Set the following attributes for the gradient in the Options bar:
    - Gradient Type = **Linear Gradient**
    - Mode = **Normal**
    - Opacity = **100%**
- Fill the selection from top to bottom with the gradient. See **Figure 8.25**.
- Choose **Edit** ➢ **Fill**. Enter the following attributes in the Fill dialog box:
    - Contents: Use = **Pattern**
    - Load the **AFX-Grids** pattern set. Select **afx-grid10** as the fill pattern.
    - Blending Mode = **Overlay**
    - Opacity = **60%**
- Click **OK**.
- Create a new layer.
- Press the **D** key to reset the foreground and background colors to black and white, respectively.
- Choose **Edit** ➢ **Stroke**. Enter the following in the Stroke dialog box:
    - Width = **16 pixels**
    - Color = **Black**
    - Location = **inside**
    - Mode = **Normal**
    - Opacity = **100%**
- Click **OK**.
- Choose **Filter** ➢ **Blur** ➢ **Gaussian Blur**. Enter a blur radius of **17** pixels.
- Click **OK**.

STEP 5: ADD A PICTURE

- Open the image **Skull.psd**, found on the CD-ROM.
- The skull image is in layers. Drag the layer containing the skull onto the interface image. See **Figure 8.26**.
- Choose **Edit ➤ Transform ➤ Distort**. Enter the following settings in the Options bar:
  - Width = **100 %**
  - Height = **60%**
- Move the upper-right point in such a way as to distort the upper-right portion of the image. See **Figure 8.27**.
- Press **Return/Enter** to apply the Transform settings to the layer.
- ⌘/**Ctrl**+click the original distorted triangle layer to generate a selection.
- Choose **Select ➤ Inverse**.
- Make sure the skull layer is selected and press the **Delete** key.
- Deselect. See **Figure 8.28**.

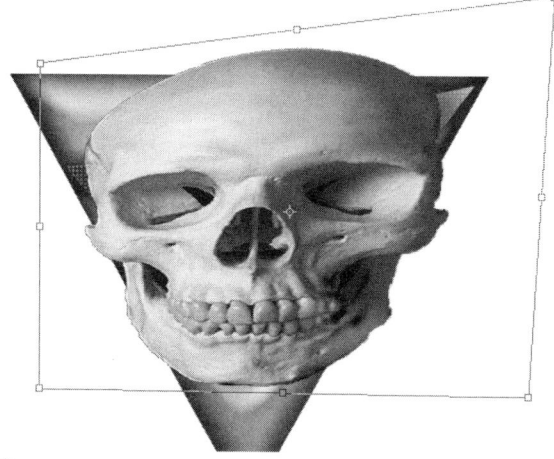

8.27

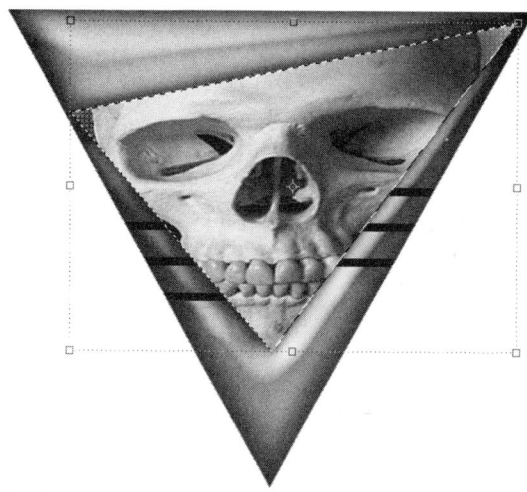

8.28

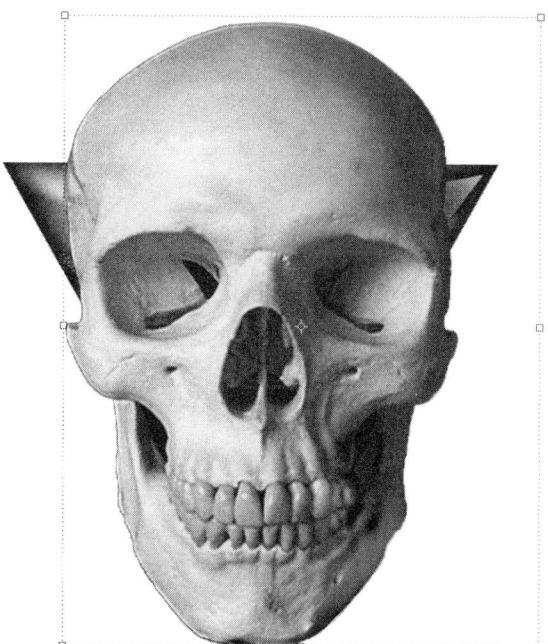

8.26

■ Set the skull layer blending mode to **Overlay**.

■ Using the ⌘/**Ctrl+I** keys, invert the colors of the skull layer.

■ Choose **Enhance** ➤ **Adjust Color** ➤ **Hue/Saturation** (⌘/**Ctrl+U**). Enter the following settings in the Hue/Saturation dialog box.

  ■ Hue = **200**
  ■ Saturation = **100**
  ■ Lightness = **0**

■ Click **OK**. See **Figure 8.29**. The skull takes on a hue that fits the theme of a monitor.

STEP 6: MAKE INTERFACE DIALS

■ Create a new layer.

■ Select the **Elliptical Marquee** tool. Set the following options on the Options bar:

  ■ Feather = **0**
  ■ Anti-aliased = **selected**
  ■ Mode = Fixed Aspect Ratio

■ Increase the zoom on the image to **200%**.

8.29

■ Create a circular selection (see **Figure 8.30**) along the top of the interface so that the dial appears to be affixed to the beveled section.

■ Press the **D** key.

■ Choose **Edit** ➤ **Stroke**. Enter the following attributes in the Stroke dialog box:

  ■ Width = **3 pixels**
  ■ Color = **Black**
  ■ Location = **Center**
  ■ Mode = **Normal**
  ■ Opacity = **100%**

■ Click **OK**.

■ Select a light gray foreground and dark gray background color again.

■ Select the **Gradient** tool.

■ Using the same gradient and settings as the view screen in Step 4, fill the selection. Start in the upper-left of the selection and draw the gradient down to the lower right. See **Figure 8.31**.

■ Choose **Select** ➤ **Modify** ➤ **Contract**. Contract the selection by 2 pixels.

■ Click **OK**.

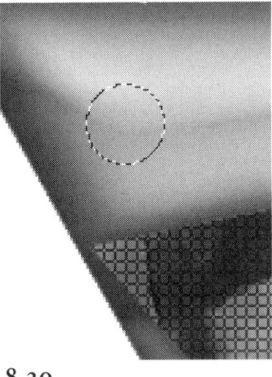
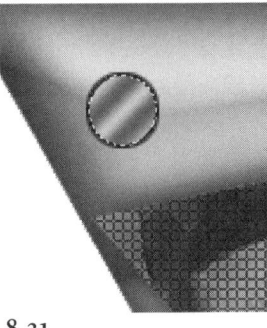

8.31

8.30

- Set the foreground color to white.
- Click the **Gradient** tool.
- Use the same gradient as before, but change the gradient style to **Angle Gradient**.
- Starting at the center of the selection, draw the gradient to the edge of the selection. See **Figure 8.32**.
- Swap the foreground and background colors.
- Choose **Edit** ➢ **Stroke**. Enter the following settings in the Stroke dialog box:
  - Width = **1 pixel**
  - Color = **Foreground**
  - Location = **Inside**
  - Mode = **Normal**
  - Opacity = **100%**
- Click **OK**.
- Select the **Layer Styles** palette. Load the **Drop Shadows** style set.
- Select the **Low** layer style to apply it to the layer.
- Decrease the zoom to **100%**.
- Deselect. This adds a bit of depth to the dial, to give the face a recessed appearance. See **Figure 8.33**.
- Select the **Move** tool.
- Hold down the **Alt** key. Click the dial and drag it to a new position. Doing this creates a duplicate dial layer, leaving the original in place. Repeat this process until you have several dials placed around the interface, as shown in **Figure 8.34**.
- Starting at the top dial layer, merge down until all the dials are on one layer.

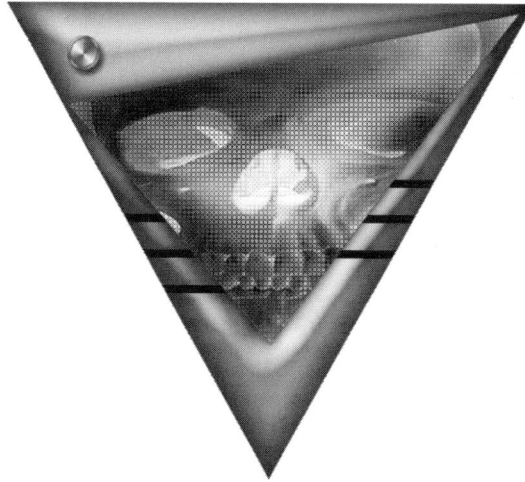

8.33

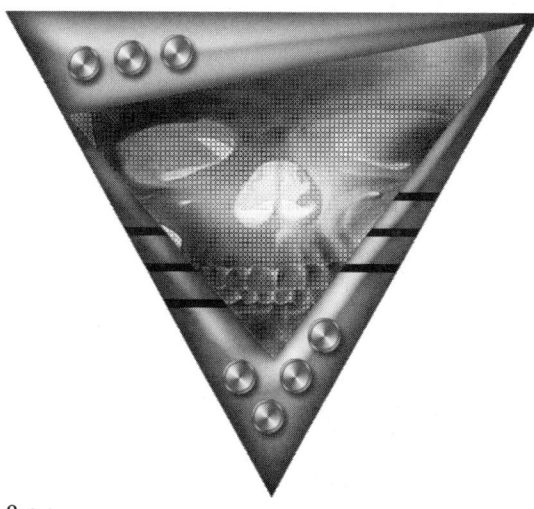

8.34

8.32

STEP 7: NEW USE FOR BLUE GEL BUTTONS

- Select the background layer.
- Select the **Shape** tool. In the Options bar, select the **Rounded Rectangle** tool, with the following attributes:
    - Radius = **25 pixels**
    - Create a new shape layer = **Selected**
    - Color = **Foreground**
- Draw a pill button shape. Place it to the left or right of the interface so that it can be clearly seen. Do not make it too large; gauge this by the roundness of the left and right sides. They should be perfectly round without any vertical space. See **Figure 8.35**.

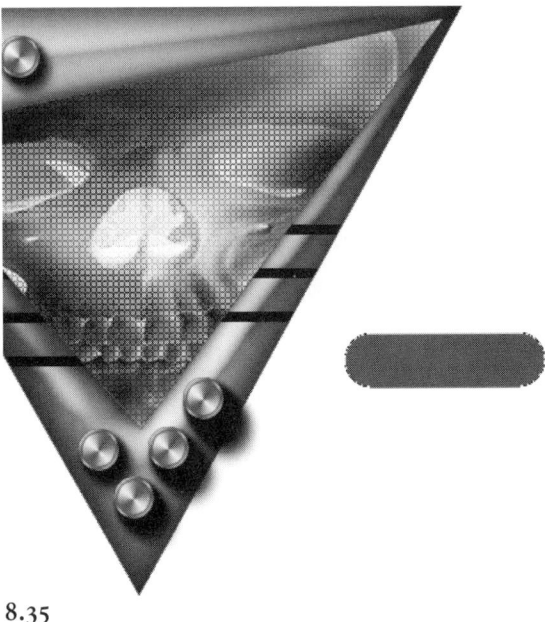

8.35

- Right-click the shape layer. Select **Simplify Layer** from the pop-up menu.
- ⌘/**Ctrl**+click the pill button layer to select it.
- Press the **Delete** key. Keep the selection active.
- Change the foreground color to **#99FOFD**, or R = **153**, G = **240**, and B = **253**.
- Change the background color to **#1C23AE**, or R = **28**, G = **35**, and B = **174**.
- Choose **Edit ➤ Fill**. Enter the following attributes in the Fill dialog box:
    - Contents: Use = **Foreground color**
    - Mode = **Normal**
    - Opacity = **85%**
- Click **OK**.
- Swap the foreground and background colors.
- Create a new layer above the pill button layer.
- Choose **Edit ➤ Stroke**. Enter the following in the Stroke dialog box:
    - Width = **8 pixels**
    - Color = **Foreground**
    - Location = **Inside**
    - Mode = **Normal**
    - Opacity = **100%**
- Click **OK**.
- Choose **Filter ➤ Blur ➤ Gaussian Blur**. Enter a blur radius of **4** pixels.
- Click **OK**.
- Create a new layer above the stroke layer.
- Press the **D** key to reset the foreground/background colors.
- Press the **X** key to swap the foreground/background colors.
- Select the **Gradient** tool. In the Options bar, select the **Foreground to Transparent** gradient.
    - Gradient Style = **Linear Gradient**
    - Mode = **Normal**
    - Opacity = **100%**

■ Starting at the top of the selection, draw the gradient straight down through two-thirds of the selection. See **Figure 8.36**.

■ Choose **Image ➤ Transform ➤ Perspective**.

■ Move the lower transform points closer together. See **Figure 8.37**.

■ Press **Return/Enter** to accept the transform. See **Figure 8.38**.

■ Merge the three layers composing the button effects together.

■ Change the layer name to **BlueButton**.

■ Duplicate the BlueButton layer and move it beneath the BlueButton layer in the Layers palette.

■ Choose **Filter ➤ Blur ➤ Gaussian Blur**. Enter a blur radius of **6** pixels.

■ Click **OK**.

■ Select the **Move** tool.

■ Move the blurred layer down and to the right a few pixels. Doing this gives the appearance of light shining through the button and casting a blue shadow. See **Figure 8.39**.

■ Merge the BlueButton and blurred layers together.

■ Place the button behind the interface, so that about half is visible.

■ As done previously with the dials, hold down the **Alt/Option** key. Click and drag the button, creating a duplicate BlueButton layer. Place this in a new position around the interface. Continue to do so until you have several buttons, as shown in **Figure 8.40**.

■ Select the original triangle-shaped layer.

■ Click the **Layers Styles Palette** tab. Load the **Drop Shadows** style set.

■ Click the **Low** layer style icon.

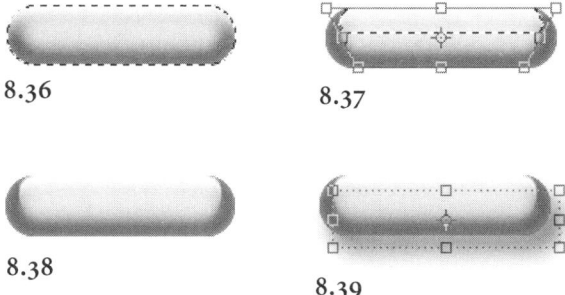

8.36　　　　　　8.37

8.38

8.39

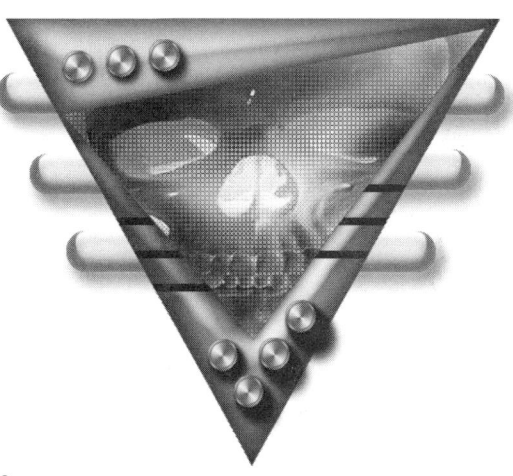

8.40

8.41 (CP24)

Figure 8.41 (CP24) shows what the completed interface may look like online.

Perhaps you have little or no use for interfaces of killer insects or skull-faced monitors. What I've tried to show you (and hope you picked up) are elements of Web design taken from a graphics approach. You will, of course, design your Web site to your particular specifications and tastes, but I hope you can take some of these techniques with you while you design. The secret to a Web page is just like any other graphic created in this book; start with a foundation and build on it. You may be surprised to see what you and Adobe Elements 2 are capable of.

CHAPTER 9

HOW CAN YOU SAY THAT? TYPE TREATMENTS

W here graphics are concerned, type treatments are my favorite pastime. Judging from the popularity of Web sites aimed at type manipulation and special effects, I'm not alone in my interest. My Web site is devoted to type effects, and I receive visitors from all over the globe.

Adobe Elements 2 is very versatile in creating effects for type. In truth, many if not most of the techniques covered in previous chapters can be altered to fit type treatments. Adobe Elements has type effects built right into the software in the form of Effects — a batch of effects just for text is included with the software. There are also the ever-popular layer styles referred to throughout this book. This chapter shows how to load, apply, and manipulate the settings for your specific project.

TYPE VERSUS TYPE MASK

T his tutorial isn't intended to set up a debate on which of these two tools has the most muscle. Rather, this chapter shows some differences between the two tools and where their specific strengths lie. Both are powerful, and each has attributes that distinguish it from the other.

TYPE TOOL

The primary difference between the Type tool and the Type Mask tool is that the Type tool is vector graphics based. Vector graphics are not founded on pixel information, but rather on mathematical formulas. Vector graphics can be resized, warped, and printed without any change in resolution or loss of information (see **Figure 9.1**).

9.1

Vector graphics are displayed as pixels, but that is simply for display, because the computer uses pixel information to show the image to you (see **Figure 9.2**).

Because the Type tool is vector based, the type functions much the same as it would in a word processing program. As such, many of the tools found in a word processing program are resident in Elements, and available for use with the Type tool. **Figure 9.3** shows the Options bar.

The Type options available are, from left to right, as follows:

- **Horizontal Type**
- **Vertical Type**
- **Horizontal Type Mask**
- **Vertical Type Mask**
- **Font Style:** Some font sets come with variations in thickness or shape, such as Bold and Italic. Verdana, Times New Roman, and other system fonts have these options. If a font set comes with

these variations, then they may be selected here. These are not to be confused with the Faux adjustments covered below.

- **Font:** Lists fonts that are installed on your computer and enables you to choose from those fonts.
- **Size:** Set or adjust the font size used. When you open the size menu (indicated by the small arrow to the right of the size window), a list of preset sizes is displayed from 6 pts to 72 pts. You may change to any size, however, by clicking in the size window, highlighting the setting, and typing a custom size. See **Figures 9.4** and **9.5**.
- **Anti-aliased:** This feature softens the jagged edges produced by displaying vector type in pixels. **Figure 9.6** shows type that has Anti-alias turned off; **Figure 9.7** shows the same type with Anti-alias turned on.
- **Faux Settings — Bold, Italic:** Some font families do not include bold or italic. Elements 2 allows you to apply these settings to those font families. Simply highlight the text in the image, and these settings become available. Please note that Warp cannot be applied to type with the Faux Bold setting applied.
- **Underline/Strikethrough:** Just like they sound, these allow you to underline your type or draw a line through the text as you would in a word processing program.
- **Justify:** Left, Center, or Right. Clicking a type layer selects the start point for these options. If Left Justify is selected, then the type starts at that point and moves to the right. To change justification, highlight the text with the mouse and click the proper Justify icon in the Options bar.

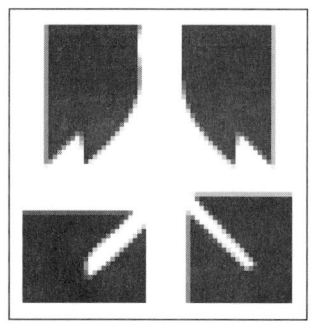

9.2

9.3

■ **Color:** Generally this is the foreground color by default. You may change the color by clicking the color window and selecting a new one in the Color Picker, or by changing the foreground color.

9.5

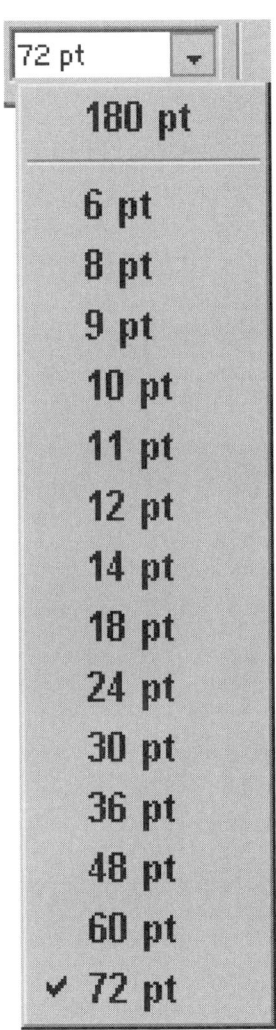

9.4

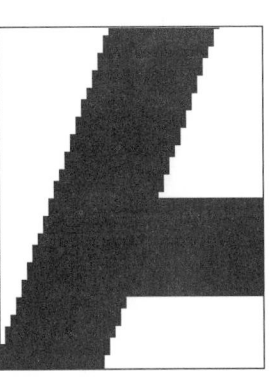

9.6

9.7

■ **Warp Text:** Allows you to warp text in a variety of ways, such as curves, waves, bloats, and so on. This tool is covered more in depth below.

■ **Change Text Orientation:** Change type from horizontal to vertical. See **Figures 9.8** and **9.9**.

9.8

9.9

WARP TEXT

This is an option exclusive to the Type tool; it is not available for the Type Mask tool. Applied to all characters in a type layer, this cool feature allows you to distort the text by using variable sliders.

First, apply warp to text.

■ Create a new image. This example uses the following settings:
  ■ Preset Size = **800x600**
  ■ Resolution = **72 dpi**
  ■ Mode = **RGB**
  ■ Background = **White**
■ Press **D** to reset the default foreground/ background colors. Doing this places black in the foreground and sets the color in the Options bar for the type.
■ Select the **Type** tool. Enter the following settings in the Options bar:
  ■ Font = **Times New Roman**
  ■ Size = **200 pts**
  ■ Anti-alias = **Selected**
  ■ Justify = **Center Text**
  ■ Color = **Black**. See **Figure 9.10**.
■ Click the **Create Warped Text** icon in the Options bar.
■ The Warp Text dialog box appears, with None selected in the Warp menu. Click the arrow to open the Distortion Style menu. See **Figure 9.11**.

9.10

- Select **ARC** from the menu. Note that you may bend the text, or warp the text in a horizontal or vertical perspective.
- In the Arc dialog box enter the following settings:
  - Bend = **30**
  - Horizontal Distortion = **0**
  - Vertical Distortion = **0**
- Click **OK**. See **Figure 9.12**.

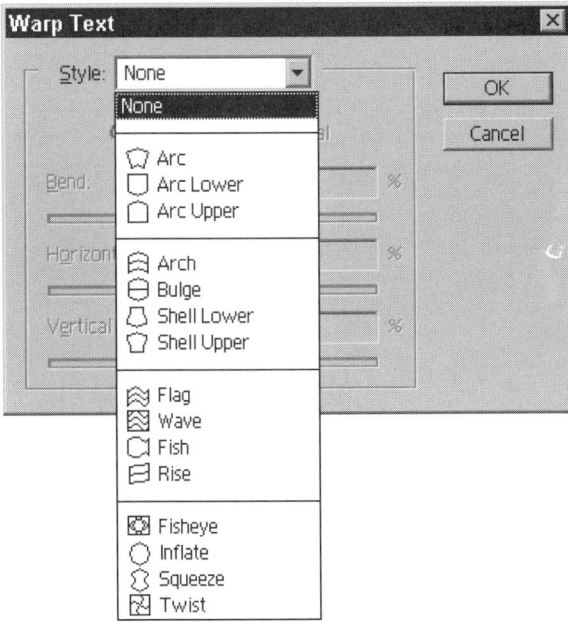

9.11

9.12

You can also change the warp distortion to another style, in this example, Flag.

- Click the **Create Warped Text** icon again.
- The Warp Text dialog box appears again, retaining the settings applied earlier.
- Set the Bend Distortion to **0** again.
- Open the Distortion Style menu.
- Select **Flag** as the distortion style.
- Set the Distortion setting as follows:
  - Horizontal = **Checked**
  - Bend = **+25**
  - Horizontal Distortion = **145**
  - Vertical Distortion = **0**
- Click **OK**. See **Figure 9.13**.

There are three Warp settings that give the appearance of applying type to a curved surface or across the face of a sphere. This step demonstrates the differences among the three.

- Click the **Create Warped Text** icon in the Options bar to bring up the Warp dialog box again.
- Select **Bulge** from the Distortion Style menu.
- Set the Bend to **+50**.
- Without closing the dialog box, move it off to the side so you can clearly see the type. The Bulge command inflates the type vertically, but there is

9.13

no curve to the sides. The Bulge command works well on, say, a cylinder. See **Figure 9.14**.

■ In the Warp dialog box, change the style to **Inflate**.

■ The type retains the +50 setting. Though it now appears curved, the left and right edges of the type are spread away from the center. This may appear to work on a sphere, but when a filled shape is placed behind the type, the distortion works best on a pill shape, as shown in **Figure 9.15**.

■ In the Warp dialog box, change the distortion style to **Fish Eye**.

■ This style combines attributes of both Inflate and Bulge, modulating the curves vertically and horizontally. **Figure 9.16** shows the type affixed to the face of a sphere. This is the best fit of the three tools.

TYPE TOOL AND LAYER STYLES

These steps require the following from the CD-ROM:

■ jul02-88-woods.asl (layer style set)

As stated before, the Type tool operates in vector format. As such, many effects, filters, and commands cannot be applied to type without first simplifying, or rasterizing (changing to raster/pixel format) the type layer first. As soon as this is done, no type settings can be changed.

However, Adobe Elements allows layer styles to be applied to vector graphics. More information on styles is covered later in this chapter, but here is a

9.14

9.15

9.16

quick demonstration of applying a layer style to a type layer.

- If not loaded previously, load the **jul02-88-woods.asl** layer style set, found on the CD-ROM. For instructions, see Appendix B, "Loading and Changing the CD Layer Styles."
- Select the type layer.
- Click the **Layer Styles** tab. Select **jul02-88-woods** from the Layer Styles menu. See **Figure 9.17**.
- Click a **Layer Style** icon. For this example Style 12 is used. The settings, pattern, and so forth

attached to the style are instantly applied to the text. See **Figure 9.18**.

- As long as the Type tool has not been rasterized (simplified), the text may be changed and warped with the layer style adapting to the altered settings. See **Figure 9.19**.

SIMPLIFY TYPE

Simplifying type converts the text from vector format to raster, or pixilated format. As soon as the type is simplified, you can no longer edit the type with the Type tool or the Warp command, but more functions become available for you to use on the type layer.

To simplify type:

- Right-click the type layer in the Layers palette and click **Simplify Layer** from the pop-up menu,

9.17

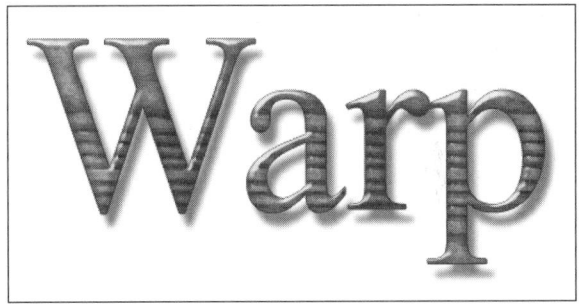

9.18

9.19

or select **Layer ➢ Simplify Layer**. **Figure 9.20** shows the type layer in the Layers palette prior to applying the Simplify command. **Figure 9.21** shows the type layer after Simplify has been applied.

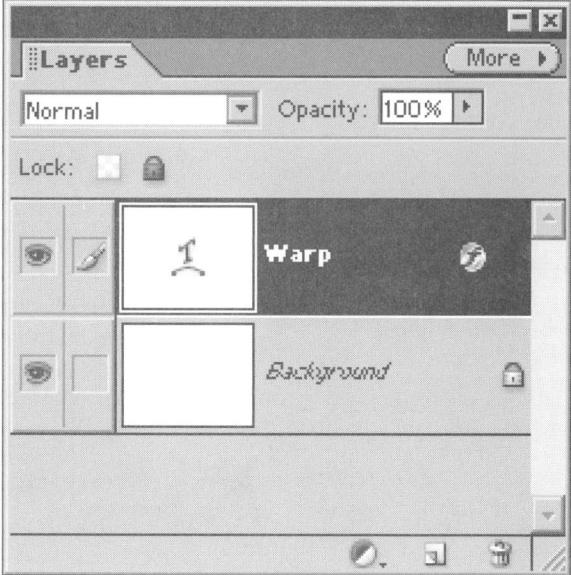

9.20

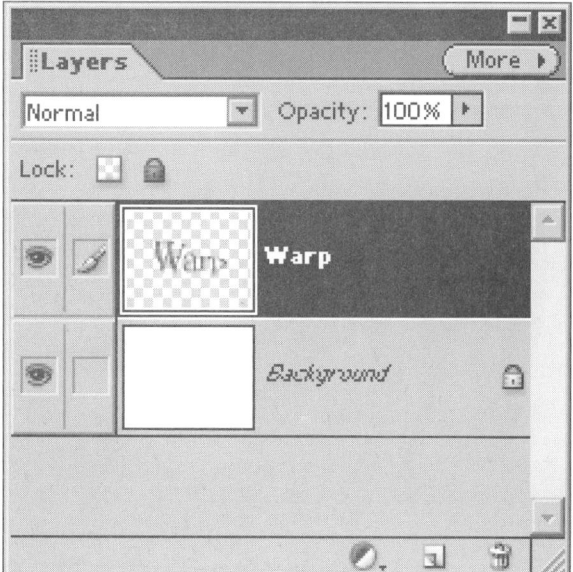

9.21

- After you apply Simplify Layer, filters, effects from the Effects palette, Transform, and other commands can be applied to the text.
- ⌘/**Ctrl**+click the type layer to generate a type-shaped selection.
- Click the Effects palette tab.
- In the Effects menu, load **All**.
- Click **Green Slime**. See **Figure 9.22**.
- Click **Apply**.
- A new layer is created above the type layer, creating an effect that looks like a slimy coat to the text. See **Figure 9.23 (CP25)**.

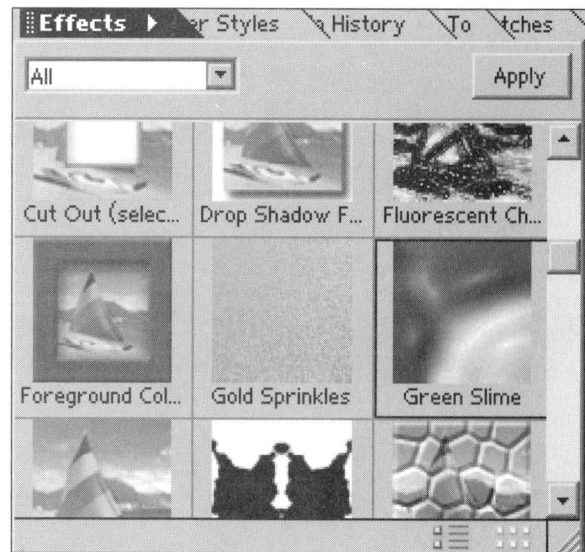

9.22

9.23 (CP25)

TYPE MASK TOOL

The Type Mask tool is different from the Type tool in that, rather creating a vector graphic, it makes a type-shaped selection. Think of the Marquee tools: they are designed to select an area of a layer. You can select a square, a rectangle, a circle, and so forth. By making the selection in Fixed Aspect Ratio, limits are set as to the dimensions of the selection.

The Type Mask tool operates on a similar basis. The font and size you select set the limits of the selection you can make, but rather than make it with the mouse, you use the keyboard. The shape of the selection is type, but when filled the type is a raster graphic rather than a vector graphic. It is defined by pixels, and not by paths (straight lines restraining the color borders) as in vector graphics.

Type selections may also be warped. The key is to apply the warp while the mask is still active. See **Figures 9.24** and **9.25**.

9.24

9.25

As soon as the selection is made, the Warp Text becomes unavailable.

TYPE SELECTION: IMAGE FILL

These steps use the following from the CD-ROM:

- Monochecks.jpg

To begin,

- Open the image **Monochecks.jpg**, found on the CD-ROM.
- Select the **Type Mask** tool. Set the following attributes for the Type Mask tool in the Options bar:
  - Tool = **Horizontal Type Mask**
  - Set Font Family = **Times New Roman**
  - Font Size = **200 pts**
  - Anti-aliased = **Selected**
  - Justify = **Center**
- Enter some text on the background layer.
- While the red mask (called rubylith) is visible, the Warp command can be used. In the Options bar, click the **Warp** icon.
- In the Warp dialog box, select **Rise** as the style and set the Bend to **–15**.
- Click **OK**.
- In the Options bar, click the **Commit** icon. See **Figure 9.26**.

9.26

- Choose **Layer** ➢ **New** ➢ **Layer Via Copy**.
- Select the background layer.
- Choose **Enhance** ➢ **Adjust Brightness/Contrast** ➢ **Brightness/Contrast**.
  - Brightness = **–35**
  - Contrast = **+20**
- Click **OK**. See **Figure 9.27**.

The last was just one demonstration of type versus type selection. As with any selection, you may fill it with a color or gradient, a pattern, apply a stroke, and apply filters as soon as the selection has been filled.

Here's another example. This time, you fill the selection with a custom pattern.

- Create a new image. Set the image attributes as follows:
  - Preset Size = **640x480**
  - Resolution = **72 dpi**
  - Contents = **Black**
- Create a new layer.
- Select the **Type Mask** tool.
- Enter your text in the new layer. Set the font to 200 px or so, just to help see the fill.
- Choose **Edit** ➢ **Fill** ➢ **Pattern**. Select one of the preset patterns or a custom pattern (your choice in this example) to insert into the selection.
- Click **OK**.
- Deselect the text. See **Figure 9.28**.

The main reason for giving a bit more description for both the Type and Type Mask tools is to serve as a lead in for the next tutorial. In the next few pages, you learn how to load custom layer style into Adobe Elements 2 and how to apply styles to your own type, filled type selection, layers, and shapes.

9.27

9.28

LOADING AND APPLYING LAYER STYLES

T hrough the course of the last few chapters you have been directed to either apply a pre-existing layer style that is included with Adobe Elements 2 when installed or been directed to load and use specific layer style sets found on the included CD-ROM. In this section of the book, I discuss loading additional items into Adobe Elements so that those presets are available for use in your work.

STEP 1: LOAD CD LAYER STYLES INTO ELEMENTS

■ Ensure that Adobe Elements 2 is closed. If the program is running, shut down Adobe Elements 2 prior to proceeding.
■ Insert the CD-ROM into the CD-ROM drive.
■ On your hard drive, open the **Adobe Elements** folder group.
■ Open the **Presets** folder. See **Figure 9.29**.
■ Open the **Styles** folder. See **Figure 9.30**.

> **NOTE**
>
> Although this tutorial focuses on loading layer styles, other presets such as brushes may be loaded in the same manner.

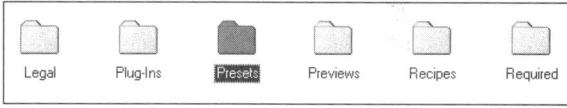

9.29

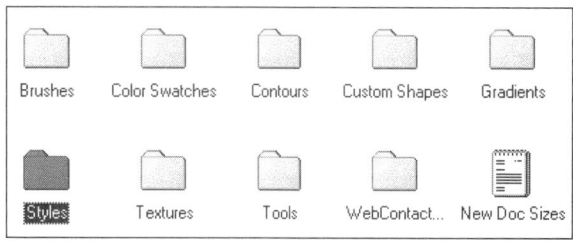

9.30

- Create a new sub folder in the Styles folder and give it a name (in this example, AFX-Styles). This is for organizational purposes only. See **Figure 9.31**.
- Open another instance of the File Browser.
- Open the **Layer Styles** folder on the CD-ROM.
- Select the style sets you want to load into Elements.
- Drag and drop the style sets into the Elements sub folder. See **Figure 9.32**.

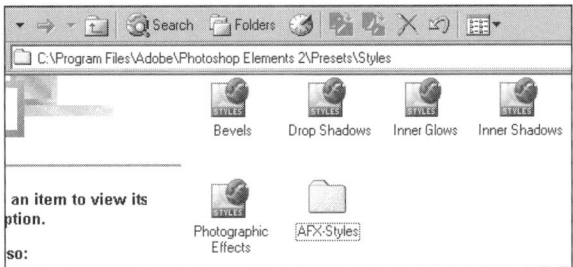

9.31

STEP 2: FIND THE NEW STYLES IN ELEMENTS

- Launch Adobe Elements 2.
- The best way to find the styles is to create something to apply the styles to. Create a new image with the following attributes:
  - Preset Size = **800 x 600 pixels**
  - Resolution = **100 dpi**
  - Mode = **RGB**
  - Contents = **White**
- Click **OK**.
- Create a new layer.
- Select the **Type** tool. Set the following attributes for the font:
  - Font = **Times New Roman** (any font will do)
  - Size = **200 pts**
  - Anti-aliased = **Selected**
  - Justify = **Center**
  - Color = **Black**

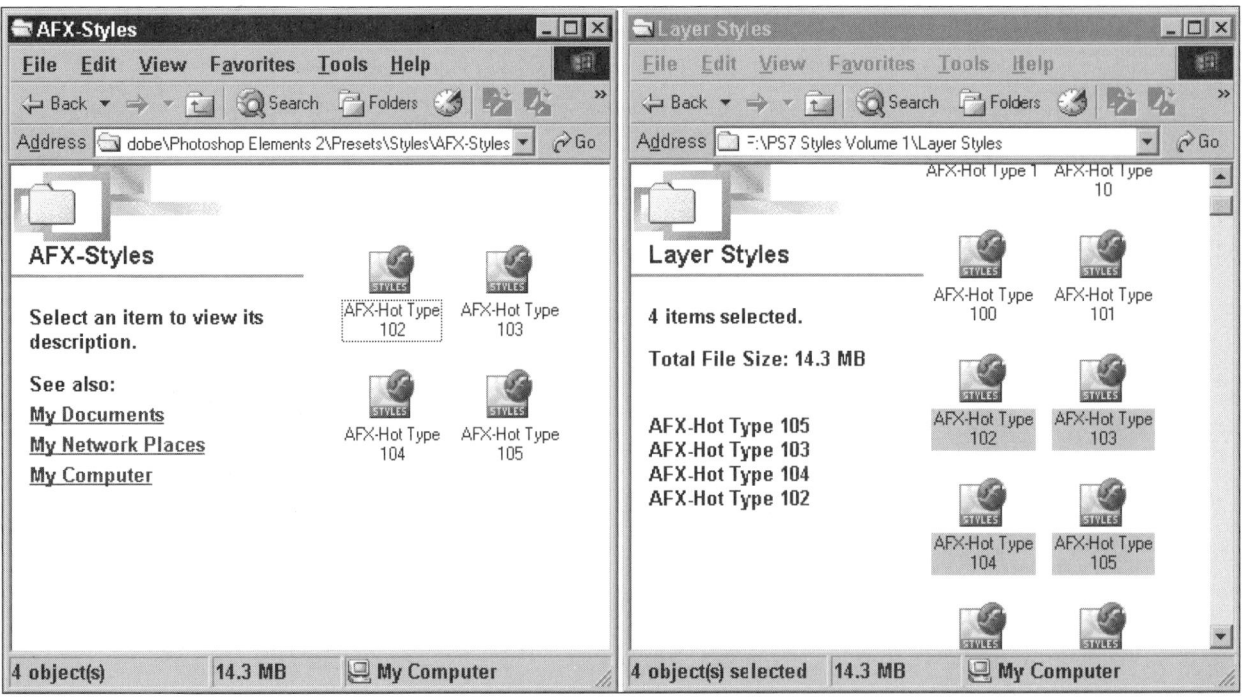

9.32

- Enter your text. See **Figure 9.33**.
- Click the **Layer Styles** tab.
- When you open the Layer Styles menu, the layer style sets loaded into the sub-folder you created appear in the list. See **Figure 9.34**.

9.33

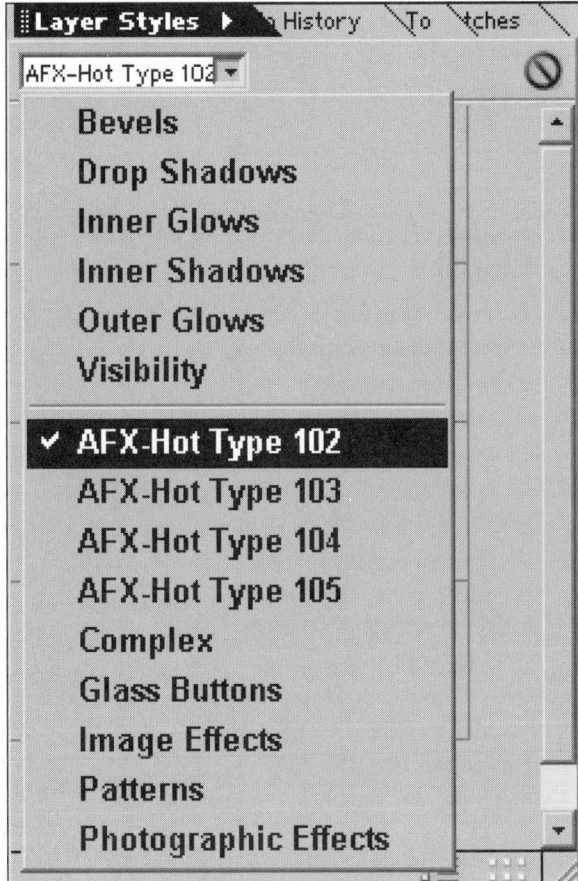

9.34

STEP 3: APPLY THE STYLES

- Select and load **AFX-Hot Type-103**.
- Clicking a layer style instantly applies those settings to the selected type layer. Click the **Style 1** icon. See **Figure 9.35**.
- As mentioned in the previous tutorial, the type can be warped while the layer style is applied, so long as the type layer has not been simplified. In the Options bar, click the **Warp Type** icon.
- In the Warp dialog box, enter the following settings:
  - Style = **Bulge**
  - Horizontal = **Checked**
  - Bend = **+50**
  - Horizontal Distortion = **–50**
  - Vertical Distortion = **0**
- Click **OK**. See **Figure 9.36**.

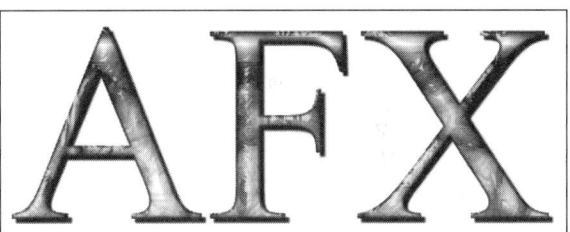

9.35

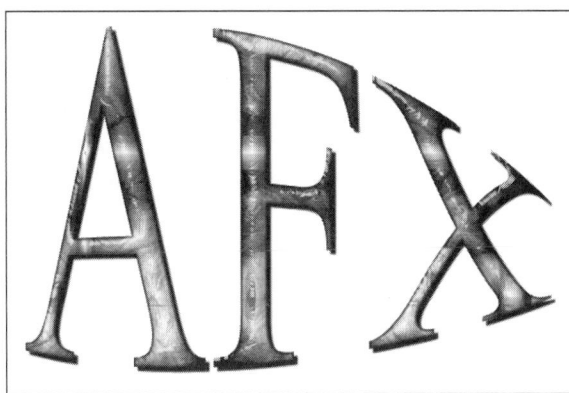

9.36

■ Even if you change the Font attributes, the layer style stays in effect. Select the **Type** tool. Highlight the text again. See **Figure 9.37**.

■ Select a new font in the Options bar.

■ Click the **Commit Current Edits** icon on the right side of the Options bar. See **Figure 9.38**.

■ The applied style may be changed by simply reopening the Styles palette, clicking the empty style in the first position to remove the previous style, and then clicking a new style icon. Though the style changes without removing the previous settings, in some examples a few settings are retained, so it is best to remove the previous settings first. See **Figure 9.39**.

STEP 4: ALTER THE STYLE SETTINGS

These steps require loading the following style set from the CD-ROM:

■ jul02-40.asl

9.37

Because the styles are recorded in advance and retain the original bevel settings for the specific image/layer for which they were created, often, when

9.38

NOTE

The layer style sets included with this book each has an empty style occupying the first position in the Style palette. If you apply a layer style, and then apply another without removing the previous style, some of the previous settings will be retained. The empty style eliminates this problem. Prior to applying a second style, you may remove all previous settings by clicking the empty style. Do this first to start fresh each time.

re-applied to other images, the bevel is wrong or the settings just don't match up to the current work. For example, say a style was originally created for use on a font, but you would like to apply it to a pill button shape. The settings for the style can be readily altered in Elements to match the current design. Here is the process for adjusting a style.

- Create a new image with the following attributes:
  - Preset Size = **800 x 600 pixels**
  - Resolution = **100 dpi**
  - Mode = **RGB**
  - Contents = **White**
- Click **OK**.
- Press **D** to reset the default colors.
- Select the **Custom Shape** tool.
- In the Options bar, select the **Rounded Rectangle** tool. Set the following attributes for the tool:
  - Radius = **25 pixels**
  - Create New Shape Layer = **Selected**
  - Style = **none**
  - Color = **Black (foreground)**

- With the mouse, click and draw a pill button shape. A new layer for the shape is created. See **Figure 9.40**.
- Click the **Layer Styles** palette tab.
- Load a style set. For this example, **jul02-40** is used.
- Click **Style 12** to apply the style to the shape. See **Figure 9.41**.

9.40

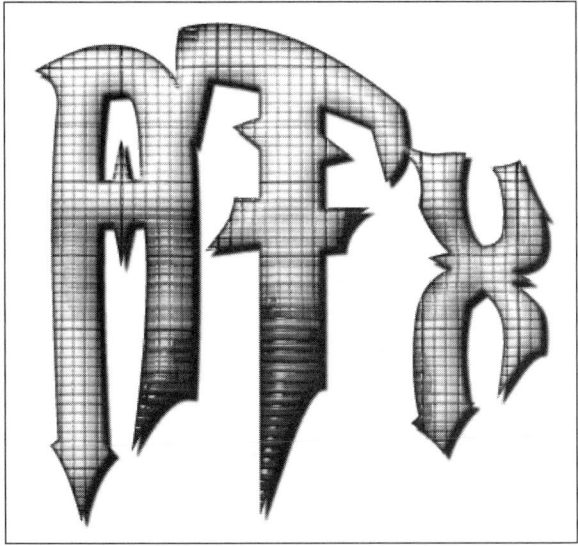

9.39

9.41

■ As you can see from the example, the style is applied, but the bevel is a little weak. The settings for the style can be altered to give the button a more pronounced curve. Choose **Layer ➤ Layer Style ➤ Style Settings**.

■ In the Style Settings dialog box, enter the following:

    ■ Shadow Distance = **15 pixels**

    ■ Inner Glow Size = **25 pixels**

    ■ Bevel Size = **45 pixels**

■ Click **OK**. See **Figure 9.42**.

■ Further manipulations can be made by using the Scale Effects command. All the style settings are changed when this command as used, rather than changes to individual settings. Choose **Layer ➤ Layer Style ➤ Scale Effects**.

■ Move the slider to **150%**.

■ Click **OK**. See **Figure 9.43**.

 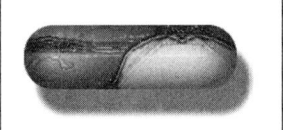

9.42   9.43

STEP 5: COPY AND PASTE STYLE SETTINGS

You may copy the style settings from one layer and paste them onto an item in another layer.

■ Choose **Layer ➤ Layer Style ➤ Copy Layer Style.**

■ Create a new layer.

■ Select the **Type** tool. Enter some large text in the new layer. See **Figure 9.44**.

■ Choose **Layer ➤ Layer Style ➤ Paste Layer Style**. See **Figure 9.45 (CP26)**.

9.44

9.45 (CP26)

TYPE VIA THE EFFECTS PALETTE

For the final tutorial, take a look at another feature for generating cool effects for type in Elements — the Effects palette.

First, you need to know some information about Effects. These handy little items are known in Adobe Photoshop as actions. These are recordings of filters and commands applied to an image and saved for later use on other images. In Elements, several Effects sets in four categories are pre-installed:

- Frames
- Image Effects
- Text Effects
- Textures

**STEP 1: APPLY THE PRESET
EFFECTS TO TYPE**

- Create a new image with the following
attributes:
  - Preset Size = **800x600**
  - Resolution = **100**
  - Contents = **White**
- Click **OK**.
- Create a new layer.
- Press **D** to reset the default colors.
- Select the **Type** tool. In the new layer, type
your text in large font size (200 pts or so). See
Figure 9.46.
- Click the **Effects** tab to open the Effects palette.
- Select **Text Effects** from the menu.
- Click the **Brushed Metal (type)** icon.
- In the upper-right corner click the **Apply**
button, and the effect is applied to the text layer.
See **Figure 9.47**.
- You can dress up the effect by applying a layer
style, such as Drop Shadow. Click the **Styles**
palette tab. Load the default **Drop Shadow** style
set and click the **High** icon. See **Figure 9.48**.

To sum things up, layer styles and effects offer a
wide range of powerful, instant effects for your work
or artistry. A bit of practice in loading, applying, and
adjusting the settings is in order, but even using a
hammer takes a bit of practice. This book and the
CD-ROM can help you get started, but your best
work will come from your own imagination and
increasing skill. These are simply tools to assist you in
the learning and developing process. As soon as you
have grasped the process of creating images from
scratch in Adobe Elements, the art you produce will
not only be better as time goes on but increasingly
satisfying.

9.47

9.46

9.48

APPENDIX A
WHAT'S ON THE CD-ROM

This appendix provides you with information on the contents of the CD that accompanies this book. For the latest and greatest information, please refer to the ReadMe file located at the root of the CD. Here is what you will find:

- System Requirements
- CD-ROM Installation Instructions
- What's on the CD
- Troubleshooting

SYSTEM REQUIREMENTS

Make sure that your computer meets the minimum system requirements listed in this section. If your computer doesn't match up to most of these requirements, you may have a problem using the contents of the CD-ROM.

FOR WINDOWS 9X, WINDOWS 2000, WINDOWS NT4 (WITH SP 4 OR LATER), WINDOWS ME, OR WINDOWS XP:

- PC with a Pentium processor running at 120 MHz or faster
- At least 32MB of total RAM installed on your computer; for best performance, we recommend at least 64MB
- Ethernet network interface card (NIC) or modem with a speed of at least 28,800 bps
- A CD-ROM drive

FOR MACINTOSH:

- Mac OS computer with a 68040 or faster processor running OS 7.6 or later
- At least 32MB of total RAM installed on your computer; for best performance, we recommend at least 64MB
- A CD-ROM drive.

CD-ROM INSTALLATION INSTRUCTIONS

To install a particular piece of software, open its folder with My Computer or Internet Explorer. What you do next depends on what you find in the software's folder:

1. First, look for a ReadMe.txt file or a .doc or .htm document. If this is present, it should contain installation instructions and other useful information.

2. If the folder contains an executable (.exe) file, this is usually an installation program. Often it will be called Setup.exe or Install.exe, but in some cases the filename reflects an abbreviated version of the software's name and version number. Run the .exe file to start the installation process.

WHAT'S ON THE CD

The following sections provide a summary of the software and other materials you'll find on the CD.

All items on the CD-ROM were created by the author for use in Adobe Elements 2. The folder name is listed in bold, with the description or the contents of that folder below.

BRUSHES

Advert-1.abr	Advert-17.abr	AFX-Blots16.abr	assorted-11.abr
Advert-2.abr	AFX-Blots1.abr	AFX-Shapes1.abr	assorted-12.abr
Advert-3.abr	AFX-Blots2.abr	AFX-Shapes2.abr	assorted-13.abr
Advert-4.abr	AFX-Blots3.abr	AFX-Shapes3.abr	assorted-14.abr
Advert-5.abr	AFX-Blots4.abr	AFX-Shapes4.abr	assorted-15.abr
Advert-6.abr	AFX-Blots5.abr	AFX-single.abr	assorted-16.abr
Advert-7.abr	AFX-Blots6.abr	assorted-1.abr	assorted-17.abr
Advert-8.abr	AFX-Blots7.abr	assorted-2.abr	assorted-18.abr
Advert-9.abr	AFX-Blots8.abr	assorted-3.abr	baby1.abr
Advert-10.abr	AFX-Blots9.abr	assorted-4.abr	ButterF-1.abr
Advert-11.abr	AFX-Blots10.abr	assorted-5.abr	ButterF-2.abr
Advert-12.abr	AFX-Blots11.abr	assorted-6.abr	festive-1.abr
Advert-13.abr	AFX-Blots12.abr	assorted-7.abr	single.abr
Advert-14.abr	AFX-Blots13.abr	assorted-8.abr	valentine-1.abr
Advert-15.abr	AFX-Blots14.abr	assorted-9.abr	wedding-1.abr
Advert-16.abr	AFX-Blots15.abr	assorted-10.abr	

CHAPTER ADD-ONS

This folder contains files referenced in the tutorials. When an image, layer style, or other element is mentioned in the tutorial (usually at the beginning), go to this folder for the source files. You can then proceed with the tutorial using the same image or custom setting as the author.

GRADIENTS

ActionFx-PipesGradient.grd
AFXGradSet1.grd
AFX-ScrewHead.grd
Experiments1.grd

Experiments2.grd
Experiments3.grd
Experiments4.grd
Experiments5.grd

Experiments6.grd
Solids1.grd
Tubes-Metals.grd
Wire Coat.grd

LAYER STYLE EXAMPLES

This folder contains example images that correspond to the layer style sets. These images give you a preview of the layer style to help you decide which layer style sets to load into Adobe Elements 2.

LAYER STYLES

AFX-BigFlat-01.asl
AFX-Digital-1.asl
AFX-EL2-Set1.asl
AFX-FancyType-1.asl
AFX-FancyType-2.asl
AFX-FancyType-3.asl
AFX-FancyType-4.asl
AFX-FancyType-5.asl
AFX-FancyType-6.asl
AFX-FancyType-7.asl
AFX-FancyType-8.asl
AFX-FancyType-9.asl
AFX-FancyType-10.asl
AFX-FancyType-11.asl
AFX-FancyType-12.asl
AFX-FancyType-13.asl
AFX-FancyType-14.asl
AFX-FancyType-15.asl
AFX-Glass1.asl
AFX-Glass2.asl
AFX-GlassPlastic-1.asl

AFX-GlassPlastic-2.asl
AFX-GlassPlastic-3.asl
AFX-GlassPlastic-4.asl
AFX-GlassPlastic-5.asl
AFX-GlassPlastic-6.asl
AFX-GlassPlastic-7.asl
AFX-GlassPlastic-8.asl
AFX-GlassPlastic-9.asl
AFX-GlassPlastic-10.asl
AFX-MetalsHard.asl
AFX-MetalType-1.asl
AFX-MetalType-2.asl
AFX-MetalType-3.asl
AFX-PatternType-1.asl
AFX-PatternType-2.asl
AFX-PatternType-3.asl
AFX-PatternType-4.asl
AFX-PatternType-5.asl
AFX-PatternType-6.asl
AFX-PatternType-7.asl
AFX-PatternType-8.asl

AFX-PatternType-9.asl
AFX-PatternType-10.asl
AFX-PatternType-11.asl
AFX-PatternType-12.asl
AFX-PatternType-13.asl
AFX-PatternType-14.asl
AFX-PatternType-15.asl
AFX-PatternType-16.asl
AFX-PatternType-17.asl
AFX-PatternType-18.asl
AFX-PatternType-19.asl
AFX-PatternType-20.asl
AFX-PatternType-21.asl
AFX-PatternType-22.asl
AFX-PatternType-23.asl
AFX-PatternType-24.asl
AFX-PatternType-25.asl
AFX-PatternType-26.asl
AFX-PatternType-27.asl
AFX-StoneMetal-1.asl
AFX-StoneType-1.asl

AFX-StoneType-2.asl
AFX-StoneType-3.asl
AFX-StoneType-4.asl
AFX-StoneType-5.asl
AFX-Woods-01.asl
AFX-Woods-02.asl
AFX-Woods-03.asl
AFX-Woods-04.asl
AFX-Woods-05.asl
AFX-Woods-06.asl
AFX-Woods-07.asl
AFX-Woods-08.asl
AFX-Woods-09.asl
AFX-Woods-10.asl
AFX-Woods-11.asl
AFX-WoodStone-1.asl
AFX-WoodStone-2.asl
a-single.asl

PATTERN SETS

AFX-1.pat	AFX-13.pat	AFX-25.pat	AFX-37.pat
AFX-2.pat	AFX-14.pat	AFX-26.pat	AFX-38.pat
AFX-3.pat	AFX-15.pat	AFX-27.pat	AFX-39.pat
AFX-4.pat	AFX-16.pat	AFX-28.pat	AFX-40.pat
AFX-5.pat	AFX-17.pat	AFX-29.pat	AFX-41.pat
AFX-6.pat	AFX-18.pat	AFX-30.pat	AFX-Fun-1.pat
AFX-7.pat	AFX-19.pat	AFX-31.pat	AFX-grids.pat
AFX-8.pat	AFX-20.pat	AFX-32.pat	AFX-Metals-1.pat
AFX-9.pat	AFX-21.pat	AFX-33.pat	AFX-Woods-1.pat
AFX-10.pat	AFX-22.pat	AFX-34.pat	AFX-Woods-2.pat
AFX-11.pat	AFX-23.pat	AFX-35.pat	a-single.pat
AFX-12.pat	AFX-24.pat	AFX-36.pat	single.pat

SEAMLESS PATTERNS

This folder contains tileable patterns for use in your designs. These make effective backgrounds for Web sites, for filling text, or for use as textures. All patterns were created by the author for your enjoyment.

TROUBLESHOOTING

If you have difficulty installing or using any of the materials on the companion CD, try the following solutions:

- **Turn off any anti-virus software that you may have running.** Installers sometimes mimic virus activity and can make your computer incorrectly believe that it is being infected by a virus. (Be sure to turn the anti-virus software back on later.)
- **Close all running programs.** The more programs you're running, the less memory is available to other programs. Installers also typically update files and programs; if you keep other programs running, installation may not work properly.
- **Reference the ReadMe:** Please refer to the ReadMe file located at the root of the CD-ROM for the latest product information at the time of publication.

If you still have trouble with the CD-ROM, please call the Customer Care phone number: (800) 762-2974. Outside the United States, call 1 (317) 572-3994. You can also contact Wiley Customer Care by e-mail at `techsupdum@wiley.com`. Wiley will provide technical support only for installation and other general quality control items; for technical support on the applications themselves, consult the program's vendor or author.

APPENDIX B

LOADING AND CHANGING THE CD LAYER STYLES

Layer styles are saved settings that enable you to instantly apply effects to the contents of a layer. In addition to the default layer styles sets that come with Adobe Elements 2, third-party layer styles may be loaded into the software for use in your designs. Layer styles sets created with Adobe Photoshop 6 or 7 may also be used in Adobe Elements.

 The CD included with this book contains dozens of layer styles sets created by the author, Al Ward. Each layer style set contains several separate styles, adding up to hundreds of instant effects at your disposal.

LOADING AND CHANGING LAYER STYLES FROM THE CD

In order to load and use the layer styles included on the CD, make sure that Adobe Elements is closed.

- Insert the CD into your CD-ROM drive.
- Open the **Adobe Elements 2** directory.
- Open the **Presets** folder.
- Open the **Styles** folder.
- Create a new folder in the **Styles** folder. Name the new folder **AFX-Styles**.

 Some operating systems only allow for 15 to 20 additional layer style sets to be loaded into Adobe Elements at a time. Too many sets result in a loss of access to the Layer Styles menu. To avoid this error, load only 15 to 20 additional layer style sets into Adobe Elements at one time. Remove some sets prior to loading new sets.

 Additional information concerning the use and editing of layer styles can be found in the Adobe Elements 2 Help Files included with your software.

ADDITIONAL RESOURCES

You can connect directly to these Web sites by clicking the appropriate hyperlink on the CD-ROM that accompanies this book.

Red Eye Adobe Elements User Group, Administrated by Al Ward and Richard Lynch:
`http://groups.yahoo.com/group/red_eye/`
`http://groups.yahoo.com/group/hpe/`

Richard Lynch's Elements Web site:
`www.hiddenelements.com`

Adobe Photoshop Elements Tutorials from Adobe:
`www.adobe.com/products/tips/photoshopel.html`

Adobe Support Knowledge Database:
`http://pshopelementssupport.adobe.com/search.asp`

The Adobe Forum:
`www.adobe.com/support/forums/main.html`

Additional Elements Information:
`www.arraich.com/elements/psE_intro.htm`

TECHNIQUES AND TUTORIALS

Although there are not many sites online specifically dedicated to Adobe Elements, many of the Adobe Photoshop tutorials can help with Adobe Elements as well.

Action Fx Photoshop Online Resources (Author's Web site): `http://actionfx.com`
Photoshop Café (Web site of Colin Smith): `www.photoshopcafe.com`
Eyes on Design Photoshop Tutorials: `www.eyesondesign.net/`
Planet Photoshop: `www.planetphotoshop.com`
PS6.com (Web site of Richard Lynch): `http://ps6.com`

About.com Elements Information:

http://graphicssoft.about.com/cs/photoshopelements/index.htm?terms=
  photoshop+elements

Design Tips and Tutorials:

www.myjanee.com
http://psworkshop.net/
www.photoshopuser.com/
http://graphicssoft.about.com/
www.sketchpad.net/photoshp.htm
www.photoshopace.com/home.htm
www.alphateck.com/
www.bobsphotoshopsource.co.uk/
www.photoshop-stuff.com/
www.mnsi.net/~jhlavac/photo/
www.fredsphoto.on.ca/linksphotoshop.htm

Downloads:

Author's Web site, with additional layer styles for use with Adobe Elements: http://actionfx.com
Adobe File Sharing Web site: http://share.studio.adobe.com/Default.asp

ABOUT THE AUTHOR

Al Ward, a certified Photoshop addict and Webmaster of Action FX Photoshop Resources (`www.actionfx.com`), hails from Missoula, Montana. A former submariner in the U.S. Navy, Al now spends his time writing on graphics related topics and creating add-on software for Adobe Photoshop and Adobe Elements. Al is the co-author (with Colin Smith) of *Photoshop Most Wanted: Effects and Design Tips*, *Photoshop Most Wanted II*, a manual of popular Photoshop Special Effects, and *Foundation Photoshop 6.0* from Friends of Ed Publishing. He has been a contributor to *Photoshop User* magazine, a contributing writer for *Photoshop Elements 2.0: 50 Ways to Create Cool Pictures*, *Photoshop 7 Magic*, *Inside Photoshop 6*, and *Special Edition Inside Photoshop 6* from New Riders Publishing, and writes for several Photoshop related Web sites including the National Association of Photoshop Professional's Official Web site, Photoshop User.Com (`www.photoshopuser.com`), Planet Photoshop (`www.planetphotoshop.com`), and the Photoshop Café (`www.photoshopcafe.com`).

Al was a panelist at the Photoshop World 2001 Los Angeles Conference, and contributes to the official NAPP Web site as the Actions area coordinator.

Al lists Scott Kelby, Editor-In-Chief of *Photoshop User* magazine as his hero, coffee as his favorite food group, and sleep as the one pastime he'd like to take up some day.

In his off time he enjoys his church, his family, fishing the great northwestern United States, and scouring the Web for Photoshop related topics.

COLOPHON

This book was produced electronically in Indianapolis, Indiana. Microsoft Word 2000 was used for word processing; design and layout were produced using Quark Express 4.11, Adobe Illustrator 8.0.1, and Adobe Photoshop 7.0 on Power Macintosh computers. The typeface families used are: Chicago Laser, Minion, Myriad, Myriad Multiple Master, Prestige Elite, Symbol, Trajan, and Zapf Dingbats.

Acquisitions Editor: Tom Heine
Project Editor: Sarah Hellert
Technical Editor: Colin Smith
Copy Editor: Beth Taylor
Permissions Editor: Carmen Krikorian
Production Coordinator: Dale White
Cover Designer: Anthony Bunyan
Production: Beth Brooks, Sean Decker, Joyce Haughey, LeAndra Johnson, Gabriele McCann, Kristin McMullan, Heather Pope, Erin Zeltner
Proofreading and Indexing: John Bitter, Richard T. Evans, David Faust, Joanne Keaton, Angel Perez, Carl Pierce, Charles Spencer

INDEX

Continued

Continued

WILEY PUBLISHING, INC.
END-USER LICENSE AGREEMENT

5. **Limited Warranty.**

   (a) WPI warrants that the Software and Software Media are free from defects in materials and workman-ship under normal use for a period of sixty (60) days from the date of purchase of this Book. If WPI receives notification within the warranty period of defects in materials or workmanship, WPI will replace the defective Software Media.

   (b) WPI AND THE AUTHOR OF THE BOOK DISCLAIM ALL OTHER WARRANTIES, EXPRESS OR IMPLIED, INCLUDING WITHOUT LIMITATION IMPLIED WARRANTIES OF MERCHANTABILITY AND FITNESS FOR A PARTICULAR PURPOSE, WITH RESPECT TO THE SOFTWARE, THE PRO-GRAMS, THE SOURCE CODE CONTAINED THEREIN, AND/OR THE TECHNIQUES DESCRIBED IN THIS BOOK. WPI DOES NOT WARRANT THAT THE FUNCTIONS CONTAINED IN THE SOFT-WARE WILL MEET YOUR REQUIREMENTS OR THAT THE OPERATION OF THE SOFTWARE WILL BE ERROR FREE.

   (c) This limited warranty gives you specific legal rights, and you may have other rights that vary from juris-diction to jurisdiction.

6. **Remedies.**

   (a) WPI's entire liability and your exclusive remedy for defects in materials and workmanship shall be lim-ited to replacement of the Software Media, which may be returned to WPI with a copy of your receipt at the following address: Software Media Fulfillment Department, Attn.: Photoshop Elements 2 Special Effects, Wiley Publishing, Inc., 10475 Crosspoint Blvd., Indianapolis, IN 46256, or call 1-800-762-2974. Please allow four to six weeks for delivery. This Limited Warranty is void if failure of the Software Media has resulted from accident, abuse, or misapplication. Any replacement Software Media will be warranted for the remainder of the original warranty period or thirty (30) days, whichever is longer.

   (b) In no event shall WPI or the author be liable for any damages whatsoever (including without limitation damages for loss of business profits, business interruption, loss of business information, or any other pecuniary loss) arising from the use of or inability to use the Book or the Software, even if WPI has been advised of the possibility of such damages.

   (c) Because some jurisdictions do not allow the exclusion or limitation of liability for consequential or incidental damages, the above limitation or exclusion may not apply to you.

7. **U.S. Government Restricted Rights.** Use, duplication, or disclosure of the Software for or on behalf of the United States of America, its agencies and/or instrumentalities "U.S. Government" is subject to restrictions as stated in paragraph (c)(1)(ii) of the Rights in Technical Data and Computer Software clause of DFARS 252.227-7013, or subparagraphs (c) (1) and (2) of the Commercial Computer Software - Restricted Rights clause at FAR 52.227-19, and in similar clauses in the NASA FAR supplement, as applicable.

8. **General.** This Agreement constitutes the entire understanding of the parties and revokes and supersedes all prior agreements, oral or written, between them and may not be modified or amended except in a writing signed by both parties hereto that specifically refers to this Agreement. This Agreement shall take precedence over any other documents that may be in conflict herewith. If any one or more provisions contained in this Agreement are held by any court or tribunal to be invalid, illegal, or otherwise unenforceable, each and every other provision shall remain in full force and effect.